# 797,885 Books
### are available to read at

# Forgotten Books

## www.ForgottenBooks.com

Forgotten Books' App
Available for mobile, tablet & eReader

ISBN 978-1-330-74952-4
PIBN 10100422

This book is a reproduction of an important historical work. Forgotten Books uses state-of-the-art technology to digitally reconstruct the work, preserving the original format whilst repairing imperfections present in the aged copy. In rare cases, an imperfection in the original, such as a blemish or missing page, may be replicated in our edition. We do, however, repair the vast majority of imperfections successfully; any imperfections that remain are intentionally left to preserve the state of such historical works.

Forgotten Books is a registered trademark of FB &c Ltd.
Copyright © 2017 FB &c Ltd.
FB &c Ltd, Dalton House, 60 Windsor Avenue, London, SW19 2RR.
Company number 08720141. Registered in England and Wales.

For support please visit www.forgottenbooks.com

# 1 MONTH OF FREE READING

## at
## www.ForgottenBooks.com

By purchasing this book you are eligible for one month membership to ForgottenBooks.com, giving you unlimited access to our entire collection of over 700,000 titles via our web site and mobile apps.

To claim your free month visit:
www.forgottenbooks.com/free100422

\* Offer is valid for 45 days from date of purchase. Terms and conditions apply.

English
Français
Deutsche
Italiano
Español
Português

# www.forgottenbooks.com

**Mythology** Photography **Fiction** Fishing Christianity **Art** Cooking Essays Buddhism Freemasonry Medicine **Biology** Music **Ancient Egypt** Evolution Carpentry Physics Dance Geology **Mathematics** Fitness Shakespeare **Folklore** Yoga Marketing **Confidence** Immortality Biographies Poetry **Psychology** Witchcraft Electronics Chemistry History **Law** Accounting **Philosophy** Anthropology Alchemy Drama Quantum Mechanics Atheism Sexual Health **Ancient History Entrepreneurship** Languages Sport Paleontology Needlework Islam **Metaphysics** Investment Archaeology Parenting Statistics Criminology **Motivational**

# LETTER-BOOK

OF

# GABRIEL HARVEY,

A.D. 1573—1580.

EDITED FROM THE ORIGINAL MS. SLOANE 93, IN THE BRITISH MUSEUM,

BY

## EDWARD JOHN LONG SCOTT,

M.A. OXON., ASSISTANT KEEPER OF MSS. BRITISH MUSEUM.

Τὰ παθήματα μαθήματα.
Satius est ἀδικεῖσθαι quam ἀδικεῖν.

WESTMINSTER
PRINTED BY NICHOLS AND SONS,
25, PARLIAMENT STREET.

[NEW SERIES XXXIII.]

# COUNCIL OF THE CAMDEN SOCIETY

## FOR THE YEAR 1883-4.

*President,*

THE RIGHT HON. THE EARL OF VERULAM, F.R.G.S.

J. J. CARTWRIGHT, ESQ., M.A., *Treasurer.*
WILLIAM CHAPPELL, ESQ., F.S.A.
F. W. COSENS, ESQ , F.S.A.
THE HON. HAROLD DILLON, F.S.A.
JAMES E. DOYLE, ESQ.
REV. J. WOODFALL EBSWORTH, M.A., F.S.A.
JAMES GAIRDNER, ESQ.
SAMUEL RAWSON GARDINER, ESQ., LL.D. *Director.*
J. W. HALES, ESQ., M.A.
ALFRED KINGSTON, ESQ., *Secretary.*
ALEXANDER MACMILLAN, ESQ., F.S.A.
STUART A. MOORE, ESQ., F.S.A.
THE EARL OF POWIS, LL.D.
REV. W. SPARROW SIMPSON, D.D., F.S.A.
WILLIAM JOHN THOMS, ESQ., F.S.A.

The COUNCIL of the CAMDEN SOCIETY desire it to be understood that they are not answerable for any opinions or observations that may appear in the Society's publications; the Editors of the several Works being alone responsible for the same.

# PREFACE.

GABRIEL HARVEY, the writer of the following Letter-Book, is better known to us than almost any other man among the literary characters who crowd the Elizabethan stage. His celebrated controversy with Nash (who raked up against him every circumstance in his life and writings in order to pour unlimited abuse and contempt upon his head) has furnished us with a vivid picture, not only of Harvey's manners and conversation, but even of his dress and physiognomy. Fortunately, there is no need for us to enter into the merits of that wordy war, as the present volume contains letters and compositions of a much earlier date, covering apparently only the years 1573-80.

Gabriel was the eldest boy, among six children, of a well-to-do ropemaker,* at Saffron Walden, in Essex. He had three brothers and two sisters. Of these we only know the names of John and Richard among the boys, and Mercy as one of the girls. The father was rich enough to send three of his sons to Cambridge, but the present volume tells us nothing of the fortunes of his brothers at college, save for one letter, at page 183, from Gabriel to

* In " The Records of St. Michael's Parish Church, Bishops Stortford, edited by

Richard, about some college scrape, into which the latter had fallen, but of which nothing precise or intelligible is said. On the other hand, the episode of Mercy's courtship, or rather persecution, by a young married nobleman, gives us a very curious insight into the manners and habits of the period.

In describing the volume, we may roughly divide it into three parts. (*a*) Letters to and from Gabriel during his residence at Pembroke Hall, Cambridge. These occupy the beginning of the book, as far as page 54, and then break off to be renewed on page 159 ; and so continue until the end at page 184. They are fair copies, written in a very neat legible hand. (*b*) Drafts of Gabriel's verses, and of his correspondence with Edmund Spenser, under the feigned name of Immerito or Benevolo. They extend from page 55 to page 143 (except seven pages of notes for Rhetoric Discourses at folios 54-57 of the MS.) These compositions are scribbled in an almost illegible and undecipherable scrawl, and, were it not that they contain so much unpublished matter of great interest and value relating to Spenser, they would certainly never repay the incredible labour and weariness of making them out. To add to their difficulty, the pages have been, at some time or other, hopelessly transposed, and in one instance it is quite plain that four leaves have been very neatly cut out, and possibly the same fatal mistake has been repeated in other parts where no mark of excision is now visible. (*c*) "A noble man's sute to a cuntrie maide" extends from page 143 to page 158. This part is written in the same elegant hand as used in (*a*). It is, of course, needless to observe that the whole volume is throughout in Harvey's own hand, though in several different styles.

The earlier division of the letters relates entirely to the dispute between the Master of Pembroke Hall and the Fellows, consequent on

PREFACE.                                    vii

their refusal to pass the grace for Harvey's degree of Master of Arts. There are eight letters in all from Harvey on this subject, of which the first, fourth, fifth, sixth, and eighth are to Dr. John Young, Master of Pembroke Hall ; the second and third are to Humphrey Tyndale, Fellow of Pembroke Hall ; and the seventh is to Harvey's own father. The dates run from 21st March to 1st November, 1573 ; and, curiously enough, the new style is used, the year beginning on 1st January instead of 25th March. These letters give us a very full and most interesting insight into every part of the life of a student at the University during the latter half of the sixteenth century.* The second series of letters, from page 159 to the end at page 184, relates almost entirely to Harvey's choice of the law as a profession, and to his attempts to be chosen Rhetoric Lecturer against John Duffield, of Peterhouse. The number of letters is seventeen, of which the first is to Dr. Young ; the second, fifth, eleventh, and twelfth are to Sir Thomas Smith, of Audley End, in Saffron Walden ; the third is to Jacob Harrison, of Christ's College ; the fourth and sixteenth are to Arthur Capel, father of the first Lord Capel ; the sixth is to Lady Smith, second wife of Sir Thomas ; the seventh to Luke Gilpin, of Trinity College, with his answer ; the eighth and tenth are to Richard Bird, Fellow of Trinity College, with his answer ; the ninth is to Richard Remington, Fellow of Peterhouse ; the thirteenth is *from* Richard Remington, inclosing one from John Duffield ; the fourteenth is to Humphrey Hales, of Pembroke Hall ; the fifteenth to a gentleman in the Queen's Court, named Wood ; and the seventeenth and last to Harvey's own brother Richard. These twenty-five letters com-

* Compare with these scenes of rebellion against the Master's authority the fourth chapter of Mr. Gosse's admirable monograph on the poet Gray, where we find the same college, just one hundred and sixty years later, going through a similar if not worse experience.

prise the first division of the volume. And now, turning back to page 55, we enter on the second, viz., that which contains the drafts of Harvey's poetical pieces and his correspondence with Edmund Spenser. It is in this portion of the book that the leaves have been hopelessly misplaced, and several cut out; and this is the more to be regretted, if we may judge the lost leaves to have been at least of value equal to those which fortunately remain. It is curious that Edmund Spenser's name does not occur, and that there is not the slightest allusion to him, in any of the twenty-five letters above mentioned, because the first half of the second division is (with the exception of some lines on George Gascoigne's death) almost made up of letters between him and Harvey. The first piece consists of Latin and English verses, composed by Harvey to the memory of Gascoigne, immediately on hearing of his death, which event took place at Stamford on 7th October, 1577. After the first leaf four folios have been cut out, but fortunately we are not left in the dark as to the matter formerly contained in them, by reason of a marginal note written on the preceding page, and evidently intended to form the heading of the first of the excised leaves. From it we gather that Harvey had written a poem on " A suttle and trechrous advantage (poetically imagined) taken at unawares by the 3 fatall sisters, to berive M. Gascoigne of his life." Pages 56-58 and 68-70 contain all that is left of this elegy, but these remaining lines are so full of quaint allusions to historical personages, and so vividly, by a few choice phrases and epithets, bring them before us, that our regret becomes all the keener that any of these verses should have been lost. We read of Chaucer, Gower, and Lydgate as " aunciente cuntrymen " of Gascoigne, whom he is sure to meet in the world of spirits; of Edward the Fourth's court fool, Scogan, " where he lawghes aloane "; of the laureate poet, Wolsey's malicious detractor, John Skelton, "that same madbraynd knave," who "knawes a dead horse boane"; of good Sir Thomas More, who "will deyne his cuntryman at first insight so curteously to interteyne"; of Henry Howard, "my lorde of Surrey"; and of Gascoigne's own "copesmates," Withipoll, Daniel, and Batt; and, last of all, Harvey tells Gascoigne he will be introduced to "Maddame Beatrice," and well content he is that they should meet, for few save "those twoe," Dante and her, do thrive there. The second part of this elegy, to be found at pages 68-70, is an outcry against the introduction of foreign matters, foreign dresses, and foreign phrases into English life; and Harvey tells Gascoigne the effect on his mind in Hades will be to make him produce "A newe Steele Glas, a second girding satyre"; but yet, after all, the world is the world, and will have its fling, and Gascoigne had better leave them to themselves, and enjoy his own pleasures above, for "where is huffcapp there is huff, and where is revell there is rowte; what marvell though a London stage with fooles be compasd rounde aboute." So ends "the epitaph to fit your tum."

On turning back to page 58, we find Harvey's rough drafts of a correspondence he held with Edmund Spenser in 1579. Whether these letters ever really passed between the friends, or whether they are the mere creatures of Harvey's imagination, it is now quite impossible to decide. It is certain they have never been printed before in their entirety, although here and there pieces of them are to be found among Harvey's published works. The first letter is from Harvey, written at Cambridge on the tenth day of an unnamed month in the summer of 1579. The subject of it is the

PREFACE.

Harvey's first attempts at English verse; or, as he himself terms them, his "Verlayes." The letter is written throughout in a bantering mood and a patronising manner, and describes the hawking of them for sale at Bartholomew and Stourbridge Fairs, in so vivid a way, that we are at once irresistibly reminded of the "Fortunes of Nigel," and the experience of Richard Moniplies' first perambulation of the streets of the southern metropolis: "What lack ye, gentlemen? I pray you will you see any fresh newe bookes? Looke, I beseeche you, for your loove, and buie for your moonye. Let me yet borrow on crackd groate of your purse for this same span new pamflett. Iwisse he is an University man that made it; and yea, highlye commendid unto me for a greate scholler. I marry, good Syr, as you saye so it should appeare in deede by his greate worke; by my faye, he hath taken verye soare paynes, beshrowe my hart else. What? will iij$^d$ fetche it? I will not steeke to bestowe so mutch in exhibition upon the University." He then proceeds to describe what will be the effect of their publication on his cotemporaries at Cambridge, and tells Spenser the only amends he can make him is to send him by the next carrier to Stourbridge Fair, "the clippings of your thris honorable mustachyoes and subboscoes to overshadow and to coover my blushinge." From these expressions we may, I think, fairly gather that, at this time (in 1579), Spenser could boast of a luxuriant growth of hair both on his upper lip as well as on his chin; and that Harvey, on the other hand, displayed a smooth and beardless face. For he goes on to say, "I hope in the heavens my chin will on day be so favorable and bountifull unto me . . . . as to minister superabundant matter of sufficient requitall to add a certayne most reverende venerable solemne grace to my Præsidentshipp when it cummes." He therefore draws up an obligation or humorous bond between Spenser and himself, by which he agrees to repay his friend one hundred and two hairs of his beard by fixed instalments. Finally, he begs him to take the greatest care that neither this letter, nor the obligation, fall into anyone's hands but his. "To be shorte," he says, "I would to God that all the ilfavorid copyes of my nowe prostituted devises were buried a great deale deeper in the centre of the erthe then the height and altitude of the middle region of the verye English Alpes amountes unto in the aier." Here we seem to have an allusion to Pendle Hill in co.. Lancaster, where Spenser's friends are supposed to have lived. The obligation, couched in Latin, follows immediately after the letter, and was intended to have been followed in turn by "The Condicion of this Obligation"; but, instead of it, Harvey breaks out into a yet more violent condemnation and pretended abuse of his friend for his unfriendly behaviour, and points out to him that had these same Verlayes or poems been composed in any other language than their own " vulgare tunge," they might have been something accounted of; but, as it is, "nothinge is reputid so contemptible and so basely and vilelye accountid of as whatsoever is taken for Inglishe." He would have Spenser understand how he has prejudiced his good name for ever in thrusting him on the stage to play Wilson's or Tarleton's part, that is, that of a mere low buffoon or mimic. Then, in a passage, which is full of interest for us, from its numerous allusions to the theatrical world of that date (A.D. 1579), he proceeds, "I suppose thou wilt go nigh hande shortleye to send my lorde of Lycesters or my lorde of Warwickes, [Lord] Vawsis, or my lord Ritches players, or sum other freshe starteupp comedanties unto me for sum newe devisid interlude, or sum maltconceivid comedye fitt for the theater or sum other painted stage, whereat thou and thy lively copesmates in London maye

lawghe ther mouthes and bellyes full for pence or twoepence.'
" And then, perhappes, not longe after, uppon newe occasion (an
God will), I must be M. Churchyard's and M. Elderton's successours tooe, and finally cronycled for on of the most notorious
ballat-makers and Christmas carollers in the tyme of her Maiesties
reigne." Here the letter breaks abruptly off, as though Harvey
had either got tired of the subject or had merely intended this
portion as a postscript to the former letter.

In his next letter, at page 70, Harvey begins by telling Spenser
that he is suddenly called upon to supply the "roome of a greater
Clarke, and play Il Segnor Filosofoes parte upon the Commencement stage"; in other words, he has to deliver the Philosophy Oration at the Commencement or Encænia, before all the
University, and the distinguished visitors who are wont to flock to
Cambridge at that time. Had he only the various qualities that
distinguished Socrates, Plato, Aristotle, Cicero, or Hortensius, he
might hope to succeed. Had he only the wise characteristics of
the Moderns; of his fellow-gownsman, M. Bovington; of Dr. Dee;
of the fine Cambridge barber, M. Williamson; of his Welsh land-
lady, nicknamed Mistresse Trusteme—truly, of the founder of
Caius College (afterwards immortalised by Shakespeare in the
"Merry Wives of Windsor"), Dr. Caius; or, lastly, of the Regius
Professor of Civil Law, Dr. Busbye, he would make shift to win
over the daye. But, failing all these, he begs his friend to lend him
" on tolerable oration, and twoe or three reasonable argumentes,"
as a set-off against his former unkindness in printing his verses
without leave. The rest of the letter, strangely enough, is from
this point onwards almost a reproduction of the former letter about
the bond, or obligation of a loan of his friend's beard, but ending at
last in a different manner and no precise date: " From my chamber
the daye after my victory."

After this Harvey introduces a supposed heading, by Spenser, to a fictitious publication without permission of two letters from Harvey, the first to Spenser himself, the second "to an old fantasticall miller, that made loove to a certayne mayde of his acquayntance," which letters, he says, "I fownde nowe perchaunce amongst a number of oulde scatterid papers." The first letter is a mere letter of thanks for some unspecified favour, but is subscribed—"He that is faste bownde unto the in more obligations then any marchante in Italy to any Jew there." This is an evident allusion to the play of "The Jew and Ptolome," then in acting at the Bull Theatre, the precursor of Shakespeare's "Merchant of Venice."\* It looks as though Spenser and Harvey had been to the Bull together—had there witnessed the play of "The Jewe," and had had it so impressed on their imaginations that they connect this comical bond of Spenser's loan of beard, and stuff their letters with allusions to it. The second epistle to the miller is not to be found *here*, but occurs on page 90 ; while, in its place, is a letter from Harvey to a Mr. Wood, of very great interest, as it gives us a clear insight to the method of study then pursued at Cambridge. He tells us that scholars are now active rather than contemplative philosophers, and have expelled Dunse and Thomas of Aquine, with the whole rabblement of schoolmen. Instead whereof they have applyed themselves to study modern French and Italian authors of late date, such as Philippe de Comines, Macchiavelli's works, and "I know not how many owtelandish boocreyes besides of the same stampe," of which he names more than a dozen. Aristotle's "Organon" he declares is nighhand as little read as Duns's "Quodlibet." Scholars are even cunning in certain gallant Turkish Discourses, too, as University men were wont to be in their

\* See *Gosson's School of Abuse*, entered at Stationers' Hall, 22 July, 1579.

Parva Logicalia, and Magna Moralia, and Physicalia of both sorts. Yet he says, for all that, they are still bound to apply to lawyers and courtiers, such as Wood, for daily fresh news, and a thousand both ordinary and extraordinary occurrents and accidents in the world. And he congratulates himself on possessing in Wood " sutch an odd frende in a corner, so honest an yuthe in the city, so trew a gallant in the courte, so towarde a lawier, and so witty a gentleman." This letter is undated. It occurs again in an abbreviated form on page 182. The next page contains a draft of part of the letter already described at pages 72 and 73. The next letter Harvey sends to Spenser, in answer to one received from him, and delivered to him " at myne hostisses by the fyersyde being faste heggid in rownde abowte on every side with a company of honest good fellowes, and at that tyme reasonable honeste quaffers." He read out the letter to them, and they decide to send a joint answer to it, the host himself acting as secretary. Spenser seems to have complained of the new world, in which they were living, as a false and treacherous world, compared with the times of antiquity. The discussion is very long, dry, and tedious, being principally carried on by two speakers, and the letter breaks off abruptly, without any definite conclusion, as though Harvey were tired of the subject. It is followed by a copy of a letter from William Fulke, Master of Pembroke Hall, to the Fellows, stating that the Earl of Leicester has made earnest request for the continuance of Harvey's Fellowship for one year ; that Fulke is not only willing but anxious to grant it, and begs their consent thereto. It is dated from Norwich, 22nd August, 1578. On page 89 is seemingly a draft of a title-page for an edition by Spenser of some of Harvey's works, with a dedication to Sir Edward Dyer, called here " owre only Inglishe poett." The works, five in number, are headed—1. The Verlayes ; 2. The Miller's Letter ; 3. The Dialogue ; 4. My Epistle to Immerito ; or, according to a further arrangement—1. The Verlayes ; 2. My Letter to Benevolo ; 3. The Schollers Loove ; 4. The Miller's Letter; and, 5. The Dialogue. The title-page is dated the 1st of August, 1580, and three out of the five works follow immediately after (with two exceptions— (1) a misplaced page of Harvey's letter at pages 82 to 88 ; and (2) seven leaves containing " Fine Notes for mie Rhetorique Discourses"). The Verlayes are now missing altogether from the volume, and the letter to Immerito or Benevolo is probably one of those above described. The Miller's letter leads the way, and is a comical " sonett " to his mistress, with an equally comical answer, " scribblid longe since by the autor (Harvey) for an honeste cuntrye mayde of his acquayntaunce," and dated " this present fryday, 1575." Next comes the Dialogue, or " A shorte poeticall discourse to my gentle masters the readers, conteyning a garden communication or dialogue in Cambridge, betwene Master G. H. and his cumpanye at a Midsumer Comencement, togither with certayne delicate sonnetts and epigrammes in Inglish verse of his makinge." The Dialogue is evidently imperfect between pages 96 and 97. On the latter page we find a draft of a copy of English hexameters, composed by Harvey, and published (as regards the latter half of them) in the well-known " Foure letters and certayne sonnetts, &c." After a few jottings down of fragments of letters and trifles comes the longest piece in the whole book, called " The Schollars Loove or Reconcilement of Contraryes." To this there are four headings ; in the first Harvey calls it " The very first English meeter that ever I made " ; in the second he gives " September, 1573," as the date of its composition ; and in the third he terms it " An owld new Cantion, ffatherid uppon Sir Thomas More, and supposid to be on of his first youthfull exercises." The gross absurdity of such an idea seems afterwards to have struck him, for he naïvely adds, " but never . . . . heard of in Sir Thomas More's dayes." The piece extends over forty-two pages, and in it the scholar first heaps every commendation on his love, and then loads her with the vilest abuse. The author criticises his composition in his fourth heading, as if he were somewhat (and justly) ashamed of it. He terms it " A few idle howers of a young Master of Art. A dayes correction woold sufficiently refine it. The meeter must be more regular, and the Inglish elocution more elegant, fine, and flowing, as in posthast. It was scribled at the first in a hurlewind of conceit."

Now we come to the strangest episode in the whole Letter-Book, where Harvey writes out at full length, with scarcely any attempt at concealment, the whole story of a young married nobleman making a dishonourable pursuit of his sister Mercy. It is true he does not give the nobleman's surname or title, but he mentions his Christian name of Phil, and talks of his aunt, my lady of W——; so that it would be quite possible to satisfy our curiosity by a slight search, if any good were to be gained by raking up old scandals. On page 152 we learn that this courtship took place during the winter of 1574-5, which, we are told on the next page, was a marvellous wet year at Christmas-tide, by reason of the rain and snow that fell together. The discovery of the correspondence by Gabriel himself seems to have put an end to the disgraceful affair; at least we hear no more of the matter after his letter to the young lord. The close of this story brings us to the second set of letters already described as part of the series of University epistles, from pages 1 to 54; and it extends from page 159 to the end of the book at page 184.

Before we close this preface, it may not be out of place to say a few words about the language used by Harvey. Being, on the one hand, the son of a ropemaker, he is a perfect master of all the vulgar slang and homely proverbs of his time ; and being, on the other hand, one of the most deeply-read men of his age, and having, evidently, a most retentive memory, he employs the most out of the-way terms and the most long-winded sentences to express his meaning. It would, I make no doubt, be easy to point to more than one hundred words (in this very volume) whose existence in the English language, for more than half a century later, has been hitherto quite unsuspected. To take but two instances ; he talks, in the year 1579, of the "intricate acumen of Aristotle," on page 71 ; but Dr. Murray's new Dictionary gives A.D. 1645 as the first appearance of "acumen" as a thoroughly English word. Again, in page 100, about the same date, he speaks of "hexameters, adonickes, and iambicks"; but Dr. Murray quotes no example of "adonickes" before A D. 1678, or a full hundred years later. In truth, Harvey's writings are a mine, out of which may be dug inexhaustible treasures to illustrate the growth and luxuriance of our mother tongue.

I have to express my most grateful thanks to Professor Hales of King's College for kindly reading through the whole of my transcript of the Letter-Book, and furnishing me with fourteen pages of invaluable notes, which have saved me from many blunders, and thrown light on many obscure words and allusions. Also I am deeply indebted to my friend and colleague, Dr. Garnett, for most useful hints and suggestions during the compilation of the Index.

## CORRIGENDA.

Page 56, line 20, *for* Dias *read* Bias, and *dele* note " c."
,, 63 ,, 3, *for* tarreeres *read* karreeres.
,, ,, ,, 15, *for* Paionius *read* Perionius.
,, ,, ,, 16, *for* Paionium *read* Perionium.
,, ,, ,, 29, *for* your shier *read* y$^e$ aier.
,, 71 ,, 25, *for* Duffington *read* Buffington.
,, 78 ,, 28, *for* Galatro *read* Galateo.
,, 98 ,, 4, *for* Galatro *read* Galateo.

# LETTER-BOOK

OF

# GABRIEL HARVEY.

# LETTER-BOOK

OF

# GABRIEL HARVEY.

To JOHN YOUNG,[a] MASTER OF PEMBROKE HALL, CAMBRIDGE.

Mi duti in most humble wise remembrid riht wurshipful, with most dutiful and harti thanks for the great frenship and special gud wil which you have alwais before and sinc mi cumming to the college shewid me: these shal be to crave leave of youer wurship that I mai bouldly and plainly declare that unto you, to mi furtheranc, which iniuriusly and spitefully hath bene offrid unto me to mi hi displeasure; nothing a whit douting but that your wisdum, uppon a reasnable vew of the matter, wil se a present redres of so wrongful delings. I am and have bene alwais veri loth to complain, if quieter mænes could have servid; but now in this extremiti, being in so slipperi a case as I am, I am enforcid to do as I do. And hereuppon I have the rather too chosen to write in Inglish, that I might the better and more fully open the matter as it standith. I beseech you pardun mi rudenes if I do otherwise then I shuld do; and blame their unkindnes that use me otherwise then they can or ouht to do. Your wurship is not ignorant, that

[a] John Young, S. T. B., was elected Master of Pembroke Hall on 12th July, 1567, resigned in 1578, on being made Bishop of Rochester. Died at Bromley 10th April, 1605.

this is mi year to commens master in[a]: and you know how ordinari a thing it is, that everi on at his time should inioie his degree, unles there be sum wunderful great let to the contrari. It is now wel ni a fortuite sinc mi grace amongst the rest was put up in the hous: when it cam to M. Osburn[b] he deniid it; and after him M. Nevel[c] said he wuld do as M. Osburn had dun; and at the last Sir Lawhern,[d] being abusid bi on or both of them, pretendid that he would give with none, unles al miht go out, but indeed intendid, as it fil out, to give against me. These thre and the rest of the fellows which were abrode were enowh, and too mani too, as it hath proved now, to stai me. Althouh in deed Sir Lawherns voie, if the vantage had bene presently takin, and I as circumspect to sê to mi self as other were hasti to set uppon me in M. Nuces,[e] and also in M. Osburns and M. Nevils iudgments too, as thei them selues have sine not steekid to tel me, did make for me, for he giving with me none had bene hindrid. Sine which time M. Nuce said unto me that if he had notid so mutch at the present, I shuld with out ani farther delai have had mi grace at that time, which if it might then have taken place, I can not se whi it miht not take place yit. The matter stud after this manner :

M. Nuce was requestid over niht to put up our graces the next morning: he made promis to do so. In the morning after praiers, as the manner litely is, we looked for it: but we had word that M. Nuce was not very wel at ease: and that he wuld dispatch the matter wel enoub before the congregation. I can not sai hou it fil out, but I am sure it fil out too il for me, that the bel began to ring to the congregation before M. Nuce began to rise out of his

[a] The word "in" has been erased and "of art" written over it by Harvey.

[b] . . . . Osborne, Fellow of Pembroke Hall.

[c] Thomas Nevil, Fellow of Pembroke Hall, Senior Proctor in 1580, Dean of Peterborough in 1591, Dean of Canterbury in 1597. He died 2 May, 1615.

[d] . . . . Lawherne, Fellow of Pembroke Hall.

[e] Thomas Nuce, *alias* Newce, Fellow of Pembroke Hall, Prebendary of Ely in 1584, and Vicar of Gazeley, co. Suffolk, where he was buried 9 Nov. 1617.

bed. In deed then he made as great speed as he wel miht and in
al the hast hiid him in to the hale. He put up mine, Sir Fars [a]
and S[r] Hoult's [b] graces togither for more spéed: thei easly were
graunted bi al, I wrongfully staiid bi M. Osburn and M. Nevil.
The reason being demaundid whi, thei saied there was now no time
to talk of it; and M. Nevil thouht that he needid not to render ani
reason: but M. Osburn saied he wuld shew the cause privately
ether to mi self or ani of mi frends. The case hanging thus doutfully, as you se, and I delaied thus unfrendly, as you have hard,
the Pensionars were also forthwith propoundid, nether were thei
so soon propoundid but thei were as soon grauntid. This was
after eiht a clock in the forenoon, and after nine (for there was a
sermon ad clerum first) was the congregation for the nomination.
Al the rest were nominatid. The congregation was continuid until
the afternoon. Thei had al their graces ad visitandum. Thus was
I kast behind twoo congregations, and yit not on good reason
alleagid whi. Mi freuds wunderid at it, and I had cause to be
greevid at it; considering how litle I had deservd it at ani of
there hands. But wilfulnes wil beare a suai, if it be not bridelid:
and thai that have the wors end of the staf shal be sure to be
wrung to the wors, if thai be not rescuid. Here your wurship
culd not choose but think me greatly to blame, if I shuld not have
endevorid mi self to assuage there coller, as far as I miht, and
reconcile them unto me, as wel as I culd: considering that the law
was now in there own hands, and miht had alreddi overcumd riht.
Therefore after the rest were nominatid, and before thai had
there graces ad visitandum, I besout M. Nevil that he wuld not
deale so hardly bi me in that whitch concernd me so greatly:
desiring him that he wuld not hinder me ani longer, but that I
miht be nominatid that dai. No intreati wuld serv: and this was
al that I culd get of him, that if I wuld cale the cumpani to

f. 3.

[a] Henry Farre, Fellow of Pembroke Hall, Junior Proctor in 1586.
[b] .... Hoult, M.A. of Pembroke Hall.

gither, I shuld se what he ment to do for me. I tould him that unles he wuld put me in sum hope, it wuld be but a trubble for them, and no pleasure to me. Wel, al wuld not suffice: M. Nevil is resolvid what to do: he hath set down his staf, and made his reckning: he wil sustain the displeasure of it, cum of it what wil. And yit we comminid so long togither, that there was no time at al left to talk with M. Osburn before the congregation. Al our hole talk concernid the causes of his staying me. Whitch seeing the matter staiith chefly uppon them, I wil truly report unto yur wurship, as thei were uniustly and scornfully laid in mi dish. I hope you wil have me excusid thouh I be trubblesum to your waihtier affaiers. He laid against me mi commun behaviur, that I was not familiar like a fellow, and that I did disdain everi mans cumpani. To this I made him anser that I was aferd les over mutch familiariti had mard al: and therefore where as I was wunt to be as familiar, and as sociable and as gud a fellow too, as ani, seing sum to be sumwhat far of, and other not to like so well of it, as it was ment, I was constrained to withdrawe mi self sumwhat the more, althouh not greatly nether, out of oftin and continual cumpani. Marri so, that at usual and convenient times, as after dinner and supper, at commenti fiers, yea and at other times too, if the lest occasion were offrid, I continuid as long as ani, and was as fellowli as the best. What thai cale sociable I know not: this I am suer, I never auoidid cumpani: I have bene merri in cumpani: I have bene ful hardly drawn out of cumpani.

f. 3 b. And as for disdaining of others, I wuld thai culd have found in their harts to have made that account of me that I have made of them, and bene as willing to accept of mi cumpani as I have bene reddi to seek theirs. And of troth this dare I avouch bouldly to your wurship, whitch sum others can testifi to be most tru, that I have not shoun mi self so surli towards mi inferiors as M. Nevil hath shoun him self disdainful towards his œquals and superiors too. For mi self, whitch in deed am an inch beneath him, as he ons made his vaunt; he can not deni it, he hath confest so mutch to me himself, that I passing bi him, and mouing mi cap, and speking unto him, he hath lookd awri an other wai, nether afording me a word, nor a cap: purposing, as I take it, to make of his inch a good long el, and to show a lusti contempt of so silli a frend. As for others, this is wel knoun, not to on, or two, but to al, or most of y$^e$ cumpani, yea and to sum of the Pensionars too. I am assured none wil nor can deni it, that both M. Nuce and M. Jackson[a] at a commenti fier in M. Jacksuns chamber this last year, did in gud ernest and in sum heat for his gud behaviur then, cale him Wil Summer.[b] In deed he was faint to put it up quietly bycaus he knew he had the wors end of the staf. At other times ful oft hath he bene at big words, and gud whot bickerings with sum other and with M. Nuce almost continually; til now of late that nu matter hath bene in bruing. And this is he that accuseth me of not being sociable, him self so sociable as you se, and wil needs bare other doun, not onli privately at home but communly abrode, amongst his cumpanions and others, that I am thus and thus insolent, when as he miht do wel to shew him self les insolent. I wuld he were but as wel bent to pluck out the beame out of his oun i as he is busi to spi a mote in an other man's i. But it is almost impossible that he shuld se him self, which is so mutch gevin to look uppon others. Nether do I speak this so mutch to accuse him, whome I use to speak wel of, and mutch better then he hath deservid, as it proovith now; as to excuse mi self whome he hath so uniustly and falsly chargid with arroganci and disdainfulnes. But it mai pleas your wurship to remember that excellent vers of y$^e$ famus poet: Quis tulerit Gracchos[c] de seditione querentes? for it were nedles for me to go about to point out his pride and

f. 4.

---

[a] .... Jackson, of Pembroke Hall.
[b] Will Sumner, *alias* Sommers, Court Jester to Henry VIII. and Edward VI. See Dr. Doran's *Court Fools*, pp. 134-144.
[c] Juvenal, Sat. ii. 24

lustines, whereas his oun gai gallant gaskins, his kut dublets, his staring hare, with sum other gudli and gentlemanlike ornaments, do and wil discri it sufficiently. And how sociablely he hath delt bi me, to deni me mi grace in the house, and to disgrace and slaunder me in the toun, I had rather leav it to your wisdums consideration to ludg then I in mine own cause be mine oun iudge.

II. The secund point that he stud uppon was, that I culd hardly find in mi hart to commend of ani man ; and that I have misliked those which bi commun consent and agrement of al have bene veri wel thout of for there lerning. I anserid, that I was alwais of this opinion that I thout it mi duti to speak wel of those that deservd wel ; and that he miht sundri times have harde me commend mani a on, but that it pleasd him now to wrangle with me. Whereuppon he tould me roundly, that that was mi fault indeed, and that 1 was evermore in mi extremites, ether in commending to mutch without reason, or dispraising to mutch without cause. To the whitch I gave him no other anser but this, that he ouht to give me and others as gud leave to use our iudgments in that behalf as I and others had givn him. Stil he harpid uppon that string, that I culd not aford ani a gud wurd. And I made him aunser, that this were great arroganci and extreme folli. Hereuppon we had farther descanting of them both, and he semid sumwhat pretely as he thout, but too flatly, and grosely indeed, to kast them both in mi teeth. In which discours, amongst other things, I hapned to kast out thus mutch, that althouh thei were both veri il, yit of the two it were better for a man to be thout arrogant then foolish. Whereuppon aris a wunderful accusation made bi M. Nevil in a gud great audienc—I mi self not being there—that sutch an on semid flatly to allow of arroganci, that he præferd it before folli, that he would not steak to sai bouldly he had rather be arrogant then foolish. And this was a great big matter, and a hie point forsooth, for them to beat there beds and whet there tungs about. So that your wurship mai here plainly se, as in a glas, how reddi thai ar to take the vantage, and how able thai ar to make sumwhat of nothing. Touching the veri accusation, I can sai no more for mi self but this, that I have commendid and discommendid men, as I thout thai deservid to be commendid or discommendid. And this wil I stand bi, and am able to proove it too, if need be, that I never haue discommendid ani of thos, that haue in the most and best mens iudgments bene thout commendable. In deed thei sai against me, that I on a time præferd M. Lewin[a] before M. Becon[b] in speaking ex tempore: which I can not deni but I miht have done, as mani others besides me have, and mai yit, for ani thing I know, do it stil, as wel as thai. I præfer Tulli before Cæsar in writing Latin: do I therefore disable or disalow Cæsar? And yit I do not so præfer Tulli nether but that Cæsar in sum on point, as in lepore, brevitate or the like mai pas and excel Tulli. I contend that M. Lewins extemporal faculti is better then M. Becons is, and yit I do not deni, and I have often said it too, that M. Becon is more sententius then M. Lewin. But thai wil sai, Comparisons ar odius: in deed, as it fals out, thai ar too odius. I am wel assured thai have gone about bi this comparrison to make me odius. How iustly I leav it to your wisdum to think of.

This I dare sai, and I can as easly proove it, that thai themselvs that wil now seme to mislike this so mutch in me, and therefore plague me thus cruelly for it, have usid mutch more liberti this wai then euer I did; and have made more odius comparrisons then euer I have, or purpose to make. I prai you let this on suffice in stead of a mani the like. We had talk not long sinc in M. Nuces chamber of M. Alin,[c] then and now senior proctor. I

[a] William Lewyn, Fellow of Christ College, Junior Proctor in 1568, Public Orator in 1570. Gabriel Harvey dedicated to him his *Ciceronianus* in 1577.
[b] John Becon, of co. Suffolk, Fellow of St. John's 1561, and Public Orator in 1571.
[c] Walter Allen, of Christ's College, Senior Proctor in 1572.

commendid him to be a riht gud schollar divers wais, and that he
was veri wel sene in the lattin and greek tung. Strait wais M.
Nevil was on mi top, and said he plaid the veri snudg then that
had so much lerning and shoud so litle: and that he did not wel
to hord it up, whereas he miht have so gud vse of it. Besides
sum other trim iests and iybes of his, as that he had givne us
mani a choke pare in his dais and the like. Here wuld I fain
know whither I bi M. Becon or Nevil bi M. Alin have delt more
reasnably, and spokin more curtuusly. But no marvel if Nevil
were sumwhat sharp set against M. Alin, when as I had givn him
so hih a commendation before: for within les then this fortniht he
tould me thus mutch to mi face, that he and sum others had dis-
praisd sum men the more bicaus I had praisd them, not so mutch
to disable them as to overwhart me, and that I miht not have
mine own wil. These ar ther sociable and fellouli delings. But I
pas mani sutch misusagis over les I shuld be over tædius to your
wurship.

III. M. Nevils third reason was, that I made but smal and liht
account of mi fellouship. That he gatherid uppon certain talk that
a litle before fil out betwixt him and me at the table. The talk
was this: he said he wuld not for a hundrith pounds but have
bene fellou of the hous: and I said merrely, that a hundrith pound
was a great deal of moni in a schollars purs. Wel, said he, it hath
savd me forti pound spending alreddi, and I wuld rather have
givn an hundrith pound then have gone beside it. I tould him
f. 5 b. plainly, that so had not I, and that I wuld rather have missid of it
then givn twenti pound in reddi munni for it: whi, saith he, it hath
bene so mutch wurth unto you alreddi: I easly grauntid him that,
but I tould him I culd have made better shift without a fellouship then I culd have made shift to pai so mutch for a fellouship.
I said also, that I made as great account of the bennefit as ethir
he or ani man els did, or coold. Marri so, that I wuld have
bene loth to have bouht it so dear as he spake of. Al this was

spokin obiter at the table, as mani things were beside : and suerly
I had thout it had bene as wel digestid as other things were.
But here was stuf gud plenti to furnish up a trim tragedi. I set
naut bi mi felloushíp : I contemn mi felloushíp: I make no count
of the bennefit : ani college in y<sup>e</sup> toun wuld have bene glad of
me : I miht have bene as wel sped in ani other place : I culd not
have wantid a felloushíp in ani place, no not in kings college, if
nead had bene. And mutch a doo had we with this I warrant
you : here was matter enouh for them to wurk uppon. So cunning ar thai to bru, and so reddi to broche debate, if a man feed
not there humor, nor sooth them up in there saiings. I tould M.
Nevil then, and said as mutch to M. Nuce sine, that I culd not
abide it in an other, and therefore did abhor it in mi self to be in-
grateful for a bennefit receivid. And that if thai bi hose means I
had obtainid this bennefit, and namely your wurship, had ever had
occasion to tri me, ye shuld have found me in al points both veri
mindful of it and riht thankful for it: finally that I did and do set
as great store bi mi felloushíp as he whoosoever made most of it.
M. Nevil was content to give me the hering, to take occasion of nu
matter, and fresh game : but when we came one to y<sup>e</sup> point to
know what he wuld do for me or against me, I was never a whit
the near, but rather farther to seek then at our first meting. For
in the end the gentleman was disposid to shew his wit, and pleasd
him self wunderfulli in blurting out sutch iests as he had gottin
togither for the nons : I wil do as men of best consciences do : I
dare make no promis : I wil not do ani thing for intreati : I wil do
as god shal put in mi hed : I minde to cum fre to y<sup>e</sup> place : And as
mani or mo in an other vain: You must lern to know your self: It
is dun for your amendment: In sum respects I coold finde in mi
hart to giv you an hundrith voicis, if I had them : In sum other
respects I must stai a while. You must put of the ould man, and
put on the nu man : You have the veni ; the game is to strive for
yit. And I cannot tel how mani mo of this stamp frivolus and

f. 6.

doggid iests. This is the wai that thes fellouli men have takin to
school and coole me, silli soul. And yit if I shuld report and re-
peat al, your wurship miht think me far wurs abusid.

IIII. It pleasd M. Nevil to use a forth reason also against me;
and that forsooth was this: that I was a great and continual patron
of paradoxis and a main defender of straung opinions, and that communly against Aristotle too. I tould him that for thos paradoxis,
as he termid them, thai were more of mine own making, but only
propoundid of me out of others to be discussid and riflid in disputation: and that I never yit tooke uppon me the defenc of ani
quæstion which I culd not shew with a wet fingar out of sum excellent late writer or other; and esspecially out of Melancthon,[a]
Ramus,[b] Valerius[c] and Foxius,[d] fower wurthi men of famus memori·
And as for Aristotle, that I have alreddi both in private talk often,
and in publick disputation almost usually commendid him as hihly
as I wel culd and purposid hereafter to commend him more, as
occasion shuld serv and the matter bare: marri not so, that I can
strait wai take it for scripture what soever he hath givn his wurd
for. Mi chefist propositions against Aristotles philosophi have
bene thes, or the like: Mundus non est æternus: Cœlum non est
quintæ naturæ: Cœlum non est animatum: Nihil est $\phi\upsilon\sigma\iota\kappa\hat{\omega}\varsigma$
infinitum potentia: Virtus non est in nostra potestate. Whereof
the first, the secund, the third, and the fift too after a sort, ar al
stoutly and mihtely avouchid of al, or almost al thos fower notable
and famus writers. In deed, the forth as far as I could yit lern,
is onli defendid of Ramus: marri so, that I for mi smal scil think
he is able to satisfi ani reasnable natural philosopher in that point.
If thes or the like be so greuus and hainus opinions as mai law-
fulli debar a man of his degre, what meen we to account the

[a] Philip Melanchthon, German Reformer, 1497-1560.
[b] Peter Ramus, French Philosopher, 1515-1572.
[c] Cornelius Valerius, Professor at Louvain, 1512-1578.
[d] Sebastianus Foxius Morzillus, Tutor to Don Carlos, 1528-1548.

tutors and fautors of them so wurthi and passing men? Unles we wil onli admit of that to be done whitch we our selvs ouli have dun, in philosophical disputations to give popular and plausible theams, de nobilitate, de amore, de gloria, de liberalitate, and a few the like, more fit for schollars declamations to diseurs uppon then semli for masters problems to dispute uppon: and more gudli and famus for the show then ether convenient for the time, or meet for the place, or profitable for the persons. Sutch matters have bene thurrouly canvissid long ago: and everi on that can do ani thing is able to write hole volumes of them, and make glorius shows with them. I cannot tel, but me thinks it were more fruteful for us and commodius for our auditors to handle sum sad and witti controversi. But I never found ani fault with them for duelling in there own stale quæstions. I wuld it miht have pleasd them as litle to envi me for mi nu fresh paradoxis. But thai fare that this singulariti in philosophi is like to grow to a shrode matter, if I one convert mi studdi to diuiniti. Belike thai are aferd les I shuld proove sum noble heretick like Arrius and Pelagius: and so disturb and disquiet the Church as I now do the Chappel. Wel, I hope thai shal have no great caus as long as I busi mi self in no other matters then I do, and if I keap mi self as upriht in diuiniti as thes men have dun whos opinions I have desirid to be thurrouly siftid I dout not but I shal do wel enoub, althouh not fully so wel as thai. And yit, bycaus thai wil nedes have me do as thai do and sai as thai sai, I care not greatly if I now take forth a nu lessun, and begin to do so in deed: and I wil lock Melancthon and Ramus up in mi studdi, and bring Osorius[a] and Omphalius[b] in to the chappel. But enouh of this, and to mutch too, but that I am drawn and drivn unto it violentli. I have in most humble manner to desier you, riht wurshipful, to bare with mi over great simpliciti

f. 7 b.

[a] Hieronymus Osorius, Bishop of Silves in Algarve, Professor at Coimbra, 1506-1580.
[b] Jacob Omphalius, Professor at Cologne, died in 1570.

and bouldnes in opening mi case unto you: and you se how the matter goith with me. I am inforcid rather to bungle up a pelting bistori then to write a set epistle. Your wurship hath harde what forcible and waiti reasons M. Nevil hath usid against me; besides certain glauncis at two or thre od things mo; (1) as at mi sitting in the chappel in the reading of my oration, whereas the use, thai sai, hath bene to kneel, and yit now as mani almost use to sit as kneel, and I think suerly everi man mai do as he himself felith most for his case : (2) and esspecialli at the putting on of mi hat at problem, which I did not twelmunth nethir. Indeed not long after mi first cumming I must needs, and do willingly confes, I having bene veri sore sick, and at the self same time waring a charcher, feeling mi hed sumwhat could (for it was in the deadist time of winter), and, faring lest I shuld take could and kast mi self in to farther sicknes, did præsume so mutch of other mens pacienc as to put on mi hat; and no man did onc seem to note it, or to think ani thing in it, that I could heer of. And a while afterward I, having thus bi reason of sicknes usid mi self to a hat and a karcher, culd not abide ani while to be barehed, without sum præsent hed ache: and therefore twise or thrise that winter and not above, uppon the cruellist could nihts, did after the same manner. No man al this while for ouht that I culd lern did onc sai black was mine i for it. The next winter, uppon a sharp frosti niht or two, being not greatly wel nethir, I was so hardi as to do as mutch; and so was M. Nevil him self too onc, by his leav, being then but batchelur as wel as I. The secund time M. Nuce veri frendly, I thank him, gave me this caveat in mine are, that it was not the custum that batchelurs shuld be coverid, and that it was offensive unto certain of the cumpani.

f. 7 b. I aunserid him as louly, I did not know so mutch; and that I wuld not do so ani more; nethir in deed did I so ani more sine. But Insipientis est dicere non putaram: and yit now am I forcid onc again to it, and cannot choose but cri out, non putaram:

Suerly it never once cam in to mi mind to imadgin that it wuld ever have cum to ani sutch ishu. If it had, I percaiv a great inconvenienc had bene better then the breach of ani custum. But it was mi il luck to bi wit at the dearist hand. And now your wurship hath, as near as I culd, harde al, or wel ni al the talk, that passid betwene M. Nevil and me at that time and how I did then unto him, and do now unto you aunser in mi own behalf. Bethat we had on this manner spent gud part of the afternoon (for we had now bene at it from immediatly after dinnar til thre a clock) the bel rang to the congregation. The other got there graces ad visitandum, as I said before; I was left at home ad miserandum as it hath proovd since.

Notwithstanding, as soone as I miht conveniently (for it stud me in hand to bestur me) I went also in like manner unto M. Osburn, and requestid him most ernestly that he wuld not kepe me back ani lenger, considering what a foul shame and foil it had alreddi bene unto me. I made him this lavish offer, whitch then I promissid, and now purpose duly and truly to perform, that if I had ani wais dun amis, or in ani point offendid ether him or M. Nevil, or ani other, that I wuld bend, and endevur mi self to the uttermost of mi power both hereafter to redres and amend it, and præsently to make ani reasnable satisfaction for it. This so moovid M. Osburn at the instant, that he semid hereuppon to be wel pacifiid: and indede I was more than half perstadid that he wuld do for me. Onli this he said, and he spake it veri mildly, that before I had talkd more with the rest and namely with M. Nevil, he miht make no prommis: and yit truly mi thout he did almost make me a pees of a prommis.

This made wel for me; I began now to be in a farther hope: and therefore I sout mi opportuniti to talk with M. Nevil a fresh, to tri if I culd find him ani whit more tractable.

M. Nevil was M. Nevil stil, the veri self same man that I left him, nether to be allurid bi prommissis, nor persuadid bi wurds,

f. 8.

nor wun bi intreati nor moovid bi *greef*.[a] In so mutch that him
self spake thus curragiusly of him self, that if the Emperur shuld
write his letters unto him in mi hehalf, that he wuld not relent: a
wurthi pattern of a noble stummock. And now he was thurrouly
furnisshid with a cumpani of gud lusti cuts and stateli scofs, and
amongst a pack of them he brake out into this iolli and brave
iybe: We have you at the suords point: we wil hould ye thare
whilst we have ye thare, les if you get ons within the half swurd
you chaunc to give us the lamskin. And straitely after (for I
let him alone, I sae him so lustely disposid); A bird in the hand is
surist. So that now he was altogither set on his merri pinnes, and
walkd on his stateli pantocles; setting al at nauht that I culd
sai unto him. And yit I am suer I wooid him so as mani a gud
man never did his wife: and I am suer he reiectid me so as few
bonist masters have dun there servants. To conclude, I talkid
and walkid so long with him, that I was so weri I culd scarce
stand, and so dri that I culd hardly speak. Al was nauht wurth:
onli he gave me this flim flam, that I had persuadid him sumwhat,
and as mutch as a man miht persuade him: marri so that he culd
not, nor wuld not as yit condescend ani thing to mi petition. And
forsooth now he had gotten a gud nu argument of singulariti, and
that was this: that I wuld needs in al hast be a studdiing in Christmas, when other were a plaiing, and was then whottist at mi book
when the rest were hardist at their cards. Here althouh there was
little need of excuse, yit, to satisfie his mind and abate his heat,
I said that I had veri urgent busines this last Christmas, more
then everi man knew of, or els I had bene man like enoub to have
dun as other did. He tould me again, na, I had dun so everi
Christmas sins I cam to the house. Wel, there was no shift of it,
M. Nevil wil and must needs have his own wurds: and thus he
and his fellows seek to pick quarrels with me, and to make huge
mountains of smal low molhils. When I had reasenid the matter

[a] Against the word *greef* is written in the margin "pitti."

up and doun mi belli ful, and my hed ful toc, I praid him most hartely, and that with mi cap in mi hand, that he wuld not suffer me to go in as great suspens as I cam: and, unles he thout too vilely and abiectly of me, that he culd not altogither set me and mi wurds at nauht, but wuld at the last put me in sum better hope. Tush, thes ar but wurds, nothing wil suffice, there is no remmedi; M. Nevil is flinti, and is M. Nevil stil; I must needes abide the brunt of his displeasure; what is a gentleman but his pleasure? And so I partid from him as wise as I cam. After this I tooke mi time to intreate M. Osburn anu: and I found him not so quiet and calme before, but I felt him as whot and boisterus, or rather pevish, and wayward now. He revilid me to mi teeth: and tould me veri flatly that he was bewitchid before, yea, and that it was mi flatteri and serviliti (for so it pleasd him now to term it) that bewitchid him: and that for an unreasnable desire of the degre I spake that whitch I never ment, and did I carid not what. What shuld a man doo, or sai, in so desperate a case? Wel, I tould him quietly, that he delt veri rouhly and uneurtuusly by me, to charg me with that which he knew not: and to interprit that so il which was dun and ment so wel: and that now I parsaivid plainly nothing culd content them; before I was arrogant and now I am servile. And he said again as fersly as before, that I went ab extremo ad extremum sine medio; so il succes had mi gentle behaviur towards them. The conclusion was this, that if the fellous were calid togither he wuld do for me as he thouht best. Thus was I doggid and dodgid on everi side; and so that in your wurships absenc I sae litle hope of amendment, sum of them being so far in with M. Nuce, as I knew. And yit in this meane while I once besouht M. Nuce also; that he wuld stand mi frend in so great an extremiti: althouh in deed I culd not be ignorant that M. Osburn and M. Nevil, mi beavi masters, had now handelid the matter wel enoub with him, and had, as we sai, forestalid the market. Notwithstanding, suerly I must needs sai, I

f. 9.

found him reasnable and frendly: but so that he culd not stur in the matter til there reasons were examinid. Whereuppon we began to reckin up sum of them: and he thouht that thos causis of being sociable, and of commending and discommending men, were no better then trifling and childish causis; and that litle better of setting so lite bi mi fellouship. We had longist and largist discoursis about mi philosophi quæstions: and he tould me that he ment not to discurrage other from doing the like; onli I seemid to be givin over mutch to nu opinions in givin so communly sutch questions. We touchid also thos other points that M. Nevil stud uppon before: but more particularly and fully certain iars that had faln out betuixt M. Osburn and me, and M. Nevil and me, long ago: thai them selvs, not I, being the beginners and continuers of them. Thes he said in deed were private quarrels and privately had with private men, and therefore to have bene forgivn and forgottin: but that it was likeli that thai went about of private grudgis to make them commun causis, and therefore desirid that the hole matter miht be harde, and iudg of bi the fellous. And that he misdeemid thai had sum sutch thing in there hed to go about to proove me contentiosum, as indeed it hath proovid sins.

For against the next morning was there an other congregation calid. Whereuppon in the morning I desirid M. Nuce to moove mi grace unto the fellous anu: He did so. M. Osburn did now as he did in y$^e$ parlur before: he being urgid to shew the cause, usid first thes veri wurds towards me: S$^r$ Harvie you have bene veri surli and too surli heretofore: and therefore if I shuld addere autoritatem, I think I shuld ignem igni addere. In the mean while M. Nevil askith leav of M. Nuce that he miht depart, alleaging his other busines, and saiing that he wuld leav M. Osburn to follow the matter for this time. M. Osburn went on, and began in deed to lai contentiusnes to mi charg. Whi? Bycaus I had bene at wurds with him, with M. Nevil, and I cannot tel with home besides;

nor he nethir, if he wil speak no more, but that he knowith and thinkith. And to sai troth, I suppose verily, a litle breach betuixt thes twoo and me was the tru and onli caus of al thes sturs.

Hinc mihi prima mali labes, hinc semper Ulisses
Criminibus terrere novis, hinc spargere voces
In vulgum ambiguas et quærere conscius arma,
Nec requievit enim, donec Chalcante ministro.[a]

Wel, I tould M. Osburn that thos matters were or shuld have bene dead and buriid long ago: And, as for his contentiusness, that I culd easly enoub clear mi self of it; considering that the plaintifs themselvs plaid the cheefist part, and bore the greatist stroke in it. Notwithstanding if he or ani other culd proove that bi me, whitch nethir he nor ani other shal ever proove bi me, that there was an ordinari deeling, præscribid bi our statuts for it, and that he culd not, nor ouht not in ani sutch respect to deni me mi grace. I trow I shuld first have bene admonnisshid privately of it, and not openly have takin ani iniuri for it. And this statute I chargid him with al. Bi that time we had talkid thus mutch too and fro, the bel range to the Congregation: and so we brake up; I thus delaiid and deludid, as you have härd. S$^r$ Far and S$^r$ Hoult were præsently admittid, and ar now Masters of Art, and I not as yit gottin mi grace in the hous, to mi great defamation in the town and hous. And now tales run up and down the town that S$^r$ Harvi of Pembrook Hale hath dun thus and thus, abusid thes men, and thes men, behavid himself after this manner and this manner and thereuppon is staid in the hous: in so mutch that thai that knew me not can not choose but think veri il of me, and thai that knew me too (unles it be sum of mi nearist acquaintanc) mai now begin to dout of me. In deed M. Thomas Nevil, a veri frend of mine at the pinch, I thank him for it, hath dun mi arrand, and bläsd mi arms abrode, and hath not offerid so mutch wrong and iniuri at home, but he hath utterid muteh more malice and spite in other

f. 10.

[a] Verg. Æn. ii. 97-100.

placis: so that I have not yit bene so courst and gald in our own hous as I am like hereafter to be pincht and nipt in the regent hous. Matters ar made wurs and wurs in the telling: and now forsooth mi not being sociable, arguith great arroganci; mi reprehending of others, arguith great arroganci; mi defending of paradoxis, arguith great arroganci; and, to be short, everi thing, mi going, mi speaking, mi reading, mi behaviur arguith great and intolerable arroganci. Nothing so commun and rife in everi mans mouth as sutch a batchelurs hautines, insolenci, stoutnes, pride, contentiusnes, and I can not tel what els: besides suteh ripping up of ould matters, and sutch boulting and sifting of mi matters as I suppose there have sildum been seen the like; I am veri suer I never felt the like. Al this, and more then al this too, if more mai be, sprung of gud M. Nevil, whitch uppon no other occasion but stummock, and an ould grudg, hinc illæ lachrymæ, whatsoever he prætends otherwise, hath now not so litle as a fortniht openly and before not so litle as a munth prively plaid his part and wrouht his feat on this manner: besides his facing and outfacing of me at y$^e$ table, in the court and in everi place els. So that I suppose verily never bare was so baitid at the stake with bandogs and masties as sum of them and namely gud M. Nevil, a gud benefactur of mine, hath baitid and tuslid and chasid me. Whitther this be procurare malum socio, to doo thus at home and abroade and in eviri cumpani sine discretione, I leav it to your wisdum to considder. Truly I cannot scil what is procurare malum socio, or iniuriam inferre socio, nae I know not what is petere iugulum socii if this be not. Suer I am it is far enoub from that, Inter bonos bene agier, and, Homo bomini Deus. I am afraid it smels to mutch of the contrari, Homo bomini lupus; and if that be ani whit more, socius socio. Wel, I douht not but I shal finde your wurship, as I have dun alwais, veri favorable and gud unto me in this ruli and miserable case. You se how greatly it concerns me: and how unkindly, nae how cruelly and fersely, I am delt with al. Nethir

can I looke for ani thing els but passing extremiti, and the
wurst thai can doo at there hands. Therefore I have most
humbely and hartely to beseech you, riht wurshipful, that you for
your wisdum wil take sum sutch order out of hand that I mai
præsently get mi grace in the hous. There is now no other wai,
thai have handelid the matter so clarkly, and armid them selvs
so strongely. So gracius ar thai that have mi grace in there
hands: and so ungracius am I, that am to seek mi grace at
sutch men's hands. Whereas almost al the toun ar gracid yea
and admittid too alreddi : and I, uules I have better luck then I
looke for, am as suer to have sumwhat a doo an other while in
the town. But thes men, for ani thing I can see, wil never
relent of themselvs, but bi your wurship's means and commandi-
ment ; and suerly I am afraid thai have vowid so mutch, in so
mutch that M. Nuce, whome thai have, as is most likeli, made
privi to al there doings, gave me this watchwurd in his own
chamber, that it miht be thai ment to make me weri of the hous,
and so caus me to commens in sum other hous. So mihtely and
valiantly thai purpose yit to set uppon me. But I trust, as it hath
likid your wurship to bestow so great a bennefit uppon me, in
choosing me fellow, so it mai pleas you to bestow as great a
bennefit uppon me in keeping me in mi felloushíp stil ; for alas
what ioi can I possibely have to continu in mi fellouship, mi
juniors being masters, as thai ar, and I but batchelur, as I am yit
like to be ; and thos other triumphing and insulting uppon me as it
pleasis them ? For God's sake wai mi caus, what it is, and considder mi case how it standith ; and as soon as you mai conveniently rid me out of sum of this greef. I am occasionid to go
abroad about Whitsuntide (and in deed it is to Sir Thomas
Smyths[a] hous in the cuntri, as I was certifiid) if it were possible

[a] Sir Thomas Smith (1514-1577) of Audley End, in Saffron Walden, a near neigh-
bour and patron of Harvey's family, Dean of Carlisle, Ambassador to France, &c.
See his Autobiography in Sloane MS. 325.

before that time to be admittid: and unles I be so (and yit there is a Gaubert[a] in the wai that wil plai his part too, as Sir Flower[b] tould me this verri morning) there must be two or thre several congregations purposely and only for me. And so muteh the harder it is like to go with me when it cums one that I must run thorouh the pikes. Therefore I wuld it miht like your wurship to take this order and I beseech you most humbely do so, that thai delai and delude me no lenger, but graunt me mi grace forthwith: and if so be there be ani thing wherein thai can sai I have offendid against ani on statute I shall be reddi ani time hereafter to stand to the trial of it with them, ether before your wurship, or the Cumpani: and I shalbe contentid to abide du punishment therefore, according to the wil and discretion ether of your wurship, or the Cumpani. But I wil leave the hole matter to your wisdums reasnable consideration: for I know I have bene too tædius unto you. Wherein I have most ernestly to request your wurship to pardun me, as also in mi over flat and homeli kind of writing.

But I culd not possibely ani other wai expres the matter as it is: nethir am I able ani wai in deed to expres it sufficiently. I trust your wurship wil bare with me. And here I rest to be trubblesum unto you, commending you in mi praiers unto God, whos you ar.

From Pembrook hal this xxi. of March. A. 1573.

## To Humphrey Tyndale,[c] Fellow of Pembroke.

Salutem plurimam. Master Tendal, I am sorie I am so litle gratius in Pembrook hal that I cannot yit, after so long and great a doo, obtain mi grace. I persaive our Master hath bene sumwhat ernest and whot in mi behalf: but I persaive also M. Osburn

[a] .... Gaubert, Pensionar of Pembroke Hall.
[b] .... Flower, Fellow of Pembroke Hall.
[c] Humphrey Tyndale, Fellow of Pembroke Hall, President of Queens' College in 1579, and Dean of Ely in 1591. He died in 1614.

and M. Nevil wil be Quarter Masters. And as for Sir Flower, cf a like he is no better then Sir Perfidus, and a veri flower in deed; and so he shal wel understand if I be ons Master. What were best to be dun in so desperat a case I se not. Ride yit to London mi self I can not. Differ the time ani longer I ouht not. Overlode mi frends with mi burden I dare not. And what other wai I shuld take I know not. You counsel me to take counsel of mi pillow; but I am aferd al the pillow counsel in Walden[a] is scarc able to counsel to so hard a case. To be plaine, I like your good Cambridg counsel best, that you take the paines to make a iorni over to London to our Master, and there to talk with him at larg in the matter. And yit I wuld be veri loth, if it miht be otherwise, to be so trubblesum unto you. But I prai you bare with me, good M. Tendal, if I make too bould with mi frends in this extremiti. If I mai ani wais stand you in the like stead, or at ani time help you with the like counsel, be you wel assurid of it, I wil be as reddi to pleasure you as you ar willing to ride for me. Few wurds shal suffice amongst frends: and I am now constrainid to be short. Wel, if you do voutsafe to ride to Lundon, I beseech you handle the matter cunningly with our Master, and use sutch means that your iorni mai take effect. You know how easely our Master mai coniure our two yung masters Flower and Lawhern. And there be other wais too, I think, to make up the matter, if need be. M. Brown[b] miht be wun before he cum to Cambridge, and before he meddle ani thing in the matter. Afterward ther wil be no deling with him, if he be ons set against me, and I had rather have ten Osburns then on Brown against me. I beseech you, good M. Tendal, use your own discretion with our Master and others: for I tel you tru I mi self was never more to seek then I am now. Only thus mutch you mai certifi our Master,

[a] Saffron Walden in Essex, Harvey's birthplace and residence.
[d] Lancelot Brown, Physician, Fellow of Pembroke Hall. See Munk, *Roll of the Royal College of Physicians of London*, vol. i. p. 86.

f. 12 b.  whitch you yourself know too, as wel as I, that what soever is dun is dun uppon spite and an ould grudg; that nothing culd have bene reprochful and infamus unto me; that thei can not convict me of ani sutch crime as miht iustly deserve ani sutch punnishment; that you have known mi mind, how desirous I have alwais bene of quietnes; that thei seek al occasions of quarreling; and other the like things, whitch you know to be veri tru, and mai honestly report. But I wil commit al sutch matters to your own consideration. And as for mi cumming to Cambridg, althouh I think it better for mi harts ease to continu at Walden stil, yit I wil do as you wil me, and I wil se Pembrook hal, God willing, ere it be long. In the meane while I commit you to the protection of God. In hast.

## To the Same.

Salutem plurimam. Master Tendal, you must impute it to the chaung of the wether that Wale[a] cummith no sooner to Cambridg. I hope mi long lingering matter is ere now quietly dispatch. I prai God it be so. But, how so ever the world goith, with me or against me, I prai you send your letter bi Wale when you think it best for me to be at home and whi. And I prai you also let me understand a part how your London triacle[b] hath wrouht against your Cambridg poisun. I am aferd the triacle is scare so mihti and effectual as the poisun is daungerus and deadli. And yit bicaus I have litle or no scil in this kind of physick mi self, I hope the best, and like it so mutch the better bycaus it is minnistrid bi an

---

[a] .... Wale. Apparently the ordinary carrier from Saffron Walden to Cambridge.

[b] Triacle. Not the modern treacle, but the old sovereign remedy against poison. See *Early English Text Society,* vol. 67, pp. 37, 38.

ould and tried physician. And as smal cunning as I have that wai mi self, I persaivid this before mi cumming to Walden, that an easi purgation wuld ease them but a litle, and therefore that sum other extreme medecine was to be souht for sutch a maladi, for main evils you know must have main remmedies.

Now if nether strong triacle can take effect, nor gentle purgations do ani good, I mai rather dispaier of curing the disseuse then hope for better phisick. Unles there be sum pretti feat wai to let them blud and so to rid them of that corrupt and dead blud whitch now hath the cours in ther vennemus boddies. And this must cum too from a more expert and scilful surgeant then I mi self am, for unles he be suer aforehand that he strike the riht vain al his hole surgeri mai hap to be in vain. I tel you tru, M. Tendal, there is so muteh the les hope ether in phisick or surgeri for that the disseasid persons ar agents, not patients: whereas phisicians and surgeans, for ouht that ever I culd heare, take only uppon them to beale there patients. But nu disseassis must have nu phisick: and unles sum busi agents of Cambridg be handsumly and houlsumly curid, on pore patient of Walden is like to be past all cure.

f. 13.

You know he hath lit uppon sutch perillus surgeans, and hath so daungerusly and unhappely bene let blud, than if he had bene ani whit fainthartid he had sundid and sundid long ere this. But I suppose he hath sum gud freuds in Cambridg that wuld gladly do him gud: and I know he hath sum fast frends in Cambridg that have alreddi dun him gud: and I hope he hath sum big frends in Cambridg that shalbe able to do him gud: and I trust he shal find thos leachis in Cambridg that can for there scil and wil for there kindnes stint the blud and ease the patient. And therefore I have wild him to be on good cheare, and tarri a while, til he heares from sum on of them: bidding him not to dout but thos il disseassid surgeans of Cambridg shal find leachchraft gud enouh amongst the other gud hail surgeans of Cambridg. So that now I dare sai he hopes for no les: but looks everi hower to be healid. And this is the worst that I can wish him, I prai God he be alreddi or præsently mai be healid.

God be with you and him, good M. Tendal, and give him now and him and you ever hereafter a præsent præservative against al sutch sores. From Walden, this xiii. of April.

## To John Young, Master of Pembroke Hall.

Mi duti in most humble sort remembrid, riht wurshipful, with veri harti and esspecial thanks for your ernest and often letters in mi behalf: thes shalbe to give yow to understand that, notwithstanding al your labor in the matter, whitch I had thouht miht have prævailid with the parties in a more unlikeli matter, mi grace hath no other succes then it had at the first, and the parties are as far, or farther of, for ouht that I se, then ever thai were. So that, whereas before I had sum occasion to be a little greevid, that mi grace had first so malitiusly bene deniid, and then mi sute so slihly and disdainfully reiectid, I have now farther and far iuster caus to be more thurrouly vexid that your wurships letters also shuld so lustely be contemnid, and your laboring in the matter so litle regardid; esspecially considering your goodnes in this point hath bene a great deale greater towards me then I could wel looke for, and fully as great as I culd possibely wish or desier. I can not but wunder that men can take sutch a pleasure in displeasuring others, and I cannot but se, that men to uphould there own iolliti care nether for frend nor fo, superior nor inferior, on nor other. I was mi self in the cuntri at mi fathers when as your letters cam to Cambridg and therefore cannot sai of mi self how and after what sort matters were handelid and debatid. Notwithstanding that whitch was reportid unto me bi letters, being abroade and whitch I have lernid mi self sinc mi cumming home, I have thouht

good to let your wurship understand of: that you reasenably and indifferently mai iudg of it. Uppon the receit of your first letters to M. Nuce, the next dai in the morning, being the iiii. of April, as I was informid, mi grace was propoundid a nu bi M. Nuce in the chappel: but so propoundid, that for mi part I could have cunnid him greater thank if he had takin les paines, and should have thouht better of him then I doo, if he had said les then he did: and in deede as gud never a whit, as never the better, for so soone as he had given the cumpani to understand that your wurship had writ unto him in mi behalf: to make the matter gud, he tould them bi and bi with out ani farther circumlocutions, that you had so writ unto him, that, whereas before he had bene sumwhat ernest to further me, he wuld now be veri indifferent only. A veri proper kind of præamble to make them benevoles whome he knew wel enoub of them selvs to be malevoli: I marvel what better wai his mastership culd have takin in a hole nihts studdi bi him self and a dais conferenc with his freuds to chaung and turn there heat into fier, and there choller into coles. A man wuld have præsupposid that the Masters letters to his præsident miht have dun somewhat with his præsident, and suerly I wuld have thouht that M. Doctor Yungs letters to M. Nuce shuld have made him better, not wurs. But sutch is y$^e$ crookid disposition of sum, that that marith al with them whitch shuld make al with them: as there is matter of poison to the spider where wuld be matter of honi to the bee. When M. Nuce had finnishid his frendli prœme, and it cam to M. Osburns cours to give his voic, he said plainly that, althouh you miht do muteh with him, notwithstanding he wuld be brouht to nothing bi threatning and forc, but bi reasun. As if your wurship had delt otherwise with them then bi reasun. And being askid, according to your letter, the caus of his denial, he alleagid his ould counterfet causis, arroganci and contention. Adding thereunto that bicaus thei had bene marvelusly extenuatid  f. 14 b.
bi sum of our hous in the toun, he purposid to stand to the trial

of them : meaning belike to set a good brasin face on the matter, and to make a great monsterus milpost of his litle pudding prick. After him followid M. Nevil, who said in like manner that your letter and wurd shuld prævail mutch with him in other matters, but in this (using as it were an epitome of thos iolli curragius vaunts that he had made to me before) he wuld nether be fearid bi wurds, nor yit allurid bi wurds: making no other account, as it seemith, of your letters then of bare nakid wurds, and purposing to let his adhærents understand how litle he did æsteme of ani letters. Reasuns he usid none against me, but only avouchid and maintainid M. Osburns. At the last it came to the two yunger ons, Sir Flower and Sir Lawhern, who had beforehand, I warrant you, bene sufficiently tauht there lesson of the two elder ons: and therefore tooke it uppon them, like two greater ons then a man wuld have takin Sir Flower and Sir Lawhern for, for the on contrari to prommis, the other contrari to his first prætenc, both contrari to al good nature, being not able to render ani reasun whi, uppon a meere cockishnes and the procurement of others, in mi absenc flatly deniid me. And, that your wurship mai the better conceive there hole dealing and dubling with me, I wil shew you in a few wurds what a pretti part on of $y^e$ yung ons plaid with me. The next dai after his return from Lundon, I tould him breefly how the matter went with me: and therefore desirid him to mak me a prommis of his voie. He made me aunser that there was no caus whi I shuld dout of him: marri yit for so mutch as the case stud, as it did, he purposd not to make ani prommis too or fro. I, seing the wind in that doore and knowing that he had line with M. Nevil that niht, left him thus for two or thre dais.

f. 15.  On Ester even in the morning he cummith to me to mi studdi of his own accord: and at the veri first he tellith me I miht think veri ill of him for that he gave me so sleeveles an aunser the other dai as he did. I tel him again, for that he miht do as he saw best

caus himself, and that his voie was his own to bestow it as he
thouht good, not I. . Wel, saith he, I am now cum purposely to
you, to make you a ful and certain graunt of it: and be you
assurid, Sir Harvi, that what I can doo in the matter I wil doo it to
the uttermost. I thankid him for his gentle and curtuus offer :
and tould him I wuld bilde uppon him. He bad me do so: and
rapping out a good big othe to that purpose said he passid not ani
thing at al of al there displeasures. After mani sutch goodli god-
morrous and namely a veri loving declaration of M. Gauberts
secret purpose against me, as I certifiid your wurship in mi other
epistle, which I was then a writing, he tould me he wuld be loth
to hinder me of mi studdi, and there with departid. I bad him
farwel, with this addition that I wuld trust to him. In the halli-
dais he tooke a iurni into the cuntri with on Sir Dorringtun of
the Kings Kollege, and, riding thurrough Walden, calid in at mi
fathers hous, and tould on of mi sisters that I wuld be at Walden
that niht. He returning back again cam on like manner veri
frendly, as I tooke it, to my fathers, and askid if I were yit cum to
Walden. Thei tould him yea, but that thei thout I was at Chireh.
Immediatly after I cam in, and thei tould me the two schollars
had bene thare again, and were now gone to suteh a mans. With
that I walkid into the town, to go se if I could liht uppon them.
And indeede bi and bi I met with them and brouht them back to
mi fathers to dinnar. After dinnar and muteh gud frendli and
merri talk in dinnar while, thai said thai must needs be at Cambridg that niht and therefore it was time for them to be sturring,
I, seing them to make so great hast awai, not knowing what præsent busines thai miht have at Cambridg, walkid a litle up the  f. 15 b.
streat with them and so tooke mi leave of them. Al this iumpid
wel togither. I doutid now Sir Flower as litle as I did ani on in
Pembrook hal: and in deed thouht him nothing les then a flower :
and yit for al this within a few dais after his cumming home,
uppon no occasion given him on mi part, or mi frends, in my

absens, with out ani reason, at the motion of two or thre
πολυπράγμονες, home he knew ful wel to be mi ennemies, to
mi great hinderans, and shame enoub to him self, plais me a pretti
iugling kast of leger de main, and gives against me; as if now
the date of peace were fully exspirid, and communion matters
quite put to bed, yea and faith, troth and god too clean forgottin.
So that Sir Flower wil needes proove him self a riht flower with
a witnis: and of so trusti a frend is becum a crusti confœderate
against me and a fals fœdifragus with me. And as for Sir Lawhern, what likehood was there but he, having ons stirrid in the
matter, wuld show him self as levis in constantia to others as others
had shown them selvs constantes in levitate to him? esspecially
being flesshid and animatid as he was bi his tutors preamble.
And thus rudely was I handelid amongst them for that time.
Whereuppon M. Tendal in the afternoone talkid privately with Sir
Flower, to lern what he ment finally to do in the matter. Sir Flower
confessid that he was not able in deed to allege ani reason against
me, marry yit nevertheles that he wuld not prommis ani thing,
until he had hard from your wurship again; and that then perhaps he wuld do for me. And this forsooth was al in effect that
culd be gottin of Sir Flower. M. Tendal had private talk also
with M. Nuce who seemid to take it in marvelus great duggin
that your wurship had written so sharply and bitterly unto him,
as he thouht, saiing he wuld not have written so to ani servant,
and saiing further in a great pelt, that he mindid not in deed to
deni me him self, marry otherwise to further me he wuld not, bicaus
it shuld seem he had bene complainid of to your wurship to be on
of the confœderats in the matter. A mihti great caus indeed to
alienate so staied a man, and a wunderful strong reasun not to
further me, yea to hinder me, and stop me too, if need be. Tam
facile est invenire baculum quo cædas canem. And yit if he were
not before and be not now a consiliis, yea and a secretis too, for al
his cullerable prætens to the contrari, not only I but sum other in

f. 16.

Pembrook hal, and a great sum in deed ar wunderfully deceivid: seing him and them daily and owerly cluster togither, as thai doo.

4. There was also a forth putting up of mi grace, as I was certifiid, uppon the return of M. Brown and M. Nevil from Lundon, the dai before M. Tendal was cum home from Lundon. Amongst the rest M. Brown prætendid that he wuld willingly talk with me before he gave me his vois: alleging also, partly to uphould the other in there dooings, partly to ad sumwhat of his own, that I had generally dispraisid al men saving physicians, and that I had greatly commendid thos whitch men call præcisions and puritanes. Two things soone spokin of M. Brown, but not so easely to be proovid as he weenith. I think if his inductions were to be seen in ether accusation that thai wuld fal out in the examining to be quarreling and captius elenchs, rather then certain and evident demonstrations. Na I am suer he wuld be as far to seek to mak his inductions good, as ever he was, sins his first practis in phisick to cure ani greevus disseas.

And to sai troth me thinks there appears a manifest ἀσυστασία f. 16 b. as it were a kind of paulsi or agu or sum the like quivering and staggering disseas in the accusations them selvs: so that it seems to me a veri profound point of phisick to rid them of it. I am accusid of a phisician to prais none but phisicians. A wunderful straung case that a phisician of al others shuld take this so greevusly: unles it goith with phisicians as it doth with beggars that on can not wel brook another: and for that I have seemid not to disalow of sum home he hath spitefully girdid behind there backs. But this is not the matter: he is a veri reasnable and indifferent man, not partial to thos of his own profession, and therefore culd find in his hart that men of other professions, as divines, lawiers, philosophers, rhetoricians, yea and musicians, fensers, and daunsers too shuld have ther du commendation as wel as thai of his own. Veri wel sed: be it præsupposid that I have praisid none but phisicians, then I have praisid sum belike, which M. Nevil præcisely deniid:

and if so be I have praisid none but them, how cummith it then to pas that I have bene so præcise a commender of I know not how mani puritanes and præcisions. If there be no puritanes but phisicians, then suerly puritanes I think mai soon be numbrid, and Ingland I beleev may soon be rid of them. But I am persuadid sum puritanes be scars gud apothecaries or surgeans, so far ar thai from being phisicians; and so is our phisician him self persuadid too. And therefore I wunder mutch what phisick he can præscribe to salv this sore, that I have bene a praiser of none save phisicians and yit nevertheles have bene a great praiser of præcisions and puritanes. Unles præcisions be no men with him, and therefore shuld count it needful to distinguish. Now if M. Phisician were first put to the proof of his first accusation, and then consequently of his second, I beleev he shuld find it the busiist pees of wurk that ever he took in hand: and I am assurid his phisick and logick too wuld fail him as muteh and more then ever thai did. And as for puritanes I wuld fain know what those same puritanes ar and what quallities thai have, that I have so hihly and usually commendid. Let M. Phisician name the persons and then shew that I have praisid them, in that respect thai ar puritanes or that ever I have maintainid ani od point of puritanism, or præcisionism mi self, and I shal be contentid to be bard of mi mastership and iointid of my fellowship too, yea and to take ani other sharp meddecine that his lerning shal iudg meetist for sutch a malidi. But M. Phisician hath left a dri hard bone at home for other to knaw uppon: and hath now found gud fat soft flesh abroad for him self to wurk uppon.

5. After M. Tendals cumming home and the deliveri of your wurships letters to M. Nuce and the bacchelers, M. Nuce made report unto the Cumpani after his manner of the sum of your letters to him: whitch he said to have consistid uppon two special points; the on to deliver sum of suspicion of certifiing your wurship that he shuld be confoederat with M. Osburn and M. Nevil in

ther doing : the other, that he shuld watch al opportunities to put
up mi grace so, that it miht be grauntid. Concerning the first he
spake litle or nothing : for the secund he said the Master culd not
commaund him so to do : for that he had left al sutch things to
his discretion : as if he ment of a like to be quarter master, and
in your absens wuld do whatsoever his mastership listid : adding
also, that in his consciens he thouht it meet that you shuld hear
there accusations, and return an aunser before mi grace did pas.
Sutch a good spocheman at al assais hath M. Nuce, I thank him,
bene of mine : and here is the goodli indifferenci that he bostith
of; a marvelus case that he that is so conscionable and indifferent
a man for both parts shuld so openly favur and incurrage the on
and so artificially and cunningly overwhart the other. I wuld be
loth to have sutch an orator to parl for me in a weitier matter.
Wel, this was a veri proper præface for them that shuld follow:
And a riht good string for al to hang on, for M. Osburn now must
needs forsooth expostulate the matter with your wurship, and set
down his articles in writing before he graunt ani thing. And so   f. 17 b.
must M. Nevil too, there is no shift of it : besides that M. Nevil
after his manner avouchid stoutly that as long as you thouht it dun
of contention (so far is M. Nevil, good man, from al contention) for
his part he wuld never yeeld. The yung cockerels, hearing thes
ould cocks to crow so lustely, followid after with a cockaloodletoo
as wel as ther strenhth wuld suffer them, and, thouh not in lowdnes yit in hardines, showid them selvs chickins of the game. Thus
your wurship hath hard what good succes I have had with mi
grace thes thre last puttings up : and I doubt not but your wurship wil iudg of ther doings, as thai ar, to tend to nothing els but
mi utter defamation, and the maintenanc of there own iolliti.
Shortly after al this adoo I cam home, thinking it hih time to
labur in the matter to sum purpose. The self same dai M. Tendal
had receivid a letter from your wurship, datid the xv. of this
munth, wherein you wil us not to sollicit M. Nuce ani more in

the matter, but to let him and the rest do as thai think good: giving me this cumfortable and ioiful watch wurd, as a dubble anchor, whereunto I mai certainly trust that you wil spi a time for the performaunc of that I desier wel enouh. Whitch saiing I did at that præsent and do now recount a soverain save gard against al incumbrancis. I thank your wurship most hartely for it. Item shortly after mi cumming home M. Yale[a] of the Queenes College sent for me to cum speak with him. I was not so soon in his chamber but he fil in hand with me to know how it shuld cum to pas that I was so far behind mi fellows. I tould him there was a certain block in the wai but I doutid not but it shuld be remoovid wel enouh. Hereuppon we began to reckin up the veri causis in deed, whitch he knew fully as wel as mi self, with a good larg emphasis, I warrant you: and said he fearid thai shuld have sum other private ant privi causis against me whitch were not to be noisid abroade: or els thai made of a gnat an elephant. I tould him he had hard al, and more then al, saving certain loud pathetical exclamations, and broad hyperboles whitch thai had veri artificially coinid to serv there turn. Whereuppon he bad me make al the frends I culd to get thurrouh in the hous: and willid me to procure Sir Thomas Smiths letters unto your wurship. I aunserid him your wurship had dun as mutch for me alreddi as ether you in your absens culd wel do or I miself culd possibely requier. Indeed, said he, so I heere: and with that made mention of your letters to M. Nuce; seeming nether to be ignorant of the contents of them nor of M. Nuces snuffing at them. And in deed thus mutch he made me partaker of, that your wurship shuld tel him in flat terms, that he did otherwise then did becum a man of his graviti or of that place, wherein he was or of on that shuld be your deputi. A pretti matter that your wurships letters shuld be blasid thus abroad in the town as thai ar: and whatsoever you have writ and dun in the matter, as wel and better known, not to on

[a] Thomas Yale, Fellow of Queens' College. *See* Cooper's *Athenæ Cantabrigienses*, vol. i. p. 379.

fellow of y<sup>e</sup> Queenes Collidg, but to a great cumpani of iunior regents of everi collidg then to sum senior fellows of our own collidg. How it cums to pas, I can not certainly sai, only I ges M. Nuce made M. Osburn and M. Nevil privie to them ; and so thai carri them abroid to y<sup>e</sup> bare<sup>a</sup> and other commun ins and make them so famus as thai ar. And whether this be revelare secreta domus your wurship knows best. The same prank, if not abroad, althouh I misdout that. too, yit at home, and in the cumpani of pensionars<sup>b</sup> have the bacchelers plaid. And first, how litle thai did æsteme of your wurships letters to them, M. Tendal can be a sufficient witnes : who sitting in his chamber, whenas thai red them togither, in the nixt chamber, hard this resolute determination of thers, that your letters shuld not moove them an inch.

So good cockerels ar thai becum alreddi, and so lusti cocks ar thai like to proove if ther comes be not cut the sooner. The Flowir talkid sins with Sir Brown, and like a trim man no douht brust out into thes wurds: Doth our master imagin he hath bois in hand, that he mai frai and scare with a wurd as he list ? And within a while after, talking pleasantly with M. Goter, amongst other things tould him your wurship wuld be at home ere long ; and then, said he, the bois must be britch : meaning him self and his fellow, for he had informid them both afore, that your wurship had writtin to them two in mi behalf. I think to the end that thai and others shuld not be ignorant what iolli fellows Sir Flower and Sir Lawhern were, that had so wurshipfully bene writtin unto bi the Master. But your wisdum can best iudg and discern of thes matters. And as for Flower and Lawhern, thai them selvs cannot dissemble it without egregius impudenci, but that they are Ministri alienæ voluntatis, and that, whatsoever thai do, thai do it uppon others provocation ; hanging al togither uppon there sleevs that ar

f. 18 b.

---

<sup>a</sup> Bear Inn in Cambridge.
<sup>b</sup> Pensioners at Cambridge are ordinary students as distinguished from sizars.

like enouh to show them as pretti a logick point, ere two yeares go about. In deed now thai steek fast togither like burs, and cluster on a bunch like a cumpani of grapes; but I hope mi grace shal not be alwais in sute, and I fear me two years can hardly slip awai without sum crowing on the on part and more overcrowing on the other. Wel you have hard now, riht wurshipful, the hole discours and bistori of mi matter sins mi other letters; a great deale more tædius, I graunt, then it ouht to be, in respect of your person, but as breef, in mi iudgment, as it culd wel be, in respect of the caus.

f. 19. Wherein your wurship mai plainely see that the two March blasts were not so bitterly sharp but that the thre April storms have bene mutch more boisterus and harmful. And if Mai proove no better with me then March and April have dun, I must needs sai, and mai sai it truly, it wilbe the worst spring, yea the wurst and rouhist winter for me that hapnid this xxii. years. But I trust April showers shal bring forth Mai flowers: and after thes turbulent raging tempests I hope verrely for caulm and faier wether. And indeed showers thai sai ar more kind and seasenable for this munth then flowers ar, or els had I bene shrodely discumfited and dismaiid ere this. And yit ons a flower began to peep out his hed, and made a show as if he purposid to start forth in al hast: but he was so wel waterid and dampid on the on side with continual storms, and so litle fostrid and cherrishid on the other side with the warm sun, that he was glad to shrink in again, and be smootherid yit a while, til he miht spi out sum whot summer dai to spring out in, for I dout not I but the flower will have his kind and bud out freshly enoub for al this ere it be long. Marri I fear me there must breath sum sweat pleasant zephyrus first, that mai quietly put to silens the trubbleus and tempestuus Boreassis that have so long and so rouhly blowid and blustrid in everie corner. And then I doubt not a whit, but ther wil insu sutch a goodli temperat caulm as I have longid and lustid for this mani a dai and niht. But I persaiv how werisum and tœdius I have bene unto your wurship, and therefore I wil now cease of to molest you ani longer. God be with you, Sir, and reward you for your singular goodnes towards me.

From Pembrook hal. this xxvi. of April.

## To the Same.

Si quis mihi unquam iucundus, ac fortunatus dies illuxit, optime et optatissime vir, cuius ego semper dulcissima suavissimaque recordatione delectari debeam : certe dies hic, in quo te iampridem desideratum aliquando tandem aspeximus, et optatus quidem in primis propter animi consolationem et salutaris etiam maxime propter ægritudinis levationem fuit. Cum enim iam totos duos menses indignissime immanissimeque tractatus sim, atque in rerum omnium quasi desperationem quandam adductus nisi tua me sublevaret, confirmaretque auctoritas : quid mihi poterat vel ad voluntatem gratius vel ad utilitatem antiquuis feliciusque accidere quam ut te quamprimum hijsce oculis viderem præsentem, cuius absentis desiderio flagrarim incredibili ? Etenim ita iam obfirmati et malevolentia invidiaque obstricti meorum adversariorum animi sunt, ut nisi præsens præsentes coargueres, et a contentionis ardore ad moderationem ab importuna nocendi cupiditate, ad meliorem mentem, quod literis non potuisti voce, vultu, auctoritate revocares, actum plane de meis rebus atque adeo etiam de meipso videretur. Stomochatur Osburnus ; Nevellus furit; Flowerus, Lawhernusque indignantur ; et prostremo Nucius atque Brownus nescio quid monstri alunt. Miserum me qui tot tantosque homines nactus sim inimicos: miseriorem, qui fere solus : miserrimum vero, si liceret illis, quicquid liberet et possent quæ vellent omnia.

f. 19 b.

f. 20.

Tantum abest ut in magistrorum collegium cooptarer, maioribusque dignitatis insignibus atque ornamentis decorarer, ut verendum mihi profecto esset, ne infra Floweros Lawhernos que constitutus, et e baccalaureorum ipsorum ordine ejectus. ad ultimas discipulorum classes detruderer, et Osburniano imperio continerer. Quid enim iam diu aliud vel publice apud omnes vel privatim apud suos machinati sunt, nisi ut me contumeliis omnibus atque calumniis obrutum in odium atque invidiam adducerent, et intra infimos omnes homines collocarent? Quid fere hosce menses egerunt, imo quid omnino cogitarunt, nisi qua potissimum ratione atque oratione cunctorum a me animos abalienarent, inimicorum etiam in me vehementius inflammarent? Ego interim obscura quadam vel potius sane desperata spe, ac cæca exspectatione pendens ne vel arrogantiæ me, vel negligentiæ insimulare possent, si meam ipse rem non agerem, convenio homines, clamo, postulo, oro, ploro atque imploro eorum fidem, ut inquit ille : sed frustra omnia. Fingunt enim causas ut ipsi affirmant gravissimas, ut æquissimi homines arbitrantur futiles ac pueriles, quibus impulsos se, atque coactos esse clamant, ut de me supplicium isto modo sumerent. Ita nimirum mecum agunt, ut cum gallo feles apud Æsopum : qui primum quidem non sine maximis iustissimisque causis se eum devoraturum dicebat, quippe quem molestissimum hominibus esse sciret, nocte vociferantem cosque e somno exsuscitantem ; ideoque gallo respondente, ad illorum emolumentum atque commodum id se facere, ut ad consueta opera atque labores excitarentur ; rursus cum feles intolerandæ cuiusdam impietatis atque flagitii accusabat, quod cum matre sororibusque contra naturam coiisset :

f. 20 b.

atque hoc etiam ad dominorum utilitatem factum esse dicente gallo, cum multa hinc illis ova pariantur ; etiamsi præclare, inquit, teipsum defendas, atque criminationes meas omnes facile retundas, non efficies tamen, ut diutius ego ieiunus existem, ipsumque continuo devoravit. Sic isti me videlicet hominem importunum eorumque somnum ut videtur, intempestivis clamoribus im-

pedientem, non quidem iniuria sunt enim viri æquissimi, sed
μετ' εὐλόγου αἰτίας scilicet, ut in eadem poene causa iisdem
ego verbis utar, si non devorare ad prædam, certe dedecorare
ad pœnam volunt. Quod si mea etiam mihi non deest ἀπολογία
et id revera utile ac fructuosum est quod illis videtur intoler-
abile, at certum est denique hominem contundere. Et cum
cætera omnia, ut sunt levissima evanuerunt, at ille murus, ut
ita dicam, aheneus, vel frons sane potius, ut vere dicam,
ferrea : Sic volo, sic iubeo, et stat pro ratione voluntas.[a] Quid
multa? ego contumelijs violatus, ego in criminationem adductus,
ego iniurijs omnibus oppressus, ego læsus, uictusque sum : et
quidem ita, vix ut ulla spes superesset, fore melius. Itaque
nunc demum gratulor, atque gaudeo adesse te cuius prudentiam
appellare, æquitatem obtestari, humanitatem etiam, pictatemque
implorare queam. Neque enim quisquam mihi crede post Deum
optimum Maximum est, cui sollicitus dolores, afflictus calamitates,
vexatus iniurias commendare malim, quam tibi, quem et semper
hactenus et nunc etiam maxime propugnatorem statuo fortunæ
meæ. Itaque quanquam non dubito sane, quin patrocinium tua
sponte oppressæque afflictæque innocentiæ sis laturus, quis enim
unquam ad bonitatem omnem propensior? tamen id ut facias,
quoniam mea tanti refert, sic a te peto, ut maiore studio, magisne
ex animo petere non possim. Moveat tua te misericordia, moveat
clementia, alliciat pietas, sapientia excitet, flectat humanitas, in
commiserationem denique adducat sollicitudinis atque mæroris mei
recordatio. Sed quid te ego appello, cum ne Hercules quidem
contra tam multos? recte sane: atque sic nimirum illi ipsi gloriati
sunt. Neque enim tam mecum profecto iam, quam tecum, ut
videtur, congredi, et concertare statuerunt. Atque id mihi Nueius
non ita pridem confirmavit: et si ille tacuisset, dicta factaque
omnia loquuntur. Quid enim, deus bone, illis omnibus animosius?
Sed novi ego prudentiam, novi moderationem tuam : nec mihi

f. 21.

[a] Juvenal, vi. 223.

dubium est, quin iactationem istam atque arrogantiam facile possis, et velis refrenare. Atque eo quidem magis quod intra domesticos ea parietes contineri se noluit, sed foras etiam prorupit, et cuneta pœne collegia peragravit. Quid enim tam omnium sermonibus hosce dies celebratum, quam brevi adventurum te ut Harvæo subvenias? sed ne tibi quidem Osburnum atque Nevellum, corumque socios obsequuturos, nisi tu illis etiam certis in rebus obsequaris. Etenim ea iam nostrorum magistrorum insolentia est, ut vel tuam etiam auctoritatem frangere atque comprimere moliantur: in eoque animorum magnitudinem familiàribus suis ostentare.

f. 21 b. Quam nisi tu ita coerceas, atque reprimas, omnibus ut constare possit, quam petulanter se gesserint, non dubium est, quin et optimis de causis se id fecisse qued fecerint gloriaturi sint, et tandem etiam honorificam de te victoriam consecutos. Sed tu pro singulari tua prudentia, quid optimum factu sit præclare tenes: in qua ego, tanquam in peropportuno quodam diversorio, acquiesco. Salve.

## To the Same.

Chilo[a] Lacedæmonius, is, quem inter sapientissimos viros antiqui scriptores numerabant, cum iam admodum senex esset, atque ætate propemodum conficeretur, dixisse fertur, Ingrati animi se nunquam in tota vita sibi fuisse conscium. Ego vero, spectatissime vir, si cum sapiente isto dixerim nunquam me hactenus in ἀχαριστίας crimen incidisse, atque constantiam etiam probatissimi hominis ita mihi proposuisse, ut sequi velim, vere profecto dixisse mihi videbor: sed nisi singulares iam tibi, mirificasque gratias, propter incredibilem erga me summamque pietatem agerem, et beneficij tanti magnitudinem perpetua memoria colerem, certe ego me, quod minime vellem, maxime, non dico ἀχαριστίας, sed pæne etiam ἀσέβειας scelere obstrinxisse videri possem.

[a] Chilo of Sparta, one of the seven sages of Greek, flourished B.C. 556.

Quandoquidem is demum ingratus esse dicitur qui gratiam bene merenti non persolvit: et sane impietatis insimulari potest, qui optime merenti maximas gratias, et beneficentissimo patrono officia summa non emetitur.

Itaque cum multa hoc tempore, si maxime velim dicere non queam, dicam id, quod et benignitatem tuam illustrare maxime, et observantiam meam non obscure testificari possit. Hic enim mihi crede sentio non minus me quidem tibi, multo etiam fortasse plus debere quam vel Chrysippo[a] suo Carneades[b] vel Theseo[c] ipsi Oedipus[d] aliquando debuit. Nec tam vere meo iudicio aut ille de Chrysippo dicere potuit; nisi tu esses, non essem ego; aut de Theseo iste apud Sophoclem;[e] ἔχω, ἃ ἔχω, διὰ σε, κ' οὐκ ἀλλῶν βροτῶν: quam ego de te. Tu enim patronus es, tu pater, si deseruisses tu, periissem. Atque eo quidem et plenius, et insignius mihi beneficium visum est, quod tantam in eo, tamque incredibilem celeritatem susceperis, quantam ego nullo modo exspectare deberem, vix etiam optare possem. Sed ita nimirum tibi placuit beneficium beneficio cumulare, et, quod per se iucundum erat, festinatione ipsa reddere iucundissimum. Bis enim gratum, ut dicitur, quod cito fit: et inexspectata solent esse suaviora. Quid quæris? Nihil omnino defuit, quod vel humanitatem tuam amplificare, vel me tibi astringere et devincire posset. Neque enim dissimulandum profecto est, quod ego verissimum esse comperi, nullam esse rem tam arduam, atque difficilem, quam tu non et consilio procurare et auctoritate tueri, et prudentia conficere queas. Quod cum tibi hoc tempore perhonorificum fuit ad laudem atque gloriam: tum mihi sane et ad emolumentum est, et ad tranquillitatem animi peroptatum. Et siquando me uti voles, uti autem potes, quantum vis, senties quam

f. 22.

[a] Chrysippus, a Stoic philosopher, B.C. 291—208.
[b] Carneades, a Greek philosopher of Cyrene, B.C. 214—129, the great opponent of Chrysippus.
[c] Theseus. *See* Sophocles' *Œdipus Coloneus.*
[d] Œdipus. *See* Sophocles' *Œdipus Coloneus.*
[e] Sophocles' *Œdipus Coloneus,* l. 1129. ἔχω γὰρ ἄχω διὰ σὲ, κοὐκ ἄλλον βροτῶν.

ista ex animo dicantur omnia, et quam præclare de excellenti virtute, atque dignitate tua sentiam. Cogor enim iam brevior esse, quam velim et quam res postulat sed malim non satis dicere videri quam omnino conticescere. Summa erit hæe: Chilonis mihi exemplum, et Cleobuli[a] consilium proposui, ut ne unquam ingratus siem. Et quod ad iniurias meas attinet, equidem ἀμνηστείας mihi ipse legem imposui, rem totam tuo arbitrio, atque moderationi relinquens, in qua mihi conquiescendum esse sentio. Gaubertus nihil me fefellit. Cæterorum voluntas fuit eadem. Vale.

## To his Father.

Althoughe you have heard alreddi, most loving father, that at y<sup>e</sup> last, in spite of all mi illwillers, I have obtainid mi sute, and as it were gottin y<sup>e</sup> victory, with shame enouh to them all, and sumwhat els to sum: yit forsomutch as y<sup>e</sup> matter hung so long as it did, and you, with y<sup>e</sup> rest of mi freuds miht think more in it then was in deed, I thouht good brefely in a word or twoe to showe you what a glorius end they had of there gudly enterprise. Our Master, seing his letters wuld take no place, and persaiving there spiteful and malicius purpose against me, cam downe himself to Cambridg uppon Thursday in Whitsunweek, being y<sup>e</sup> xiiij. day of Maye, for no other purpose that any could persaive but only to stenche this strife, and to rid me out of trubble. Thay lookid presently for sum nu fresh putting up of mi grace in all hast: but he let them alone til Munday, never almost making any mention of any suteh matter: in so mutch that thay wunderid greatly what he ment, being not able to coniecture what purpose he should have in his hed. Uppon Mundy in the morning there was a congregation, that is, an assembly and meeting togither of thos in y<sup>e</sup> publique schooles that have to do in thes matters, after thay ar ons passid

---

[a] Cleobulus, one of the seven sages of Greece, B.C. 694—564.

yᵉ howse. At which time, as yᵉ manner is, I was openly nominatid as we call it: which is as mutch as can be cumpassid yᵉ first Congregation.

This geere semid verie straung and marvelus to mie heavi Masters; nether culd thay tel in the world what to say unto it, as well as thay thouht them selves ar$_{mid}$ in al respects. The Congregation was continuid til yᵉ afternoone, and then had I mi grace ad visitandum, as we terme it; that is, to visitt all yᵉ Masters in the towne of five yeares, whereunto we ar inioined by statute, which is all that can be dun at yᵉ secund meeting. That afternoon and yᵉ next day wholy, and uppon Weddensday in yᵉ morning, I trudgid upp and down yᵉ towne a visiting, as gossups in sum places do a gaddinge.

But that is our manner; and to say troth I was full glad I was cum so far, mie thought it was even yᵉ gudliist and pleasauntist progresse that ever I made. In yᵉ afternoone was there a third Congregation: at which in spite of yᵉ pie (albeit there was a certain busi boddi—a lusti pensionar of our own howse, on Gawber, a knave for yᵉ nonse sett on, as is most probable by yᵉ Masters of yᵉ Mischeif, whenas thay durst do nothing themselves for feare of afterclaps—that playd his part sumwhat egerly against me before mie face, first in charging me that I had not visitid his Mastership, as I was bownd, and then in going about to disable the doing of mi acts for that I had disputid being suspendid); at this Congregation, I say, notwithstanding this sore and fierce enditement, I was forthwithe admittid Master of Art. And thus in thre dayes were all things dispatchid thurrouhly that had now wel nih thre munths hangid so doutfully. Which was not so commodious for me to mie great cumfort, as it was inglorius for them, to ther wunderful greif. But it was now verifiid that M. Tyndal ons tould them, and often said unto me, that a foolish enterprise wuld have a foolish end; so that whereas thay thouht by there great words and big looks to have made there own parts gud and mine

wurs then nauht, thay have now by on mans reasnable and
upright dealing showid themselves what thay ar, and openid
there cancrid stummocks to y<sup>e</sup> whole town. And as for gentle
M. Gawber, his Mastership may go shake his eares elswhere, and
appoint his diet at sum other table. Pembrook hall fare is not for
his tooth. The truth is, our Master chargid him to be packing,
and willid M. Tyndall to put him out of Commins, and indeed so he
is, I warraunt him, although otherwhiles he lingerith about y<sup>e</sup>
Colledg like a masterles bowne, bycause he wuld not seem to be
thrust out: but in deed lookith like a dog that had lost his taile,
or, to make y<sup>e</sup> best of it, like an unbidden geste that knowes not
where to sitt him downe. A iust reward for sutch a companion to
shuffle him self out of dores, and a meet game for sutch a gamster
to play Wylye beguile him selfe.<sup>a</sup> Thus good M. Doctor Yunge,
to his great commendation and mie furtheraunce, handelid mie
matter at Cambridg, and forthwith returnid back to London. Since
which time I have oft thought with mieself howe great thanks I
owe unto God that shapid me so soveraine a savegard at y<sup>e</sup> last,
whenas he had chastined me a while for mie demerittes. And this
it was, as I take it, if it were any thing, that was tould me above
x yeares agoe for mie fortune, that I should go allwaies to lerning,
and go well enough forward in lerninge, but never take any high
degree in schooles; that is, very hardly and with mutch difficulty,
which mie mother putt me in minde of, at mie last being at Walden,
being quite and cleane forgottin of me. And as for good M. Yung, a
very notable instrument of Gods singular goodnes towards me, and
in deed a worthi man in divers respects, I recount mi self so mutch
bownd unto him in this behalf, that I suppose verely I cannot any
wayes possible be thankfull enough. Who as he was for his place
bownd, for his autority able, for his benevolenc desirus, to suceur

---

<sup>a</sup> "Wylye beguile himself." A comedy called "Wily Beguiled." *See* Hawkins'
*Origin of the English Drama*, vol. iii. pp. 288-377.

me, so for his wisdum he was as reddy, for his equity as forward, to repres there insolensy as ether I culd wish or he himself culd be.

His will was so pliable to better my bale:
And his scill so forcible to quitt me of ale.

And thus mutch concerning my gud and prosperus successe, after so greate and greevus trubbles: as commenly after boisterus and bitter stormes there insuith a pleasaunt caulm.

Sins mie admission M. Senior Proctour,[a] of his owne accord, without any labouring at all on mie part (whereas sum other and sum iolly fellowes in deed had said unto him in that behalfe), desirid me verry frendly to be senior Master.

---

Notes in his Diary relating to the above Letters.

Our Master gave M. Osburn and M. Nevel an admonition for deniing me mj grace.

Talk about y<sup>e</sup> admonition when M. Tindal was chosen Taxtor.[b]
1573. Die Mensis, 17 Octobris.

Further talk in our Master's own præsenc, when he willid the fellowes to name sum to be fellows: which M. Nuce, M. Jackson, M. Brown, M. Osburn, M. Nevel refused to do, bycaus as thei said, thos that were now fellows had not bene usid like fellows, whi? bycaus he went about to abridg that liberti of being abroade, which was allowid bi statute: bycaus he forcid mens voices, as namely, when I was chosen to y<sup>e</sup> Greek lecture, he said unto sum, you shal comprimit, not suffring M. Osburn to give with him self, and yit bestowing mine owne voice uppon mi self: and then

---

[a] Dr. Lancelot Brown. *See* page 21, note b.
[b] Taxor. An annual office, like the Proctors', now discontinued. *See* Hardy's *Le Neve's Fasti*, vol. iii. pp. 635-649.

choosing me, having but even voices, bycaus he gave them an admonition for giving ther voices in y$^e$ chappel, and putting M. Gaubert so long out of Commins for giving his voice freely in the schooles.

The greatist talk was about y$^e$ admonition, whether it was lawful or no. Our Master said he would not revoke it for a thousand pound, bycaus he knew he should do veri ill if he did so. Thei urging that it could not tak place, he said it could, and should take place; offering to pawne an hundred pownd to five pownd, if the matter were hard of ani wise iudg in Ingland.

In farther talk thei said our Master did not only give on admonition, but said, if thei deniid me y$^e$ next time, he would give them the second admonition, and so y$^e$ third time, y$^e$ third admonition, saiing furthermore, that thai miht as good eate whot coales as deni me agajn.

---

## To Dr. Young, Master of Pembroke Hall.

f. 27.    Althouh I am loth, at this præsent, riht wurshipful, ether to trubble you with reading or mi self with writing of letters, yet having now at the lenght so fit a barer as I have, and seing matters fal out sins your departure as thai doo, I culd not but give you intelligens thereof. And yit suerly the short time I have wil scars suffice to make a simple and bare narration of things, so far am I from amplifiing and exaggerating of them. And, therefore, I am to desier your wurship not to look after ani set or curious epistle, but to take in good part whatsoever and howsoever I write. First, I know not whither it were your pleasure that M. Gawber shuld be in commins again or no: for mi part, althouh you were then amongst us, yit I take it you were never ons made privi to it. Notwithstanding, uppon Sundai at dinnar, præsently uppon the talk that M. Proctor had of him with your wurship in the parlar the niht before, and ever sins hath he cum continually to the table. Indeed, I remember wel M. Brown, before he was Proctor, the veri self same time that M. Tendal was chosen Taxtor in the hows, amongst other of his iollj vaunts, wherein he semith greatly to delite himself, made this bost, that if thurrouh others absens it cam ever to his ccurs to be Præsident, he would venture the putting of him in commins, put him out again whos wuld. And, therefore, it mai verri wel be that he now of him self being M. Proctor, in a iolliti willid him to cum to the table. For it is wel known to sum in Pembrook hal, that M. Brown hath this properti, to be commonly as bould and hardi, as ether wise or circumspect in mani of his doings. Uppon Mundai, the same dai that your wurship took your iurni towards Lundon, even immediatly before I should go to read the Grek lecture (for the whitch, as for mani things mo, I recount mi self infinitely bownd unto you, and the rather, by caus it was frely offrid of yow, not ambitiusly souht of me) being inded fully purposid, and providid to read, mi father sent for me of the sudden to go præsently to him to the Griffin. Whereuppon the bel being tould to yᵉ lecture, as I had willid the butler before, I cam by and by into yᵉ hall, and tould yᵉ schollars mi business was sutch that I could not in ani wise read that dai, willing them to provide themselvs of bookes against yᵉ next dai, and telling them what book I intended to read unto them. Al this while a fower or five of the fellows, and Gawber, clusterid togither about the hall dore, as if there had bene sum muster towards. And M. Osburn amongst the rest, as I hard sins, in the hearing of sum schollars, like a tall fellow stept forth, and avouchid manfully that if I wuld never so fain have red, I shuld not. I was not so soone gon into the town but M. Nuce in al hast sent about for the follows to meet togither in the chappel forthwith; and al were reddi, as thei said sins, saving I and Sir Flower. The next morning after praiers, we being al togither in the chappel, M. Nuce

f. 27 b.

affirmid that you were content we shuld proceed to a new election of the grek lecturer, so that a met man were chosen to it. Whereuppon he and M. Jackson went strait wais up to the table, to cal for our voices in scrutinie. M. Hales[a] being calid up to make the third, made this answer, that he wuld not ons stur or meddle in y$^e$ matter until he hard first from you. Thai proceedid on, and calid M. Proctor to make the third in his steade. He never made ani bones at it, but trudgd up roundely, to work the feat. M. Tendal refusid, as M. Hales. M. Osburn, and M. Nevil went and gave ther voices. M. Nuce urging no man any farther, nether me nor ani after me, calid for M. Hales and M. Tendal again; and, seing thai could not be brouht in ani case to go up, cam down him self again into his place; whereat M. Proctor chafid and frettid like a proctor, and askid M. Nuce in a rage if he went about to mock him, for as it appeerid he was now marvelous desirous to be lecturer him self; and so mutch he confessid unto me even then in the chappel, and of a like had cumpassid it alreddi bi voices, as he thouht, and therefore took it the more greevusly that his enterprise took no better succes. M. Nuce, being in his place, took a corporal othe that it was your mind the lecture shuld be chosen anue, and semid to make prommis it shuld fal out so that thai and I should have occasion to like of it wel enouh. Where$^a$t thai grauntid by and by to give there voices; and M. Jackson going up again with M. Nuce to the table, M. Hales followid as third in the scrutini. M. Proctor being calid of them, Now, saith he, wil not I go up. Nether could he in ani case be intreatid to go up. M. Tendal without ani more adoo gave his vois. M. Osburn stud uppon this chrotchet, that he had bene ons there alreddi, and therefore willid them ether to go on with thos that were after him, or else if thai began again there was an other before him. Whereuppon M. Nuce and M. Osburn him self too laid hard at M. Proctor to go up; but his mastership could not possibly be over treatid. So that M.

[a] . . . . Hales, Fellow of Pembroke Hall.

Nuce was now inforcid, do what he could, to break up again, using these words in sum anger, as did appear, that on trubblid al the rest. Whitch was the Epiphonema, and as it were the windupal of that meting. Straite after dinnar I willid Sir Jackson to toul ye bel to the lecture at twelv a clock. And having partly an incling what Tragædies thai ment to make, as soon as the bel was towld, I went præsently unto M. Nuce to know whether he, or ani other he knew of, were purposid to hindir mi reading. M. Nuce made me answer, I miht read, as appointid bi you for the time, until we did heare from you what were to be dun. Marry that he for his part likid of it verry well, that I, rather then any other, shuld be lecturer, and therefore that he gave me his consent at the first, only he wisshid the form of the election miht be reformid. And so willid me hardly to go and read. I was not so soon in the haul but M. Proctor, being calid down out of his chamber bi M. Osburn, as I lerned sins, cummith swelling in, like sum greater man then the Junior Proctor, and commaundith y^e schollars from the table; saiing in his Proctors vois that I shuld read no lecture there; as he bi his Proctoral autoriti had suspendid me before, and I as yit had not bene absolvid. Whereuppon the schollars rose me strait wais from the table, and clusterid al togither about the scren, to hear and se what would insu; for of so forcible an antecedent it was most likeli there wuld follow as effectual a consequent. And I wis so there did: for by and by M. Proctor, sumwhat snappishly after his manner—I shuld have said currishly had it bene of ani but M. Proctor—bad me if I wuld neds be showing mi Grek, to read me a Gods name sum lecture in mine own chamber: for it shuld be to whot reading there for me, yea if it were but to mine own pupils, if I wuld fors them thither at that hower, unles I were first orderly chosen to it according to statute. And being carried a great deal farther then a wise man wuld, with a furious and outragious heat of words, which is no great straung thing in M. Brown, in the hearing of al the schollars, in despite calid me Sir

f. 28 b.

Harvi, and to mend the matter said flatly, that I shuld wel understand inded that I was but batcheler of art, and that he wuld stand in it, I was no more, and that he wuld pronouns me so openly in the schools, when mi cours shuld cum to dispute; with a mani of sutch glorius brags and malitius words, utterid of purpose, and for the nons, as is most likeli, to let the schollars understand what a trim terrible man thai had to be Proctor. Al this I put up quietly, desiring him only, that if he wuld neds fal into that vain, that he wuld wil y<sup>e</sup> schollars to be gon, or else here wuld be matter gud plenti, both for them to grate uppon and to brute abroad in the Town. Na, said he, let them hear a Gods name, if thai wil, it is like to go farther then so; professing that he wuld not speak on word the les, bycaus it was in there hearing. Indead I think verrely now he spake mani words the more bycaus of them, to outfase and disgrace me before them. Besides al this, sum that stud bi, report about the hows that he calid me boi, and that I durst not gev him on word again, whitch it is likeli enouh M Brown miht do; for I remember the time when, and cannot forget the manner how, in the behalf of a few schollars, as he is marvelously given to be popular, for a show matter and nothing els, he calid M. Tendal, in M. Nuces, M. Fars, and mi præsens, both knave and boi, and wuld have gone farther too had not M. Nuce willid him to take heed what he did. And so he in stead of a Commedi gave us a Tragedi, and for want of a plai had like to have made a frai. But if he boied me now, as the rumor goith, suerly I hard him not: if I had, it mai be I shuld have said more to that, then I did to the rest. When M Proctor had plaid this gudli and famus pageant on y<sup>e</sup> stage, he trots me strait wais in to the Town, like a iolli curragius man as he was, or rather like on that had bound bares or dun sum the like mihti act. When he was gon, M. Nevil and I fil a reasning and debating the matter. M. Hoult intrudid himself, as his accustomid manner is, and forsooth accusid me of I know not how great præsumption for that I tooke uppon me to bid y<sup>e</sup> butler toul y<sup>e</sup> bel.

But I knew this to be M. Hoults properti, he must evermôre·make on, if there be ani talk towards, hosoever be the other: nether was it the first time I have notid it in him, he wil be suer to take uppon him, whosoever be præsent, as if he only were appointid to sit in commission of the matter. And therefore I made the lihter account of his grave and severe censure. In the mids of our talk I was calid awai bi on that cam out of the cuntri to speak with me. What talk thai two and ther Gawber (for he was a looker on al this while) had afterward God knowith: I am wel assurid thai were so lowd that al y<sup>e</sup> Colledg rung of them. With in an hower or two after al this hurli burli, I talkid privately with M. Proctor, and in deed I fownd him a great deal cooler and caulmer then before. Now he culd sai, that he went not so mutch about to put me bi the lectureship as to remmedi this, that he and the rest were not usid at your hands like boies. Which phrase of speach you remember when and where he usid it, odly, as you tould him about the same, and the like matters, verri horrible and hainus misuses in there judgmentes. Amongst a number of other things he said he had written so unto you ons, when as it was, as he wuld never write unto you again whiles he lived. He tould me he could not like of this, that you shuld give Osburn and Nevil an admonition, only for giving there voices against me; for so he said you tould him flatly, that you did it only for this, and for no other thing. In sum he semid to charg you esspecially with over mutch stummock. Notwithstanding he swore unto me that he for his part would nether now nor at ani time hereafter harm you if he miht: only that he could not brook and put up so manifest misorders. Marry, he affirmid plainly, there were sum fellows in the hows that wuld harm you too, if thai were hable, and could tel how. Whcme he shuld meen I cannot certainly sai, unles it shuld be the two πολυπράγμονες Osburn and Nevil; for thes two I know (and I have paid for mi knowledg) (for al ther faier gloses, whitch thai can and wil other whiles use to serve there turns) have both wit to invent, and wil to

f. 30.

practis mischif, if there power were according to accomplish it. Suerly I coniecture thai have bene a coining of articles against you, and packing up stuf togither to furnish up a perfit Tragœdie.

Now I se Aquila non capit muscas. I am to base mettal for them to work uppon. Of a like thai purpose to pluck Jupiter out of heaven or, as Momus wunt was, to cal the gods to a strait account, and to controwl them at ther pleasures. No dout sum wunderful stout matter thai have in bruing: what it wil proove in the drawing I know not. It is reportid abroad in the town (and M. Wilks of Triniti Colledg, on verry great with M. Nuce and M. Brown, is said to be the autor of it) that it shuld be enactid and agreid uppon amongst them, not to have ani election whiles you were Master.

But when al is said and dun, I am perswadid Momus himself wil sooner be shouldrid out of heaven, if ned be, then he shal be hable bi his waiwardnes to bring al heaven in aw of him. Esspecially if he go on to disturb and disquiet the gods, after his ould crookid unmannerli manner. But suerly I wish it with al mi hart that he and his partners wuld pacifi and content them selvs with out ani faither broiles; and suffer others to inioi that quietnes whitch thai mai have at ani time when thai wil, and sum wuld fain have if thai miht. Marry if Momus continue the same man stil, and can never think him self wel, but when he is iangling, I fear me our heaven hath not floorishid so mutch heretofore thorouh peasablenes, the onli nurs and foundres of lerning, as it is like shortly to decai thorouh contentiusnes, the verri poison and bane of al. And therefore, seing that is so perillus, whitch is so likeli, and yit curable too, I hope thorouh discret handeling, it is your wisdum only and nothing els, whitch can expell this daungerus and deadli poisun. Althouh I am aferd thai wil put you to it to use the extremiti (thai ar so wilfully bent), and so to drive out on poison with an other: whitch kind of phisick M. Proctor knowith is sumtimes præscribid. And yit of mi troth I hartely wish so wel for them and others, that almost against al hope I stil hope the best of them towards others. But, to return to gentle M. Proctor again, he that not ful two bowers before, in the hale, had bene as whot as a tost against me, was now in his own studdi, and in privi conferens mutch more reasonable with me, then I could thus soone look for after so terrible cracks and thunderboults. Now his Mastership could find in his hart to sai, that uppon condition I wuld not offer any more to read, whitch nevertheles I shuld not if I did offer, he wuld not ani time hereafter, ether in the hows or in the town, ether openly or privjly give me an il word: and ere long, as he sae occasion, I shuld find him a caulm frend: and in time, bi his troth, for ani thing he knew, we miht proov as great frends as anj in Cambridg; for this verri gradation he usid himself with me at that time. It was sumwhat straung to me at the first to se so sudden a chaung: but I considderid sins the gentleman stud uppon his reputation before the schollars, and, as he was abroad in the schooles, so wuld neds seme a moderator at home too in the haul; and therefore in there siht wuld be thouht to rule the rost, and beare a swing in the howse, when other pore silli sowles shuld go for no better then ciphers in algorism. Whitch were sutch matter for them and others to chat of, as wuld be meat and drink to M. Proctor. I suppose verrely that same, οὗτος ἐστὶ Δημοσθένης, wuld do him more gud at the hart then half the gaines of his Proctorship: and yit I dout not but he wil make as mutch of it as ani Proctor did this seaven year. But if he wuld but take the chainid book in his hand, whitch his man carrith after him, and take the pains to run over the title concerning the Proctor's office and charg, I beleev he shuld find his autoriti wil scars stretch so far as to order, or rather disorder, matters at his pleasure, and to others shame, in private collegis.

As for other autoriti, I se not what he culd have more then I, or ani other fellow. But I take it M. Proctor was beside his book, as he wilbe now and then, bi his leav, as cunning a man as he is.

f. 31 b.

f. 32.

And as for that sudden passion of curtesi, it put me in mind of a pretti Greak vers that I had red not mani weks before εἴ με φιλεῖς, ἔργω μὲ φίλει καὶ μὴ μ' ἀδίκει συ. I wuld have him that prætendith to loove me, to loov me in deed, and not to injuri me. This is a frendship of al frendships with al mi hart, to break a mans hed, and then sai he wil uppon farther liking, and at his laisure, give him a plaster. Althouh in verri deed even that is more then M. Proctor for al his phisick is hable to perfourm : his big and swelling words running now in everi mans mouth as thai doo. But I culd tel you of an other manner of tragœdi that fil out betwene M. Nuce and him within this few munths, whereof there ar a gud mani witnesses that can testifi it, as wel as I : but that it were over long to run thorouh the circumstancis, and I have bene alreddi constrainid to be sumwhat tedius. Notwithstanding thus mutch I wil tel you: Marchant, and Marchant, were too quiet and soft words for them. M. Brown must be at his knave, and slave, and sumwhat more. But *an* ["sum" in margin] other time shal serv to open the hole matter unto you if nead be : for this time thus mutch, or rather thus little shal suffice, to give you a tast of M. Proctor's vain this wai. Uppon Weddensdai before dinnar I talkid with M. Nuce again, and askid him if he thouht it best I shuld proffer again to read after dinnar.

f. 32 b. M. Nuce willid me to let them alone, and not to kindle ani more coales til we hard from you : saiing it was most likelj thai wuld go on as thai had begun. Whereuppon I have not ons made the offer to read sins that time : nor dare not now give the on set, till we hear sum word or other from your wurship. In deed I know it is the smalist matter of an hundrid with them, for the schollars to want a Greek lecture a fortniht or thre weeks togither besides non termjnus. Na, I think verrely, if sum miht have there wils thai shuld have nether Greek nor Latin nor ani thing els red unto them : but shuld run at randon to whatsoever thai lustid ; studdi tungs that wuld for them, and I am deceivid if I have not hard,

quicunque vult, to that end. Thus within a few years al shuld be
turnid topset tirvi; and Pembrook Hal shuld set forth as mani
good schollars as it hath now good students: and that is as few, I
beleev, as ever you knew in the hows, sins you were first fellow.
But, as Juvenal[a] said of Traian, the good emperor, Et spes et
ratio studiorum in Cæsare[a]: so I hope verrely in the end, if God
send you life and helth, not I only but the hole collidg shal have
just cause to sai of you, which ar to our exceeding bennefit set over
us, as it were our Cæsar: how liht account soever sum of our
yung Masters wil seme to make of you. And therefore as within
the cumpas of that worthi Emperors reign, or thereabouts, there
were for orators Quintiljan and the two Plinnies; for historio-
graphers, Plutarch, Suetonius, and Tacitus; for poets, Juvenal
him self, Martial, Stella, and Silius; for philosophers, all thes or
most of thes, besides an infinite cumpani mo of excellent lernid men,
sutch as al ages have scars affourdid the like: so I trust yit, for
all these tumults, bi your quiet means and discretion, in the time
of your Mastership, this little collidg shal breed up sum great and
notable schollars in everi faculti; sutch as you yourself mai remember
to have bene of the hows within this twenti years or there about, not
a few. I mean thos singular men, the late ornaments of Cambridg,
and the glori of Pembrook Hal, Bisshop Ridli,[b] Bisshop Grindal,[c]
M. Bradford,[d] Doctor Car,[e] M. Girlingtun,[f] Doctor Hutton,[g] and
sum other that I culd name. And yet suerli I am perswadid
if thes them selvs were amongst us now, and did yeeld as gud frute

f. 33.

[a] Satires, vii. 1.

[b] Nicholas Ridley, Bishop of Rochester and London, martyred 1555.

[c] Edmund Grindal, Bishop of London, Archbishop of York and Canterbury,
1519-1583.

[d] John Bradford, Prebendary of St. Paul's, London, martyred 1555.

[e] Nicholas Carr, M.D. Regius Professor of Greek, 1523-1568.

[f] Anthony Girlington, Proctor in 1560, and Public Orator, 1560-1561, afterwards
Rector of Tilney, co. Norf.

[g] Robert Hutton, Rector of Little Braxted and Wickham Episcopi, co. Essex, and
Vicar of Catterick, co. York, died 1568.

of there studdi and lerning as ever thai did, thai wuld nothing so be æstemid and made of, as thai were by thos dais, esspecially if thai were never so litle owt of sum Momies books; as I think certainly thai culd not otherwise choos if thai had there continual abode amongst us. Notwithstanding, for al this, I trust yit to se the dai, and I hope shortly, and. I think bi your means, as I said before, when we shall al go quietly and rowndly to our books, and so in time grow to that ripenes of lerning, wisdum, and eloquens whitch thos our prædecessors grew unto: that at lenght it mai pas for a gud consequent, he is a Pembrook Hal man, ergo a good schollar, whitch I prai God we mai al ons doo, with this effect, to our own præferment and the commonwelths bennefit. And this is the verri worst in good faith that I wish the worst of them. God be with you sir, and, for the bestowing of the lecture, do in it as you shal think best for the behoof of the collidg. For mi part, I am the more desirus of it, I must needs confes, bicaus of the stipend, whitch, notwithstanding is not great; and yet suerly I wuld refuse no pains to do the schollars good, and to help forward lerning in the meanist, if there were no stipend at al. I know and confes I am able to do litle, but that whitch I am able to do bi mi private studdi I wilbe reddi to do to y$^e$ collidg proffit; and everi dai more and more as I shalbe better and better hable. Only I wuld desier men to think the better, not the wors of me, for so doing: as suerly I shuld do of them, if it miht like them to take ani pains that wai. But thus I forget both mi self and you, whilst I talk so mutch of mi self and others to you. And therefore I wil now ons again commit you to God, whos you are.

From Pembrook Hal, this first of November 1573.

---

Here the letterbook ends for the present, but is continued at f. 85. The intervening leaves contain *holograph* drafts of Harvey's verses and correspondence with Edmund Spenser.

In effigie Gascoigni [a]

Gascoignus Mercurium atque
Martem suum innocat
Illi verbo respondent.

G. Mercuri ades : M. Venio. G. Mars adsis : M. Protinus adsum.
G. Quid datis ? M.M. Ah, miser est, qui petit. G. Ecce miser.

Gascoignus solus, seipsum cum Hercule [b]
Strozza comparat, homine Italo
Eodemque viro generoso ac poeta nobili.

In eo discrimen notatur quod cum Mars et Venus utrique dominaretur, hæc tamen illum, hunc potius ille perdiderit.

Mercurius linguam : Mars dextram : Cypria mentem :
Et parvam mentem parve Cupido dabas.
Scilicet ista isti dederant eadem omnia iidem
Strozza tibi : nec aquam sic aqua pura refert.
Ambo infælices : sed erat discrimen in illo
Incidit tibi Mars : Cypria falsa mihi.
G. H. invita Minerva F[ecit].

A neue Pamflett conteininge a fewe delicate poeticall devises of Mr. G. H., extemporally written by him in Essex, at the ernest request of a certain gentleman a worshipfull frende of his, and made as it were under the gentlemans owne person, immediatly uppon y[e] reporte of y[e] deathe of M. Georg Gascoigne Esquier, and since not perusid by the autor.

Published by a familiar frende of his, that copyed them owte præsently after they were first compiled with y[e] same frends præ-

---

[a] George Gascoigne, the poet, died at Stamford, 7 Oct. 1577. *See* Coopers' Athenæ Cantabrigienses, vol. i. pp. 374-378.

[b] Hercules Strozzi, an Italian poet of Ferrara, 1471-1508.

face of dutifull commendation, and certayne other gallante appurtenances worth the readinge.[a] . . . . . . . . . . . .

A suttle and trechrous advantage (poetically imagined) taken at unawares by the 3 fatall sisters to berive M. Gascoigne of his life, notwithstandinge a former composition solemely and autentically agreid uppon betwene Mars Mercury and them to the contrarye. His lively and vitall spiritts grauntid and (by allegoricall interpretation) restorid unto him of [b] . . . . . . . . . . . .

f. 35.

   And if with pleasure thou delightes
    To feede thine eie, injoye thy fill;
   Here mayst thou gratis vewe the gostes
    That Socrates surveyith still.

   He longd to dye, thou wottst it well
    To looke ould Homer in the face
   And to dispute with Hesiode
    Queinte mysteries towchinge Poets grace.

   To marke withall Ulisses sleites,
    And heare Sir Nestors eloquence,
   And Hercules countenaunce behoulde,
    And note sage Dias[c] sapience.

   Methinkes thow gleekiste many a lorde
    And spees out maddames for the nonce
   And sporte thyselffe with this and that
    And specially with ther deinty bones.

   And all that glorious cumpany
    Of parsonages heroicall,
   To greete with salutations
    Divine and metaphysicall.

[a] Here four leaves have been cut.
[b] The above paragraph is written on a blank space in f. 34 b. and was evidently intended to come in somewhere on the recto of the first of the excised leaves.
[c] Dias of Ephesus, a Greek philosopher, *circ.* 350 B.C.

Of purpose framed longe before,
   And kennd be heart as many yeares,
As Horace would have poems kepte
   Before in printe on worde appeares.

This pleasure reape: and shake thou hands
   With auncient cuntrymen of thine:
Acquayntaunce take of Chaucer first
   And then with Gower and Lydgate dine.

And cause thou art a merry mate
   Lo Schoggin [a] where he lawghes aloane
And Skelton [b] that same madbraynd knave
   Looke how he knawes a deade horse boane.

Perdy thou art much to reioice
   That good Syr Thomas More will deyne
His cuntryman at first insight
   So curteously to interteyne.

And loa my lorde of Surrey [c] tooe
   What countenaunce he shows to the
O happye and thrise happye man
   That fyndes sutch heavenlye curtesye.

But preythe see where Withipolls cum
   Daniel and Batt both atonse
In soothe their odd copesmate thou werte
   Else would not they voutsafe the onse

---

[a] Scoggin, *alias* Scogan, Court Fool to Edward IV. *See* Doran's *History of Court Fools*, pp. 123-130.

[b] John Skelton, Poet Laureate, died 1529.

[c] Henry Howard, Earl of Surrey, 1516-1547.

Tis marvell if they have the nott
  To Maddame Beatrice belive
Well for this once I am content
  A fewe there save those twoe do thrive.

Ar ye so soone dispatche in deede
  And will not yet no better be
Well take thyn watcheworde and go proove
  What sightes and wightes bee ther to see.

Hese fast enoughe, I warrant him,
  For giving them or me the slipp:
Hese in for ever, and a daye:
  Not thence to sayle in anye shipp.

I may gesse wronge of Heavnly states
  And yet tis best to hope the beste
But whether those be there or not
  My frende, and George dwells there I trust.

And then he ioyes as goodly sightes
  And goodlier then I can conceive
Lett these my leude coniectures seeme
  And saye, false poets we deceive.

Most soer I am I have triumph
  Of them and all their auncetrye:
Be where they may be: deade they ar
  And followe must posterity.

---

f. 35 b.

To his very unfrendly frende
that procurid ye edition of his
so slender and extemporall devises.

Magnifico Signor Benevolo,[a] behoulde what millions of thankes
I recounte unto you, and behoulde how highely I esteeme of your

[a] Edmund Spenser, whom Harvey in this volume sometimes calls "Benevolo," sometimes "Immerito."

good Mastershipps overbarish and excessive curtesy, first in publishing abroade in prynte to the use or rather abuse of others, and nowe in bestowing uppon myselfe a misshapin illfavorid freshe copy of my precious poems, as it were, a pigg of myne owne sowe. Truste me, there ar sundry weighty and effectuall causes why I should accounte it the very greatist and notabliste discourtesy in good erneste that ever heretofore was offerid me by ether frende or foe : and truly there never happend any on thinge unto me that did ever disorder and distraute the power of my mynde so mutche. Alasse they were hudlid, and as you know bunglid upp in more haste then good speede, partially at the urgent and importune request of a honest goodnaturid and worshipfull yonge gentleman who I knewe, beinge privy to all circumstaunces, and very affectionate towards me or anye thinge of my dooinge, would for the tyme accept of them accordinglye: esspecially considering they were the very first rimes in effect that ever he perusid of mine in Inglishe: and so I remember I then excussid the matter, terming them my fine Verlayes,[a] and first experiments in that kinde of fingeringe and goodly wares. It is Italian curtesye to give a man leave to bee his own carver. And nowe forsoothe, as a mighty peece of worke not of mine own voluntarile election, which might have chosen a thousand matters both more agreable to my person and more acceptable to others, but they muste needs in all haste no remedye be sett to sale in Bartholomewe [b] and Stirbridge [c] fayer, with what lack ye Gentlemen? I pray you will you see any freshe newe bookes? Looke, I beseeche you, for your loove and buie for your moonye. Let me yet borrowe on crackd groate of your purse for this same span new pamflett. I wisse he is an University man that made it, and yea highlye com-

---

[a] Verlayes or vaudevilles, so called from Vire, a town in Normandy, south of Bayeux, where the first inventor of them lived.

[b] Bartholomew Fair. See *Memoirs of Bartholomew Fair*, by Henry Morley, London, 1859.

[c] Stourbridge Fair. See *Bibliotheca Topographica Britannica*, vol. v. p. 73.

mendid unto me for a greate scholler. I marry, good syr,
as you saye, so it should appeare in deede by his greate worke
by my faye he hath taken verye soare paynes, beshrowe my hart
else. What? Will iij$^d$ fetche it? I will not steeke to bestowe
so mutch in exhibition uppon the University. Doist thou smyle to
reade this stale and beggarlye stuffe in writinge that thy eares have
so often lothid and so disdaynefully abhorrd in the speakinge?
Am not I as suer as of the shirte or gowne on my backe to heare
and putt up these and twentye such odious speaches on both sides
of my hede before on fayer day be quite over paste, and nowe I
beseeche your Benivolenza what more notorious and villanous kind
of iniurye could have bene devised againste me by the mortallist

f. 36.  enemy I have in this whole world? Besides, if peradventure it
chaunce to cum once owte whoe I am, (as I can hardly conceive
howe it can nowe possibely be wholye kept in, I thanke your good
mothers eldist ungracious sonne) nowe, good Lorde, howe will my
right worshipfull and thrisevenerable masters of Cambridge scorne
at the matter? Tell me in good soothe, as thou art an honest
gentleman, doist thou not verelye suppose I shalbe utterlye dis-
credditid and quite disgracid for ever? Is it not a thinge neerelye
impossible ether still to mainetayne or againe to recoover that
præiudiced opinion of me amongste them, that heretofore, by means
of good fortune and better frendes and I knowe not what casualtye
else, was conceavid? What greater and more odious infamye for
on of my standinge in the Universitye and profession abroade then
to be reckonid in the Beaderoule of Inglish Rimers, esspecially
beinge occupied in so base an obiecte and handelinge a theame of
so slender and small importance? Canst thou tell me or doist thou
nowe begin to imagin with thyselfe what a wunderfull and exceed-
inge displeasure thou and thy Prynter have wroughte me? In good
faythe, I feare me it will fall oute, to the greatist discurtesye on
thy parte and the most famous discreddit on mine that ever was
procurid by a frende towards his frend. If they hade bene more
than excellentlye dun, flowinge, as it were, in a certayne divine

and admirable veyne, so that a good fellowe moughte well have saide, Did you ever reade so gallant passionate geere in Inglishe? What greate notable fame or creddit, I pray you, could they worke me, beinge still to bee reputid but for fine and phantasticall toyes, to make the best of them? Nowe, beinge on the contrarie side so farr otherwise, as all the worlde seithe, and I must needs confesse, howsoever it pleasith your delicate Mastershipp to bestowe a delicate liverye uppon them, and christen them by names and epithites, nothinge agreable or appliante to the thinges themselves (purposinge of all likehood to give me that as a plaster for a broakin pate), what other fruite is hereby reapid unto me, but displeasure of my worshipfullist dearist frences; malitious and infamous speaches of my professid and secrett enemyes: contempte and disdayne of my punyes and underlings? finally what but dislikinge, murmuring, whisperinge, open or cloase quippinge, notorious or auricular iybinge on every hande? In faythe, you have showid me a very frendly and gracious touche, I beshrowe your kyinde harteroote for your labour. Howbeit perforce I must nowe be constraynid (the wounde being so far past all remedy and incurable) to make a vertu of necessity as many poore honest men have dun before me, and if not sufficiently contente and satisfie myne owne phansye (which is simplye unpossible) yet to countenaunce oute the matter as easely as I can: seting the best and impudentist face of it that I can borrowe here amongst my acquayntaunce in Cambridge, havinge none such of myne owne. And herein onlye to saye trothe and to be playne, thou maist make me sum litle peece of amendes if so be your good mastershippes worshipp woulde deigne the voutesafynge me by the next carrier that cummith downe to Sterbridge fayr ether so reasonable quantity of your valorous and invincible currage or at the leste the clippings of your thrishonorable mustachyoes and subboscoes to overshadow and to coover my blushinge against that tyme. I beseech your goodlinesse ·lett this ilfavorid letter suffize for a dutifull sollicitor and remembrer in that behaulfe (and esspecially in the other œconomi-

f. 36 b.

call matter you wott of for the very greatist parte and highest poyute of all my thoughtes at this presente) without farther acquayntinge my benefactours and frendes with these pelting scholastical sutes and I præsume of our oulde familiaritye so mutch that I suppose it needlesse extraordinarilye to procure any noblemans petitory or commendatorye letters in any sutch private respectes. For the on I hope in the heavens my chin will on day be so favorable and bountifull unto me by meanes of sum hidden celestiall influence of the planettes and namely a certayne prosperous and secrete aspecte of Jupiter as to minister superabundant matter of sufficient requitall to add a certayne most reverende venerable solemne grace to my Præsidentshipp when it cummes: and as for the other it were but lost labour to reiterate the selfesame promisses and warrants that were so fully and resolutely determined uppon at our last meeting, and shall as largely and assuredly be perfourmid at the place and feaste appointid. In the meanwhile I knowe you may for your habilitye and I trust you will of your gentlenes affourde me so much of your stoare ether wayes as shall reasonabely serve to be imployed on so available and necessary uses. Rathere then fayle, I requeste you most hartelye lett me borrow them both upon tolerable usurye; I can forthwith give you my obligation for repayment of the principalls with the loane made in as forcible and substantiall manner as you or your lernid counsell can best devise.

Marry, on this condition, that your worship will be so good and favorable master unto me as give me leave to covenant and indent with you aforehand that you would voutesafe to suffer your selfe solemnely to be bownde in like obligation that nether this miserable letter nor my foresayd obligation (according to the usuall manner of this age and your owne late Præsident) be now or hereafter putt oute in print by you or yours, your advice or advices, procurement or procurements, labour or labours, meane or meanes, sollicitation or sollicitations, motion or motions, or such like, by what name or names, title or titles, appellative or appellatives, substantive or substantives, worde or wordes, so ever they have bene, bee or may be callid, termid, specified, declarid, or denominate, &c. In good erneste, and to leave thes same stale tarreeres, you knowe full well that woulde doutlesse and in very deede go to mar all and kutt off cleane all possible hope of recoovery if ether the on or the other by sum unluckye accident should so infortunately miscarry as to lighte uppon sum other men's fingers, and so consequently cum to farther scaming.

And then sum circumstances over præcisely examinid and ag- f. 37. gravatid according to sum men's pleasurable humors, especially this last most necessary discourse cf taking the paringes of thye mustachioes to loane, it would iumpe fall owte with me in respecte of y$^e$ former poems and this wofull letter with the obligation, as M. Carlill wrote once in a peece of Aristotle his Politiques, as I remember, touchinge Grouchius Newe Correction of Paionius translation—" Grouchius Paionium dum corrigere voluit depravavit." And so, contrary to our rule and maxime in bothe lawes, thou shouldist afflictionem addere afflicto cum sit potius ipsius miseriæ miserandum, accordinge to the charitable and fatherly glosse of Innocentius tertius. You see nowe what homely and ridiculous stuffe I still sende abroade amongste my frendes, accordinge to my wontid manners, rather desiringe continuaunce of entier frendshipp and ould acquayntaunce by familiar and good fellowlye writinge then affecting the commendation of an eloquente and oratorlike stile by over curious and statelye enditinge. To be shorte, I woulde to God that all the ilfavorid copyes of my nowe prostituted devises were buried a greate deale deeper in the centre of the erthe then the height and altitude of the middle region of the verye English Alpes amountes unto in your shier. And as for this paultinge letter I most affectionatelye praye the, mi best belovid Immerito, retourne it me back againe for a token, fast inclosid in thye verye next letters all to be torne and halfied in as manye and as small peeces and filters as ar the motes in the Sonne. Thus recomendinge my foresaid obligation when it cumeth to your gentle worshipps favorable and secrett tuition, I most humblye and serviceablelye, after my dutifull manner, take my leave of your Excellencyes feete and betake your gracious Mastershippe with all your right worshipfull and honorable posyes to the mightye protection of the Hyyest. Into whose bandes withall I comende myselfe and myne owne goodly devises, consideringe that (de facto) it will nowe no otherwise be, the starres and your most provident wisdum so disposinge, to whose invincible and fatall resolutions I humble and submitt my selfe. From Cambridge in hast; where, bycause we have no other newes that thou greatelye regardiste, I will not steeke to participate with the thus mutch of my private estate, that in a thousande respectes I am no lesse behouldinge to the person you wotte of, myne ould benefactour and reverend frende, then this goodlye fayer daye is unto the sun, beinge the 10 of this present, and as bewtifull a sunnye daye as cam this summer—1579.

G. H., as affectionate towards your Mastershipp as ever heretofore, conditionallye that nether this palting letter nor that tell tale obligation cum forthe in printe.

Alias, in steade of the oulde G. H. reade Grandis Hostis, as you redd once in my Greate Ostisses parlour, Grandis Hostis.

f. 37 b.
The foresayd obligation.

Noverint universi et universæ per præsentes, etc., me G. H. de Cambridge in comitatu eodem, Master of Arte, teneri et firmiter obligari E. S.[a] de London in comitatu Middlesex, gentleman, in cii crinibus sterling, de sua propria berda solvendis seu numerandis eidem E. S. de London, &c., aut suo vel suis certo vel certis atturnato vel atturnatis, hæredi vel hæredibus, executori vel executoribus, &c., seorsum vel divisim ad placitum eiusdem E. S. de London, &c., in forma subscripta, viz., in festo Annunciationis beatæ Mariæ Virginis proxime futuro xxv. in festo Pasche tunc proximo sequente

---

[a] Edmond Spenser.

xxv. in festo beati S. Johannis Baptistæ tunc proximo sequente xxv. et in festo vulgariter nuncupato festo Omnium Sanctorum xxvii. et sic de festo in festum, &c., viz. in quolibet festo trium festorum priorum xxv., et tunc in ultimo, viz. in festo Omnium Sanctorum xxvii. quousque dicti cii. crines sterling de sua propria berda, plenarie et totaliter sic persolvantur seu numerentur. Ad quas quidem solutiones, seu numerationes et quamlibet earum (ut præmittitur) bene et fideliter in forma prædicta faciendas, solvendas, seu numerandas, obligo me aut meum certum vel certos atturnatum vel atturnatos, hæredem vel hæredes, executorem vel executores, &c.

The Condicion of this obligation  f. 38.

(which haply my yunge Italianate Seignior and French Monsieur will objecte).

What thoughe Italy, Spayne, and Fraunce ravisshed with a certayne glorious and ambitious desier (your gallantshipp would peradventure terme it zeale and devotion) to sett oute and advaunce ther owne languages above the very Greake and Lattin, if it were possible, and standinge altogither uppon termes of honour and exquisite formes of speaches, karriinge a certayne brave, magnificent grace and maiestye with them, do so highly and honorablely esteeme of their countrye poets reposing on greate parte of their sovraigne glory and reputation abroade in the worlde in the famous writings of their nobblist wittes? What though you and a thousand such nurrishe a stronge imagination amongst yourselves that Alexander, Scipio, Cæsar, and most of ower honorablist and worthyest captaynes had never bene that they were but for pore blinde Homer? What thoughe it hath universally bene the practisse of the floorishingist States and most politique commonwelthes from whence we borrowe our substantiallist and most materiall præceptes and examples of wise and considerate governement, to make y$^e$ very most of ther vulgare tunges, and togither with there seignioryes and dominions by all meanes possible to amplifye and enlarge them, devisinge all ordinarye and extraordinarye helpes, both for the polisshinge and refininge them at home, and alsoe for the spreddinge and dispersinge of them abroade? What though Il Magnifico Segnior "Immerito" Benivolo[a] hath notid this amongst his politique discourses and matters of state and governemente that the most couragious and valorous minds have evermore bene where was most furniture of eloquence and greatist stoare of notable orators and famous poets? What a goddes name passe we what was dun in ruinous Athens or decayid Roome a thousand or twoe thousande yeares agoe? Doist thou not oversensibely perceive that the markett goith far otherwise in Inglande wherein nothinge is reputid so contemptible, and so baselye and vilelye accountid of as whatsoever is taken for Inglishe, whether it be handsum fasshions in apparrell, or seemely and honorable in behaviour, or choise wordes and phrases in speache or anye notable thinge else in effecte that savorith of our owne cuntrye, and is not ether merely or mixtely outlandishe? Is it not cleerer then the sonne at noonedayes that oure most excellent Inglish treatises, were they never so eloquentlye contrived in prose, or curiously devised in meeter, have ever to this daye, and shall ever hereafter, be sibb to arithmetericians, or marchantes counters, which nowe and then stande for hundreds and thousands, by and bye for odd halfpens or farthinges and otherwhiles for very nihils? Hath your monsieurshipp so soone forgottin our long Westminster conference the verie last Ester terme touchinge certain odd peculiar qualities, appropriate in a manner to Inglishe beddes, and esspeciallye that same worthy and notorious βριταννικὴν ζηλοτυπίαν, that Erasmus[b] prettily playeth withall in a certayne gallant and brave politique epistle of his, written purposely to an Inglish gentleman, a courtier, to instructe him howe he mighte temporize, and courte it best here in Inglande? Is not this the principall fundation and grande maxim of our cuntry pollicy, not to be over hasty in occupying a mans talent, but to be very chary

[a] Spenser.
[b] Erasmus' *Epistles*, cxlii. Leyden, 1706. Folio.

and circumspect in opening himselfe and revealinge his gifts unto others? Is it not on of the highest pointes of our Inglish experiencid wisdum, and, as a man would saye, the very profoundist mystery of our most deepe and stayd hedds, to have every on in continuall ielouzye, lest he sitt over neere there schirtes or have familiar insighte in ther commendable and discommendable qualityes? Doth not silence cover and conceale many a want, and is it not both an easier and far surer way to maynetayne and nurrish the opinion of a mans excellency by noddinge and countenauncinge oute the matter ether with tunge or penne withoute thessame discoursing vagaries after a certayne solemne manner then by speakinge or writinge to purchisse creddit? Esspecially in Inglishe where Inglishe is contemnid or in meeter where meeter goith a begginge? And canst thou tell me nowe, or doist thou at the last begin to imagin with thy selfe what a wonderfull and exceeding displeasure thou and thy prynter have wroughte me, and howe peremptorily ye have preiudishd my good name for ever in thrustinge me thus on the stage to make tryall of my extemporall faculty, and to play Wylsons[a] or Tarletons[b] parte. I suppose thou wilt go nighe hande shortelye to sende my lorde " of Lycesters,[c] or my lorde of Warwickes,"[d] Vawsis,[e] or my lord Ritches[f] players, or sum other freshe starteupp comedanties unto me for sum newe devised interlude, or sum malt conceivid comedye fitt for the Theater,[g] or sum other paintid stage whereat thou and thy lively copesmates

f. 38 b.

[a] Thomas Wilson, one of the Queen's Players. *See* Stowe's *Annales*, ed. 1615, p. 697.

[b] Richard Tarleton, Court Jester to Queen Elizabeth, died of the plague in 1588. *See* Shakespeare Society's Publications, *Tarltons Jests*, ed. by J. O. Halliwell, 1844.

[c] Leicester's Players. *See* F. G. Fleay's *Shakespeare Manual*, pp. 76-81.

[d] Warwick's Players. *See* as above.

[e] Vaux' Players. Not in Fleay's *Manual*.

[f] Rich's Players. Not in Fleay's *Manual*.

[g] This was the theatre near Shoreditch; being the first regular theatre in London it was called The Theatre *par excellence*.

in London maye lawghe ther mouthes and bellyes full for pence or twoepence apeece? By cause peradventure thou imaginest Unico Aretino[a] and the pleasurable Cardinall Bibiena,[b] that way esspecially attraynid to be so singularly famous. And then perhappes not longe after uppon newe occasion (an God will) I must be M. Churchyards[c] and M. Eldertons[d] successours tooe, and finally cronycled for on of the most notorious ballat makers and Christmas carollers in the tyme of Her Maiestyes reigne. Extra iocum. In good troothe, and by the fayth of a most faythfull frende, I feareme exceedinglye thou haste alreddy hazardid that that will fall owte to your greatist . . . . . . . . .

*Cætera desunt.*

A.B. Me thinkes I see the bite y<sup>e</sup> lipp,
At queinte newfanglid vanities,
At strange outlandishe forreyne wares,
At monstrous disguised guises.

Me thinkes I see the hange y<sup>e</sup> browe,
At periuryes and blasphemies,
At payntid vizardes and wizards,
At highe and deepe hypocrisees.

Me thinkes I see the shake y<sup>e</sup> hedd,
At such and such collusions,
As these and these have putt in me,
To his and her confusions.

---

[a] Unico Aretino = Pietro Aretino. *See* Mazzuchelli, *Vita di Pietro Aretino*, Milan, 1830.

[b] Bernardo Bibbiena, 1470-1520. *See* Paolo Giovio's *Elogium Bernardi Bibbiennæ*, f. 40 b. Venice, 1546.

[c] Thomas Churchyard, the Poet, 1520-1604. *See* Wood's *Athenæ*, vol. i. p. 727.

[d] William Elderton, Master of the Westminster Boys Company, died about 1592. *See* Wood's *Athenæ*, vol. i. p. 499.

Me thinkes I see the make a mowthe
  At certayne Tuscane brave conceites,
And so thou doist, and so thou maiste,
  At many Florentyne receytes.

(Whuist, not a worde nor halfe a worde
  Of perfumes or the pike sauce,
Or Fico foistid in thy dishe,
  Or thy first P. or Batts first pawse.)

And sithe I am nowe in the veyne
  Me thinkes ten millions of deceiptes
Must nedes amounte to greate huge summes
  Of iestes and laughtures and sutch baytes.

Me thinkes I heere a comicall scoff
  Against sum persons tragicall,
Upbraiding the of tyrannyes,
  And outrages and divell, and all.

Me thinkes thou sckornist seigniores,
  And gibist at thrise mightye peeres,
And maakst a ieste of monumentes,
  And caarst not for a thousand yeeres.

Me thinkes I see a newe Steele Glasse,
  A second girdinge satyre,
Not sutch a sainete againe in heaven
  Do moove us silly sowles to ire.

What George?[a] I pray the spare the world
  And give men leave to temporize;
Our tyme is shorte, weele lawghe with the,
  If once to heaven we take our rise.

[a] George Gascoigne.

Inioye thine owne pleasures aboove,
   Lett us aloane with ours beneathe,
And yet ifaythe sum fooleryes
   Will Sumner moughte to Patche [a] bequeathe.

Those frumpe a gods name to thy fill,
   Good leave thou haste such toyes to skoffe;
But thinke in worlde a worlde must be,
   And swine you wott will to y$^e$ troffe.

And where is huffcapp there is huff,
   And where is revell there is rowte.
What marvell, thoughe a London stage
   With fooles be compasd rounde abowte?

I did longe since drawe to an ende,
   But to what pleasure pleasures have,
Your ioyes no sooner cam to minde,
   But they a fresh discourse did crave.

My only purpose was to quote
   A epitaph to fitt your tum;
If for the iest a name you will:
   Call it A. C.'s memorandum.
        FINIS.

---

A thousande recomendations presupposid unto your good wisdum, and twise as many to your goodly worshipp. I certified your goodlines the last weeke as well bi letters as by my factour in that behalfe, M. Umphrye,[b] howe litle corne was shaken in y$^e$ late greate outragious tempest you wott of; and nowe forsoothe approachith y$^e$ solemne and grand feaste of Pennycoste, I wisse

---

[a] Patch, Jester to Cardinal Wolsey. *See* Doran's *Court Fools*, pp. 132-134.
[b] Humphrey Tyndale. *See* p. 20, note [c].

a greater plague than y<sup>e</sup> former, and farr more terrible privately unto my purse then that other publickly præiudiciale agaynste my good name. And may it please your good Mastershipp to heare all? Marry, Syr, the very worst and most unlookid for newes is yit behinde. Forsoothe my poore selfe for wante of a better must be faynte to supply y<sup>e</sup> roome of a greater Clarke and play Il Segnor Filosofoes parte uppon the Comencemente stage. A most suddayne and strange resolution in all respectes. O that I were a compounde of all the sciences as well speculative as active and specially those that consist in a certayne practicall discourse ether of speach or reason (notwithstanding ther excessive vanitye) that the ilfavorid coniurer Agrippa[a] so furiously and outragiously cryeth oute uppon. It were a fitt of frenesis moria I suppose to wishe y<sup>e</sup> morall and philosophicall wisdum of Socrates, y<sup>e</sup> divine notions and conceites of Plato, y<sup>e</sup> suttle and intricate acumen of Aristotle, y<sup>e</sup> brave eloquence of Tully y<sup>e</sup> gallant pronunciation of Hortensius, and so forthe, after y<sup>e</sup> manner of thessame greate learnid scholarissimi scholares that rowle so trimly in there antiquityes, whereas we knowe not for cerzainty whether any sutch creatures and apotheoses were ever in the worlde or noe, or, if peradventure they were, who seeith not they must needes be rotten above a hundrith thousande ages agone, not so mutch as the lest signification of an ould ilfavorid tumbe or any peece of a rustye monumente remaining behinde to helpe colour the matter. But would to God in heaven I had awhile for there sake the profounde lerninge of M. Duffington, the mysticall and supermetaphysicall philosophy of Doctor Dee,[b] the rowlinge tongue ether of M. Williamson, ouer fine Cambridge barber, or of Mistrisse Trusteme-trulye, mye Welche ostisse, the trim lattin phrases and witty proverbes of him that built Caius College[c] and

---

[a] Henry Cornelius Agrippa A Nettesheim, 1486—1535.

[b] John Dee, 1527—1604, the famous wizard, Fellow of Trinity College, Cambridge.

[c] John Caius, M.D., Founder of Caius College, 1510—1573.

made Londinensis Booke de Antiquitate, y^e audacity of my cuntryman M. Atturnye and Clarke of ouer towne, and lastly, the disputative appetite of Doctor Busbye,[a] with the like affectionate zeale to the Commencement groates and afternoone seavenaclocke dinnars, which persons according to ther severall quality do all still floorishe and karry the creddit at this daye. Kunninge would nowe be, I perceive, no burden, and eloquence, if a man had it, were more worth then a crackd testerne in his purse or a payer of tatterid venetias[b] in his presse. Had it not nowe bene a point of wisdom to have layed upp against a deere yeare? And to have furnisshed myselfe a yeare or twoe since of sutch necessary howsehowlde provision as is requisite at such a droute? Good Eloquence and gentle Philosophy, and ye loove me pittye my case and helpe me this once, and I will never be assuredlye hereafter soe farr to seeke agayne. Ye have holpen sum I knowe owte of the same place to fayer riches and good mariages and I knowe not what secrett likinge else: I beseech ye nowe extende your favorable curtesyes thus far towards me as to afforde me on tolerable oration, and twoe or three reasonable argumentes, and lett me aloane agoddes name to shifte for the other myselfe. I am not to trouble y^e often: goodnowe be a litle compassionate this once. I have no other meanes or staye in the whole worlde to repose my affiaunce in, being heggid in on everyside with so many pore bankerupte neyghbours, that ar a greate deale reddier, Godd wott, to borrowe abroad of every on then to lende at home to any on. And yet have I on suer frende as harde as the world goith (I meane my familiar, the Pheere of that which attendid uppon M. Phaer[c] in Kylgarran[d] Forest when he translatid Virgils Æneidos) [by his familiar it is most likely he

[a] Humphrey Busbye, LL.D., Fellow of Trinity Hall, Regius Professor of Civil Law, died *ante* 1580.
[b] Venetias, a kind of hose or breeches made to come below the garters.
[c] Thomas Phaer, a Welsh physician, of Kilgerran, co. Pembroke, the first English translator of Virgil. He died in 1560. See Wood's *Athenæ*, i. 316.
[d] Kilgerran Forest, on the River Teifi, two miles south of the town of Cardigan.

menith his paper booke],[a] that never yet faylid me at a pinche; peradventure he would not greately steek to shewe me a taste of his office and " disburse "[b] sumthinge for me if I could assure him once to sett a good surlye countenaunce on the matter and face it oute lustelye as sum other good fellowes doe. The wante whereof is the speciallist defecte that he comonly reprehendith in me. And therefore here I am most humbely to request your good Mastershippes favorable advise howe I mighte best attayne that same excellent vertue and most divine prædominante qualitye which I nowe speake of. The only vertue in effecte in the whole crissecrosse rowe ether of morall or intellectuall vertues that nowe adayes karrieth meate in the mowthe. The rest in amanner ar owte of fasshion and overstale for so queynte and queasye a worlde: your delicacy would haply have delighted your self in overturning ye proverbe upsyedowne and terminge them more artificiallye, mowthe withoute meate. I knowe a wise and worshipfull gentleman that giveth this for on of his posyes, O Temperantia Dea: That is no commencement posye, when ypocrasse and marchepane and all ower apothecary delicacyes runne a begginge. O Dearum dea impudentia would fitt sum of our turnes amongst a number of singular odd devises and emblemes where in he excellithe and serve our purpose a greate deale better. The worse ilfavorid lucke his that must ether putt upp his pipes and helpe to furnishe upp a dum showe, or else goe a borrowinge or begginge where it is that wantith a certayne thinge so necessarilye behoovefull: in very deede the soverayne ladye and supreme goddesse of vertues and in a manner the only foundrisse and defendresse as well of the theoricks as practicks in all sciences and professions, and namely the very mother and nurse of our most mysticall and profondist morall naturall and supernaturall philosophy. And herein only to say trothe and to be playne thyselfe mayest make me on generall grande amendes for all the particular petite iniuryes and despites that ever thou hast ether trechrously

f. 40 b.

[a] The words within square brackets are written in the margin.
[b] The word "disburse" has been scored through, and an unreadable equivalent written beneath.

devised or ungraciously practised against me to this daye if so be
your good masterships worshipp would deygne the voutesafinge me
by the nexte London karrier that comith downe to Midsomer fayer,
ether sum reasonable quantity and portion of your valorous and
invincible currage, or at the lestewise the clyppinges of your
thrise honorable mustachyoes and subboscoes, to overshaddowe and
cover my blushinge agaynste that tyme. I beseech your gallantshipp lett this stammringe letter suffize for a dutifull sollicitour
and rememberer in that behalfe (and esspecially in the other oeco-
nomicall matter you wott of, the very greatist parte and highest
poyute of all my thoughtes at this præsente notwithstandingē yᵉ
residue ar as you see) withoute farther acquayntinge my benefactours and frendes with these peltinges scholasticall sutes. I
præsume of our owlde familiarity so mutch that I supposd it
needles extraordinarily to procure any nobleman's petitory or
comendatory letters in any sutch private respectes. For the on I
hope in the heavens my chin will on daye be so favorable and
bewntifull unto me by meanes of sum hidden cælestiall influence
of the planets, and namely, a certayne prosperous and secrete
aspecte of Jupiter, as bothe to minister superabundant matter of
sufficient requitall; and to add a certayne solemne venerable grace
to my most reverend Regenteshipp when it cumes in actum. And
as for the other, in my fansye it were but lost labour to reiterate
the selfesame promisses and warrantes that were so fully and resolutely determined uppon at ower last meetinge; and shall as
largely and assuredly be perfourmid at yᵉ place and feaste appointid. In yᵉ meane space I knowe you maye for your hability,
and I præsume you will of your gentlenes, affourde me so mutch of
your stoare other wayes as shall reasonablely serve to be imployed
on so avayleable and necessary uses. Rather then fayle, I request
you most humbly let me borrowe them bothe uppon tolerable
usurye. I am forthwith to give you my obligation for repayment
of the principalls with the loane at the daye appoyntid, contrived
in as forcible and substantiall manner as your selfe or your lernid
counsell can best devise. Marry on this generall condition that

your worship wilbe so good and favorable Master unto me as give me leave to covenant and indente with you aforehande that you voutesafe to suffer yourselfe to be bownde in like obligation that nether this miserable letter nor my foresayde obligation (according to the usuall accustomid manner of this prægnant age, and the late notorious præsident of a frende of ouers that publishethe abroade every childish ridiculous toye which I shall never forgett, beinge so utterlye beyounde all exspectation and likehood) be nowe or hereafter wholye or by peecemeale severally by themselves or iointlye with sum other pamflett copied oute or putt forthe in prynte by you or youers, youer advice or advices, procurement or procurements, labour or labours, meane or meanes, sollicitation or sollicitations, motion or motions, permission or permissions, or sutche like, by what name or names, title or titles, appellative or appellatives, substantive or substantives, worde or wordes, so ever they have bene, bee or may be callid, termid, specified, denominate or declarid, &c. Not forgetting youer oulde Autenticall Rule, that you were wunt to saye you lernid first of ower Master Rydge, Cautela superabundans non nocet. Extra iocum, and to leave thessame stale karreeres you knowe fullwell it woulde suerly quite mare all, and utterly discredditt me for ever beyonde all possible hope of recoverye if either the on or the other by sum unlucky accidente should so unfortunately miskarrye, as but once to lighte uppon sum other mens delicate fingers, and so consequentlye cum to farther skanninge. And then sum circumstaunces over præcisely examined and aggravatid accordinge to sum mens pleasurable humors, esspecially this laste most necessary discourse of takinge they wott not what to loane, it would iumpe fall oute with me, in respecte of sum former matters, and this wofull letter with the telltale obligation, as M. Carleile wrote once in a peece of Aristotle (his politiques, as I remember), towchinge Growchius newe correction of Perionius' translation : Grouchius Perionium dum corrigere voluit, depravavit. And so contrary to the gentle and pitifull maxime in both lawes, thoue shouldist afflictionem addere afflicto ; cum sit potius ipsius miseriæ miserandum, accor-

dinge to y^e charitable and fatherly glosse of Innocentius Tertius.
You see howe the burnt childe dreadith fier; and he that once
smartid for Nifilles and sum prætendid oversightes will not lightely
incurr the least ieopardy, seeme the offence never so pardonable,
and his defence never so reasonable and effectuall. I beseeche,
you in good ernest, have speciall regarde to the præmisses, and
whatsoever I comunicate privately with yowe or howe merrely so
ever I write unto you, lett it be Mum to all the world beside, and
reckonid in secretis non revelandis.

f. 41 b. You see I reteyne my accustomid manner in sendinge still
abroade amongst my frendes such homelye ridiculous stuffe as I
was wonte, and as my pen is yet best acquayntid withall; rather
desiringe continuaunce of entier frendshipp and owlde acquayntaunce by familiar and good fellowly writinge, then affectinge the
comendation of an eloquent and oratorlike style by overcurious
and statelye enditinge. In deede it makith no matter howe a
man wrytith untoe his frends so he wryte frendlye: other præceptes
of arte and stile and decorum, and I know not what, ar to be
reservid for an other place. And truly in my conceyte where
argumente of gravity and matter of importaunce is wantinge, y^e
more conceited toyes and devises all the better. What ar letters
amongst frendes but familiar discourses and pleasante conferences?
and what Stoick or Eremite will bar them of any merriments and
jestes that are not ether merely undecent or simply unhonest?

Thanke my good Masters of Cambridge for this apologye. You
knowe I was not wonte to truble myself or others greately with
any sutch kindes ether of maydenlye excuses or schollarlye defence.
But since all things ar becum haynous and scandalous, at every
man's pleasure, it standith us poore sowles in hande to answer for
ower selves as well as ower silly wittes and simple tunges will give
us leave.

God be praysid the thinges themselves for the greater parte ar
not so offensive to quèsy consciences, but they **are as defensive**
against cavillinge obiections. Thus commendinge and recomend-

inge mye poor sutes with yᵉ foresayd obligation when it cummes to your gentle worshippes favorable consideration and secrett tuition, I most humbely and serviceablely after my oulde dutifull manner take my leave at your Excellency's feete and betake your gratious Mastershipp with all your right worshippfull and honorable posyes to yᵉ mighty protection of yᵉ highest.

From my chamber the daye after mye victorye. But see a fitt of my arte memorative. I had quite forgotte the odd embrodered token that M. Pumfrittes man deliverid me from your good Mastershipp the other daye. Ower courtinge manner is nowe to give the choyce of a thousand thankes for every gewegawe; and sumtymes tooe for very meere Nifilles as it were only pro forma tantum. Go tooe then, seinge thankes, to speake præcisely, ar but wordes.

---

Twoe pleasaunte and merry conceitid letters, on to my self immediately before his Masters Comencement, the other to an odd fantasticall Miller that made loove to a certayne mayde of his acquayntance; which twooe letters I fownde nowe perchaunce amongst a number of myne oulde scatterid papers, and in sum considerations thought it not greately amisse (notwithstandinge yᵉ levity of yᵉ argument in bothe) to crowde them in for cumpanye sake amongst yᵉ reste; præsuminge, as in the reste, of yᵉ Autors pardon, if any trespas be committid herein, or matter of iuste offence any waye ministrid.

f. 42.

　　　　The letter to my sellfe
　　　　　　verbatim, as
　　　it was deliverid unto me in an Inne of Courte
　　　　　　in his owne hande.

I shalbe contente after a newe fasshion to lende you the choyce of as many gentle wordes and loovelye termes as we in Inglande use to deliver ower thankes in. Choose whether you will have them given or yeeldid, renderid or recontid, impartid or repayde, kutt owte of the whole cloathe, or otherwise powrid owte in the bravist most gallant phraces that ar ether nowe allreddy takin upp or shall hereafter be devised amongst the finest discoursinge tunges.

A rehitall not so phantasticall in shewe as playne and simple in deede. The very payment of a bankerowte; and the only token you are like to receive from me at this presente besides a farewell or twooe of the largist size. A mysticall and thrise happy worde, wherein is cowchid the mightiest and sovraingist name (Ell y<sup>e</sup> name of God) under or above the heavens. On of the highest and divinist poyntes, that I leruid oute of Aggrippaes supernotable fourthe booke de Occulta Philosophia. And saye nowe, I have once in my life bestowid uppon the a Byenote for thy lerninge; and so once again take Ell with the.

He that is faste bownde unto the in more obligations then any marchante in Italy to any Jewe there.

---

f. 42 b and 43.

Concerninge y<sup>e</sup> cheefist generall poynte of your Mastershippes letters, youerselfe ar not ignorant that scholars in ower age ar rather nowe Aristippi then Diogenes: and rather active then contemplative philosophers: coveting above alle thinges under heaven to appeare sumwhat more then schollars if themselves wiste howe; and of all thinges in the worlde most detestinge that spitefull malicious proverbe,<sup>a</sup> of greatist Clarkes, and not wisest men. The date whereof they defende was exspired when Dunse and Thomas of Aquine with the whole rablement of schoolemen were abandonid ower schooles and expellid the Universitye. And nowe of late forsoothe to helpe countenaunce owte the matter they have gotten Philbertes<sup>b</sup> Philosopher of the Courte, the Italian Archebysshoppies brave Galatro, Castiglioes fine Cortegiano,<sup>c</sup> Bengalassoes

---

<sup>a</sup> *See* Arber's reprint of Ascham's *Scholemaster*, p. 37.

<sup>b</sup> Philbert of Vienne. *The Philosophy of the Courte.* Englished by Geo. North. London, 1575. 8vo.

<sup>c</sup> Balthazar Castiglione. *Il Cortegiano; or, The Courtier.* Translated by Thomas Hobby. London, 1556, 1561. 4to.

Civil Instructions to his Nephewe Seignor Princisca Ganzar: Guatzoes[a] newe Discourses of curteous behaviour, Jouios[b] and Rassellis Emblemes in Italian, Paradines in Frenche, Plutarche[c] in Frenche, Frontines Stratagemes,[d] Polyenes Stratagemes,[e] Polonica, Apodemica, Guigiandine,[f] Philipp de Comines, and I knowe not howe many owtlandishe braveryes besides of the same stampe. Shall I bazarde a litle farther: and make you privy to all our privityes indeede. Thou knoist Non omnibus dormio et tibi habeo non huic. Aristotles Organon is nighhand as litle redd as Dunses Quodlibet.[g] His oeconomicks and politiques every on hath by rote. You can not stepp into a schollars studye but (ten to on) you shall litely finde open ether Bodin de Republica[h] or Le Royes Exposition[i] uppon Aristotles Politiques or sum other like Frenche or Italian Politique Discourses.

And I warrant you sum good fellowes amongst us begin nowe to be prettely well acquayntid with a certayne parlous booke callid, as I remember me, Il Principe di Niccolo Macchiavelli, and I can peradventure name you an odd crewe or tooe that ar as cuninge in his Discorsi sopra la prima Deca di Livio, in his Historia Fiorentina, and in his Dialogues della Arte della Guerra tooe, and

[a] Stephen Guazzo. *Of Conversation;* in four books; into English by G. Pettie and B. Young. London, 1586. 8vo.

[b] Paolo Javio's *Ragionamento sopra i Motti e Disegni, d'Arme d'Amore.* Milan, 1559. 8vo. Con un Discorso di Ruscelli.

[c] *Plutarchi Vitæ gallice,* par Jacques Amyot. 1565. Folio. *Plutarchi Moralia gallice,* par Jacques Amyot. Paris, 1572. 2 tom. folio.

[d] Frontini's *Stratagems.* Translated into English by Richard Morysine. London, 1539. 8vo.

[e] Polyænus' *Stratagems.* I can find no English translation of this work before 1793.

[f] Francisco Guicciardini's *History of Italy.* Translated by Geoffrey Fenton, 1579. Folio.

[g] *See* Mullinger's *University of Cambridge,* pp. 629-631.

[h] Jean Bodin's *De Republica libri sex.*

[i] Louis le Roy *alias* Regius, Professor at Coustances; died in 1577.

in certayne gallant Turkishe Discourses tooe, as University men were wont to be in their parva Logicalia and Magna Moralia and Physicalia of both sortes; verbum intelligenti sat; you may easily coniecture y<sup>e</sup> rest yourselfe; esspecially being on that can as soone as an other spye lighte at a little whole. But, howesoever, most of us have exspired the settinge downe, or rather settinge upp of this conclusion towchinge the exspiringe of the foresayde date as a most necessary Universitye principle and mayne foundation of all our credditt abroade; me thinkes still for sum speciall common welthe affayres and many particular matters of counsell and pollicye, besides daylyə freshe newes and a thousande both ordinary and extraordinary occurrents and accidents in the worlde we ar yet (notwithstanding all and singular the præmises) to take instructions and advertisements at you lawiers and courtiers bandes, that ar continuallye better traynid and more livelye experiencid therein, then we university men ar or possibely can be, or else peradventure when we shall stande most in our owne conceites we maye haplye deceyve and disgrace ower selves most, and in sum bye matters when we leaste thinke of it, committ greater errors, and more fowly overshoote ower selves then we be yet aware of or can coniecturally imagin. For my selfe, I recounte it on soveragne poyute of my feylicitye in genere and sum particular contentement of mynde that I have sutch an odd frende in a corner, so honest an yuthe in y<sup>e</sup> city, so trew a gallant in y<sup>e</sup> courte, so towarde a lawier, and so witty a gentleman, that both can sufficiently for his rare pregnancy in conceyte, and will gladlye for his singular forwardnes in courtesye—I wuld fayne ende this periode, were it not that a certayne extraordinary passion, and on suddayne most effectuall conceyte will needes curtoll it of in y<sup>e</sup> midste. And nowe, good syr, you get nott halfe a worde more of me towchinge this article, savinge my ould coolinge carde, Item, a litle to abate your Mastershippes currage that, as we graute you y<sup>e</sup> superioritye in sum speciall particularityes concerning ower owne cuntrye, so you must needes acknowledge us your masters in all generall poyntes of governement, and the great archepollycyes of all ould and newe common welthes. As for those other particulars you write of concerning my private estate, and namely, mye commencement matters, when I am better resolvid my selfe you shall heare more. In the meane, I crave pardon.

---

then[a] to lende alsoe to any on. Save that my familiar that never yit faylid me at a pinche and once taughte me a generall polilcy for all, whensoever I should have any goodly and notable peece of worke in hande, to imitate wise gentlewoomen that, being desirous to bringe forthe fayer and amiable children when they goe abowte that worke, and esspecially at y[e] tyme of ther conceivinge and afterwarde tooe, being greate with childe, have for the nouse ever before their eies the delicate pictures ether of most beautifull and diamonde wenches as Hebe, Daphne, and Io if they looke for dawghters or else the goodlyest and wellfavoriddest boyes that ever were in the worlde, as Adonis, Ganymedes, and Cupide, if they make ther counte of sunnes; that the continuall and delightfull sightes of so amiable and gallant obiectes taking deepe impression in ther imaginations, and both passionately workinge and strongelye setlinge in ther fansyes, mighte cause, and as it were ingender a certayne like delicate conformity and resemblaunce of sutch and sutch bewtifull and loovely graces in there infantes.

f. 44.

Since which tyme A gat me the lively counterfaytes of Socrates, Plato, and Aristotle, with certayne notable epigrammes and emblemes of them all, to behoulde continually when I should have any deepe philosophy matter in hande: of Demosthenes, Tullye, and Hortensius, against I were to playe the orator; of Homer, Aristophanes, Virgil, and Horace to serve for my præsidentes, and patternes, if I must needes putt on the poets vizarde awhile; and so likewise of certayne others, as excellent and passinge in there

[a] Folio 44 evidently contains corrections of and additions to the former letter at f. 40, but there is no mark to show where they were meant to be inserted.

kyndes, for sum severall uses and propertyes, wherewith I purpose not to acquaynte all the worlde. But alasse this devise I see is over generall, and will not nowe I feare me bould oute at so greate a distance to serve the turne. I must in hande with my familiar for a newe stratageme.

---

f. 45.   As many and as fewe salutations as you liste. Will you beleeve me? Your lastweekes letter, or rather bill of complaynte was deliverid me at myne hostisses by the fyersyde, beinge fastebeggid in rownde abowte on every side with a company of honest good fellowes, and at that tyme reasnable honeste quaffers. I first runned it over cursorilye to my selfe, and spyinge the argument so generall (savinge in on pointe onlye, where I layed a strawe), and withall so fittinge the humor of that crewe, after a shorte preface to make attention, began to pronounce it openly in the audience of the whole assemblye in sutch sorte as the brave orator Aeschines is reportid on a tyme to have redd owte with a wonderfull greate grace (in the hearinge of y$^e$ Rodians, amongst whome he then soiornid,) that noble oration of Demosthenes in defence of Ctesiphon.

Shall I be playne with you? It was solemely agreeid uppon, that the letter for the manner of the enditinge was very hanssomly penid and full of many proper conceiptes, but y$^e$ argumentes whereuppon y$^e$ libell of complaynte studd, were definitively condemnid, as unsufficient. To be shorte, ower finall resolution was, that an answer should incontinentlye be contrived amongst us all, savinge that on was to be dispensid withall, to playe the secretarye. The matter most specially concerninge me, I toulde them I was contente to beare twoe partes, and to playe bothe a quarter answerer and whole secretarye. My service being accepted of, y$^e$ first began, as followith:—

Sir, yower newe complaynte of y$^e$ newe worlde is nye as owlde as Adam and Eve, and full as stale as y$^e$ stalist fasshion that hath

bene in fasshion since Noes fludd. You crie owte of a false and
trecherous worlde, and therein ar passinge eloquent and patheticall
in a degree above the highest. Nowe I beseeche you, Syr, did not
Abell live in a false and trecherous worlde, that was so villanouslye
and cruelly murtherid of his owne very brother? Na, did not
ould Grandsier himselfe live in a false and trecherous worlde, that
was so suttellye and fraudulentlye putt beside so incomparablely
ritche and goodlye possession as Paraside (*sic*) was?

The storyes to this effecte—Tower of Babel, Sodome—ar notori-   f. 45 b.
ouslye knowne; there be infinite thousands of examples to proove
that the first men in $y^e$ worlde were as well ower masters in villanye as ether predecessours in tyme or fathers in consanguinitye.
Lett us not be so iniurious to remaender antiquitye as to deprive
$y^e$ fardist of, of his due commendation, nether must we be so
parcially affectionate towards any as, against ower owne consciences, to conceale these notorious and infamous trecheryes. Un-
dowtidlye the very worlde itselfe millions of yeares before the
Creation was predestinate to be a schoolehowse and shopp of all
villanyes, and even then I suppose the ilfavoritid sprites and divells
that nowe so truble and infecte the world were a devisinge and
premeditatinge those infinite severall kindes and varietyes of
wickednes, that immediately after the Creation and ever since they
have so basely blowne abroade and so cuninglye plantid in everye
quarter and corner of the worlde.

The fyer is a queynte subtile element beyonde the reatche and
capacity of our divinist and most mysticall philosophers (I excepte not
Hermes himselfe, whom they terme $y^e$ very perfectiste philosopher
nexte unto God himselfe), and I knowe not by what extraordinarye
and secret meanes $y^e$ knowledge thereof shoulde desende into the intelligible and reasonable parte, but by the ministry and mediation
of owtewarde and externall sences and be cabalistically conveyid
over from age to age; which biinge utterlye absurde (for who ever
sae or felte the veryo pure firye element unlesse it were perchaunce
Prometheus or sum like imaginarye wonder of the worlde?) why

maye not that which they call fyer for any thinge that is certainely knowne to the contrarye be the very local place and seate of Hell, where is sutch horrible fierworkes and sutch continual burninge flames as both the formiddiste Catholique divines and most excellent profane writers threaten against the wickid? or at lestewise why maye it not be a certayne excessive and everlastinge beate, proceedinge from the whott breathes of so many divellishe fierye sprites and scaldinge feindes, as ar there inhabitinge, and bye a forcible burninge influence inflaminge the alreddye furious and boylinge minds of tyrants and whott impatient divellish fellowes (wherwith the fowre partes of the worlde are nowe sett on fier, and which finallye according to the most aunncient divine oracles and fatall destinyes must necessarilye consume and destroye all) to all kindo of colerick passions, extreame outrages and horrible crueltyes as well for pleasure as revenge or otherwise? And then, as for the aier or winde, not the profondist philosopher that ever wrote to this daye can tell me or dare undertake to determine what it is. Maye it not be, trowe you, a compounde of aierye, wyndie, raynie, snowye, frostye, coulde, whott, fayre, fowle, howlsum, contagious caulme and blusteringe tempestuous sprites? replenishinge everye place where it entrith (and it enterith at all aventure in every place beinge not allreddie fulfilled with sum other corpulent bodye) with diversitye of like qualities and effectes, and whirlinge into every mans cares infinite blasts of aierye conceiptes, and levityes, sutch as light women and fantasticall beddes ar puffid upp withall; and specially diverse frantick herittiques that ar the fonders and ringleaders of newfanglid opinions and vayne ridiculous sectes? I will not desier you to creddit magicians but even ower best and most allowid philosophers themselves to go forwarde with the reste, graute there be innumerable legions of waterishe and earthlye sprytes. And who can tell but the erthe itselfe maye be a compacte and condensate bodye of the grosser and quarrier sorte of them? And so the water, **both lande and water** bendinge themselves **and all the power they can make so** spitefullye and divelishlye against the heavens, and so cunninglye bewitchinge there inhabitants with a certayne superstitious and incredible admiration of there comodityes and treasures for the cumpassinge and obteyninge whereof so many trecherous and villanous practises ar dayly and howerlye putt in execution. Sure I am fierye, aerye, watrishe and erthely divels ar y$^e$ onlye absolute monarches of y$^e$ worlde, if they be not y$^e$ very worlde itself, and have amongst them a most sovrayne and predominate regimente over all elements if they be not the very elementes themselves. And on thing maketh me vehementlye suspecte that the physicians and philosophers imaginid no lesse but durste not so flatly utter it, in that they howlde it as a naturall principle in there physickes, that y$^e$ elementes ar not mixte and compounde, but pure and simple, and as a man would saye bodyes, whereas to spirituall thinkinge and in naturall reason they sensibelye appear very compoundes. What marvell nowe (consideringe the præmisses and per consequences what maye [be] inferd of the præmisses) thowghe the world from the very begininge to this daye, and manelye at this daye (as everye age hath allwayes complaynid of the present age) hath ever bene and still remainithe so maliciouslye sett and so ungraciouselye disposid beinge ever since the Creation and shall always continue thorowhowte and on every side so throngid and invironid in and cumpassid with such infinite huge ostes of miserable wickid creatures, and moste subtle enemyes, that knowe as well ther owne advantage and where the shooe pinchith us most, as the begger knowith his dishe?

The next complayninge of the foremans tædious discourse, and withall tellinge me I had y$^e$ best office that was so thoroughly employed, wente forwarde in this wise:

Give me leave, Syr, to run a good longe course in so large a feylde.

You make a wonderfull greate matter of it, that reason, contrarye to all reason and y$^e$ custom of former ages is forcibely constraynid to yeelde her obedience, and to be in a manner vassal unto appetite. See, I beseech you, howe you overshoote yourselfe and mistake the matter, in beinge over credulous to beleeve whatsoever is unadvisedly committid to writinge. Here is righte a newe comedye for him that were delightid with overthwarte and contrary Supposes.[a] You suppose the first age was the goulde age. It is nothinge soe. Bodin defendith the goulde age to flourishe nowe, and owr first grandfathers to have rubbid thorowghe in the iron and brasen age at the beginninge when all thinges were rude and unperfitt in comparison of the exquisite finesse and delicacye, that we ar growen unto at these dayes. You suppose it a foolish madd worlde, wherein all thinges ar overrulid by fansye. What greater error? All thinges else ar but troble of minde and vexation of spiritt. Untill a mans fansye be satisfied, he wantith his most soveraigne contentement, and cannot never be at quiet in himselfe. You suppose most of these bodily and sensual pleasures ar to be abandonid as unlawfull and the inwarde contemplative delightes of the minde more zelously to be imbracid as most commendable. Good Lord, you a gentleman, a courtier, an yuthe, and go aboute to revive so owlde and stale a bookishe opinion, deade and buried many hundrid yeares before you or I kuewe whether there were any worlde or noe! You are suer the sensible and ticklinge pleasures of the tastinge, feelinge, smellinge, seinge, and hearinge ar very recreative and delectable indeede. Your ether delightes proceedinge of sum strange mellancholy conceites and speculative imaginations discoursid at large in your fansye and brayne ar but imaginarye and fantasticall delightes, and but for names sake might as well and more trulye be callid the extremist labours and miserabeliste torments under the sunne. You suppose us students happye, and thinke the aire præferrid that breathithe on thes same greate lernid philosophers and profonde clarkes. Would to God you were on of there men but a sennighte. I dowbte not but you would sweare ere Sundaye nexte, that there were not the like wofull and miserable creaturs to be fownde within y$^e$ cumpas of

[a] Alluding to Gascoigne's Comedy "Supposes."

the whole worlde agayne. None so injurious to themselves, so tyranous to there servantes, so niggardlye to ther kinsfolkes, soe rigorrous to ther acquayntance, soe unprofitable to all, so untowarde for the common welthe, and so unfitt for the worlde, meere bookeworms and verye idolles, the most intolerable creatures to cum in any good sociable cumpanye that ever God creatid. Looke them in the face : you will straytewayes affirme they are the dryest, leanist, ill-favoriddist, abiectist, base-minddist carrions and wretcheckes that ever you sett your eie on. To be shorte, and to kutt off a number of sutch bye supposes, your greatist and most erronious suppose is that Reason should be mistrisse and Appetite attend on her ladiships person as a pore servante and handmayden of hers. Nowe that had bene a probable defence and plausible speache a thousande yeares since. There is a variable course and revolution of all thinges. Summer gettith the upperhande of wynter, and wynter agayne of summer. Nature herselfe is changeable, and most of all delightid with vanitye ; and arte, after a sorte her ape, conformith herselfe to the like mutabilitye. The moone waxith and wanithe ; the sea ebbith and flowith ; and as flowers so ceremonyes, lawes, fasshions, customs, trades of livinge, sciences, devises, and all thinges else in a manner floorishe there tyme and then fade to nothinge. Nothing to speake of ether so restorative and comfortable for delighte or beneficiall and profitable for use, but beinge longe togither enioyed and continued at laste ingenderith a certayne satietye, and then it soone becumeth odious and lothsum. So it standith with mens opinions and iudgmentes in matters of doctrine and religion. On fortye yeares the knowledge in the tunges and eloquence karrieth the creddite and flauntith it owte in her sattin dobletts and velvet hoses. Then exspirith the date of her bravery, and everye man havinge enoughe of her, philosophy and knowledge in divers naturall morall matters, must give her the Camisade and beare y$^e$ swaye an other while. Every man seith what she can doe. At last cumith braverye and iointith them bothe.

Anemographia. Not the greatist clarke and profondist philosopher that ever was in the worlde can tell the certayne cawse of the windes? What can they be but huge legions and millions of invisible tumultuous and tempestuous spirittes? What cause can there be in the erthe of such blowinge and blusteringe in everye place, be the qualityes and dispositions otherwise never so repugnant and contrarye? What matter so everlastinge and endles?

Melancholye sprites ingender melancholye passions in men, affections colerick, colericke passions, &c. Mens bodyes ar disposed and qualified accordinge to the spiritts that have the predominant regiment over them, and all philosophye saith that the temperature and disposition [and] inclination of the miudes followythe the temperature and composition of the bodye. Galen, &c.

Customarye and cabalisticall by tradition.

*Cætera desunt.*

---

WILLIAM FULKE,[a] MASTER OF PEMBROKE HALL, TO THE FELLOWS.

f. 48.    After my very harty commendacions, &c.

Whereas my lorde, the Earle of Leycester[b] hath made ernest request for y<sup>e</sup> continuance of Mr. Harveyes fellowshipp for one yeare, and that y<sup>e</sup> tyme of y<sup>e</sup> exspiringe thereof is very neere, this is to certify you, that I am not only well contente as mutch as lyeth in me, to dispense with him for one yeare longer, but also am becum an ernest suter for him unto you, that you will graunte your consente unto y<sup>e</sup> same dispensation, as you will require y<sup>e</sup> like curtesye of me in any of your reasonable requestes. Thus I committ you to God. From Norwitche, this 22nd of Auguste, 1578.

Yours in Christe,

WILLIAM FULKE.

(Doctor Fulke, then Master of Pembroke Hall.)[c]

To my loovinge frendes the fellowes of Pembrooke Hall in Cambridge.

---

[a] William Fulke, D.D., *circ.* 1538—1589. Appointed Domestic Chaplain to Lord Leicester about 1569, and elected Master of Pembroke Hall, 10 May, 1578.

[b] Robert Dudley, Earl of Leicester, K.G., *circ.* 1532—1588.

[c] These words are written in Harvey's hand in the margin.

<sup>a</sup> To the right worshipfull gentleman     f. 48 b.
And famous courtier
Master Edwarde Diar,
In a manner oure onlye Inglishe poett.
In honour of his rare qualityes
And noble vertues,
*Quodvultdeus* Benevolo
J. W.
           Commendith the
Edition of his frendes
    Verlayes, together with certayne other
Of his poeticall devises;
  And, in steade of a Dedicatorye Epistle,
Præsentith himself, and the uttermost
Of his habilitye and value,
To his good worshippes
Curtuous and favorable likinge,
This first of August, 1580.

    1.              2.
The Verlayes.      The Millers Letter.
    3.              4.
The Dialogue.     My Epistle to Imerito.

    The Verlayes ;
    My Letter to Benevolo ;
    The Schollers Loove ;
    The Millers Letter ;
    The Dialogue.

<sup>b</sup> water rulid first, thereuppon cam the diluge wherewith the    f. 49.

---

<sup>a</sup> This page seems to be a draft of an intended edition of some of Harvey's compositions with a dedication to the poet, Sir Edward Dyer, born 1540; died 1610. The words " Quod vult Deus " are written in the margin against the word " Benevolo," and seem to have been intended (by " J. W."—whoever he was) as an alternative expression for " Benevolo."

<sup>b</sup> This page is evidently out of place, and is part of the speech which broke off so abruptly on ff. 47 and 47 b.

worlde was overflowid; then fier when Sodom and Gomor, and the neygbour cityes, were destroyed with fyer; aier in greate infections, and plagues which are sturrid uppe of divells, as magicians reporte, and as is manifest by Agrippa.

The raynebowe, the signe of y$^e$ regiment of bothe; the redd colour in it signifyth fier, and the greene mundation, abundance of moysture. And therefore it is sayd in Plato, in his Cratylus, to be callid in Greeke Iris, as a foreteller and prophetesse of thinges to cum as well for the change of the worlde generallye as for the change of the wether dailye.

---

f. 49 b.    [a] An answer to a Millers vayne letter, and foolish absurd sonett, scribblid longe since by the autor for an honeste cuntrye mayde of his acquayntaunce.

Her sonnett and letter all in on.

   Firste for your acre of commendacions
   I resende you a furlonge of salutations;
   And then to requite your gallonde of godbwyes,
   I regive you a pottle of howedyes.
   And withall owte of the quiver of good likinge,
   On burboulte of truste, worthe the shootinge.
         Nowe I pray you
   Shutt upp the wyndowes of your eies awhile,
   And open the gates of your eares a myle.
   But by your leave a litle her must firste goe pisse,
   And then that her pen hath to say is this:

    My soveraine joye,
    And pretty pigges nye,
    I receivd yesternight,
    By candle lighte,
    A litle before bedd,
    When heavy was my hedd,

---

[a] Folios 49 b—51 evidently contain the piece marked No. 2 on f. 48 b.

Your soverayne toye
And trym Lullabye;
By my trulye the very finest,
And in Tom Nortons ernest
Hayghehoe hallidaye.
Who ever sae thinge so gaye?
The divells damme me take quick from hence,
Ifte bee not worth a pokefull of pence.
By Fyssle and Jynkin my hoonye,
I would all y<sup>e</sup> mill moony
Were thine and mine;
We ar so passing fyne,
Byth roode this geere
Hath noe peere.
Thou arte so queyntefelt
In thy rondelett;
Thou arte so good and better
In enditing a letter.
Truste me truly every peese
More fine then any Banberry cheese;
More sweete then sweetist boony come;
More brave then bravist cocks kome;
More gallant then the goulden soverayne
That you pickd once from Mistrisse Rayne,
And liked that so well of it belike
That all is soverayne in your site.
I kisd my hande, and lickd y<sup>e</sup> paper
Wherein was conteined such soverayne matter.
And loe the goodliest suugercandye style
That ever cam neere me a mile.
I pray Godd amightye mebe not sick
After so hoonysweete a licke.
I weene liccorisse had the name

92    LETTER-BOOK OF GABRIEL HARVEY.

f. 50.    The millers letter had no superscription,
The maydens superscription was this:

To my nameles Nick Nobody,
At y<sup>e</sup> Winde Mill.

My soverayne ioye, I receyvid your soverayne toye, the verye finist and soveraynist corne, I trow, that ever was grownd in your horrible masters mill; a greate deale finer in good soothe then ouer moste finist wheate meale here in Storforde [or] Chesterton.[a] Wherein your finall requeste, proceeding from an inflamid passionable minde and harte, afflictid thorowgh ardente concupiscible appetite (for in sutch gallant bravadoe termes runnith your mill crusadoe rhetorick) fallith owte in y<sup>e</sup> ende to be nawght else but a benigne answer, which you do, you saye, most serviceabely and affectuously attende. Good Lord, O my soverayne goodman, howe can your owne soverayne joye, unless she would be accountid more flintye then flynte itselfe, or more pittilesse and senseles then the verye stoanes that she treadithe under her feete, but shape a benigne answer to so benigne and superbenigne a replye. Marry, I hope in the ardoure of your concupiscible appetite your goodman soverayneshipp will pardon me, thowgh I use not those same fine and superfine soverayne milltermes wherewith your mealemowthe letter and whitebredd sonett ar in most superabundante measure decorate, and illuminate. For methinkes it doth my harte good, my soverayne Syr, to use your soveraynetieshippes gaye and new-fashionid words. Happy and thrise happy is y<sup>e</sup> mistrisse, and above all other terrestriall and mundane bodyes creatid to obtayne y<sup>e</sup> soverayne crowne and supreme principallity (you maye easely discerne your own wordes from myne by y<sup>e</sup> fasshion), uppon

f. 50 b.    whome fortune in steade of all the fælicities hath bestowed so trim

[a] Chesterton, co. Cambridge, a mile and a half north of Cambridge. Walden was first written, then Trumpington, but both scored through, and Storforde. Chesterton. written instead.

and tricksy a fellowe, and so eloquent, so dapper and so miniken
a yunker, a man to be her most affectionate and devoute servante; whose inflamid colericall minde, and languisshing extraordinarye melancolicall corps, loove above all animatid creatures
houldith in his tyrannicall domination by the violent celestiall and
peremtorye influence and aspect of so incomprehensible a ladye;
that is an other fitt of your mill, violent, celestiall, incomprehensible, peremptorye superfinesse. Unlesse haply it be as on of
my frendes, hearing your letter redd, in greate ernest imagenid
that the owtlandish and farfett words you use, be ether certayne
wisardlye charming spelles, or divelish coniuring termes of enchaunte-
ments, and sorcery to intangle and betwitche your pore silly soverayne incomprehensible mistrisse withall whether she will or noe.
And truly (myne owne good windemill, M. Coniurer), when I
first heard that same terrible powchemouthe and uplandish, I
meane, owtelandish worde, Eclypsation of my absence, amongst a
meny of $y^e$ same block; creddit me, I began wonderfull straun-
gelye to quiver and tremble and faynte all on $y^e$ suddeyne, as if
verilye I had bene coniurid or inchauntid therewith all. O goodly
God, I marvell, Servant, at what fayer or markett your good-
faced goodlinesse bowte upp thessame goodly Spanish, Venetian,
Babylonian, Turkishe, Muschovy, and Bonaventure termes that
have made you sutch a coniuringe and charminge creature. If
they were browght you to your mill in a kocme or quarter sack
(for a poake of ii or iii busshels will not conteyne the hugenes of
them, they are so quarry bigg and righte Babylonian like), or if
sum hobgoblin sprite or familiar did heave you them in at your mill
doore (for the least of them is a greate deale longer and broader
then your whole wyndowe) you did not well, Servante, to sende them
abroade till you had grined and trimmed them a little pretty deale
finer and made them sumwhat more Storteforde like then they
now appeare. I imagin if they were bowltid, kneadid, and bakid,
they would make bredd fitter for your blinde mill horse, that same
soverayne illfavorid Bayarde then for me. And truste me truly,

Coniuringe Servant, I beleeve he conceivithe and understandith them as well and perhaps better tooe; being better acquaintid with his masters cælestiall tearmes then I am with my servants incomprehensible style.

f. 51.  It was never my good luck to be browght upp in a winde mill, and if this be winde miller's language I must tell you playne, Servante, I was never so clarkely and profoundlye schoolid, to conster your wind millshippes language, your brave intolerable eloquence so far surpassith, surmountith, and transcendith the simplicitye and humilitye of my intelligence. If you use any other then playne Inglish and flatt Storteford speache with your soverayne mistrisse and incomprehensible ladishipp, the benignist answer I or she can answer you is, in good fayth and by my soveraineioyshipp and by my maydenhedds virginitye tooe, I can no skill, Servante, of your superabundant abominable fineshipp. As litle scripture as I have, I think I have heard thus mutch or thus litle of master Vicar in the pulpitt, where $y^e$ preyste speakith in an unknowen tunge, there cannot $y^e$ people answer, Amen. And this, Servante, is even $y^e$ benignist answer and soverainigst remedy, that my soveraineioyshipp can shape to your lowtelandish, I should saye, your owtelandish unknowen malady. I meane $y^e$ afflicted colericall inflammation of your amorous passionable minde, and $y^e$ ardent concupiscible appetite of your melancohiall languissing corps; which words or witchcraftes, whether they be, my brother Nedd, being a grammer scholler, can not finde, he saythe, in all his dictionary, which kost my father at the least xx. good shillinges and twoe, and therefore I can saye litle to them unlesse I should make Mr. Vicar, or Mr. Schoolemaster, privy to your violent inflamid amorous concupiscible ardent peremptorye passion which I knowe not howe your soveraineioyeservantshipp would take, withoute whose terrestriall and mundane advizemente I dare presume nothinge amongst sutch animatid creatures.

I have layd upp my inkehorne uppon $y^e$ shelfe.

If you will any more you must write it your owne [s]elfe.

At y^e most you gett but a sluttish worde,
In your sluvins teeth a sloovenly torde.
Thus recommendinge your suaddes skin to good-wife sowe
Farewell and be hanged, goodman cowe.

From the castell of my 'soverainecrowne supreme violent celestiall peremptory incomprehensible mistresse Ladyshipp this present fryday 1575.
The millers superscription
Your good mistresseshippes frende and frendlye without any name.
His Mistresse's subscription,
Your gentle wind millshipps frende and frendly and frendlyer and frendlyest of all terrestrial mundane and animated creatures.

Nan. Nobodye, afflicted in minde, inflamid in harte, and languisshinge in corps, thorough peremptory compassion of your passionable amorous concupiscible humour.

---

A short poeticall discourse to my gentle masters the readers, conteyning a garden communication or dialogue in Cambridge betwene Master G[abriel] H[arvey] and his cumpanye at a Midsumer Comencement, togither with certayne delicate sonnetts and epigrammes in Inglish verse of his makinge.    f. 51 b.

I am so loth, my good masters, to depryve you of any thinge that I can possibely communicate with you of this autors dooinge in whom nothinge is vulgar but ether in respecte of the manner or matter to my seeming very singular that, calling to remembrance a certayne afternoones garden discourse wherat my poore mastershipp was present betwene him and certayne gentlefolks very frendly and curteusly assemblid there togither at a Midsumer Commencement tyme, I resolvid to disclose so mutch thereof as præambles, or be playing, as it were, with myne owne shaddowe, after the manner of our ordinary Inglish writers. The occasion and originall of all was (as I remember uppon) this:—Ou of y<sup>e</sup> gentlemen straungers, a right staydd and moderate personage, by mere chaunce, as appearid uppon some small occasion sounding that waye, tost out on y<sup>e</sup> suddayne that common pentameter of Ovid—

Res est solliciti plena timoris Amor.

Whereuppon on of his companions, a boone companion in deede and lively amarous gentleman, would needes straightewayes have beene tempering with jelouzie, amongst other words of discourse pleasantly calling it thessame ordinary passion, or a subtimorous but a zelous loove, and withall making great semblaunce, as if he made no accounte at all of any other kinde of whottish loove, were it never so cunningly countenauncid or colorably intendid, saving that only, and theruppon terming it the king of looves, and all others mere counterfayte glozinges and faynid pretendid flatteryes. Oh, then we shall neever have dun, Master Charles, quoth a proper wise gentlewoman and prettely lernid; her Christian name was M<sup>ris</sup> Katharine, if you be once enterid in to that owlde zelous veyne. I beseech you reserve your king of looves for the courte or the cuntry; it is no university peece of lerning. We be all of us nowe schollars; and you, I remember, were once accountid as deepe a profonde great lernid clarke as y<sup>e</sup> beste. I would God you doctors would enter into sum good substantiall matter of lerninge, or sum witty schoolpoynte, that were not aboove my sonne Antonyes, and my capacity. Now, I praye you, gentle neygbour, propounde y<sup>e</sup> theame, quoth he, your owne selfe, and then I hope it will please your good mistrisshipp. I am glad that I have lernid thus mutch by y<sup>e</sup> waye that you had as leeve have hearde other talke, as on that poore neygbour of yours, Master Charles, had y<sup>e</sup> last weeke at your house about a certayne kinde of suspitious and chary, but very affectionate, and zelous loove, nowadayes commonly callid of men and women jelousye.

And nowe, quoth he, to returne to mye miserable Mistrisse, Verse, which, notwithstandinge her huge summes, and infinite millions of most honorable comendacions, is oftentymes driven very harde, pore sowle, for her vittales and lodginge. I passe not if I bee a litle pleasurable awhile, and for this once playe even the very right phantastic poett in deede.

And thereuppon feeling himselfe nowe, as he sayd, in his extemporall veyne of makinge notwithstanding.

> See Venus, archegoddess, howe trimly she masterith owld Mars.
> See litle Cupide, howe he bewitcheth lernid Apollo.
> Bravery in apparell, and maiesty in hawty behaviour,
> Hath conquerd manhood, and gotten a victory in Inglande.
> Ferse Bellona, she lyes enclosd at Westminster in leade.
> Dowtines is dulnes; currage mistermid is outrage.
> Manlines is madnes; beshrowe Lady Curtisy therefore.
> Most valorous enforced to be vassals to Lady Pleasure.
> And Lady Nicity rules like a soveran emperes of all.
> O tymes, O manners, O French, O Italish Inglande.
> Where be y<sup>e</sup> miudes and men that woont to terrify strangers?
> Where that constant zeale to thy cuntry glory, to vertu?
> Where labor and prowes very founders of quiet and peace,
> Champions of warr, trompetours of fame, treasurers of welth?
> Where owld Inglande? Where owld Inglish fortitude and might?
> Oh, we ar owte of the way, that Theseus, Hercules, Arthur,
> And many a worthy British knight were woonte to triumphe in.
> What should I speake of Talbotts, Brandons, Grayes, with a thousande

Such and such? Let Edwards go; letts blott y^e remem-
braunce
Of puissant Henryes; or letts exemplify there actes.
Since Galatro came in and Tuscanismo gan usurpe
Vanity above all; villanye next her; Statelynes empresse,
No man but minion: stowte, lowte, playne, swayne, quoth a
lordinge.
No words but valorous, no works but woomanish only,
For life magnificoes; not a becke but glorious in shewte,
In deede most frivolous; not a looke but Italish allwaies.
His cringeinge side necke, eies glauncinge, fisnamy smirkinge,
With forefinger kisse and brave embrace to y^e footewarde.
Largbellid kodpeasid dubletts, unkodpeasid halfehose
Streyte to the dock like a shirte, and close to the britche like a
Divelinge
A litell apish hat chowchd faste to y^e pate like an oister,
Frenche camarike ruffes, deepe with a witnesse starched to
the purpose,
Every on A per se A; his tearmes and braveryes in printe,
Delicate in speeche, qweynte in araye, conceitid in all poyntes.
In courtely guises a passinge singular odd man,
For gallants a brave myrrour, a primrose of hounour,
A dimond for nonse, a fellowe peereles in Ingland.
Not the lyke discourser for tongue and bedd to be fownde owt,
Not the lyke resolute man for greate and serious affayres.
Not the like linx to spy owte secretis and privities of states,
Eied like an Argus, earde like a Midas, nosde like a Naso,
Wyngd lyke a Mercury, fit of a thousande for to be employde,
This neie more then this doth practis of Italy in one yeare.

f. 52 b. Nether will I here kepe from mi gentle masters on other sonett
utterid by Master H. in supper while, (but not made as he prætendid of himselfe, howbeit I remayne still so persuadid and dare
warrant it was of his owne dooinge) to fitt sum parte of y^e talke

that was then occasionid by good Mistrisse Katryne, I since obtainid of him with mutch adoo to copye it owte of a litle table in his studdye wherein it was written very faier on the on syde, which syde was alwayes to the wallwarde; a certain wise and ingenious Latin epigramme being as faierly written on the other. The sonnet was this :—

>Hungry vertu
>Verbally praysid,
>Horrible vices
>Really worshipd,
>Lazarus all prayse
>Lack sily cryple
>Epulo none prayse,
>Roome for a rufler,
>Faythfulnes all prayse
>From the teeth outwarde,
>Craftines askith
>Who but her owne selfe?
>Spy ye the daye light
>At litle window?
>What do I meane then
>Thus many words use?
>Tell me nowe gentles.

Nowe tell me, I beseech you, if this be not a noble verse and politique lesson, M. Christof, in effecte conteyninge the argumente of his curragious and warly[k]e apostrophe to my lorde of Oxenforde[a] in his fourth booke Gratulationum Valdinensium, and had for title nothing but this short exclamation in greate Romane letters: O Providentia Dea. Lady, Oh excellently dun by my Maiesty.

In an Inglishe abridgment he made of Aristotles Politiques, Mr.

Christopher, it seemith to be the voyce and oracle of nature herselfe, the very best and wisest fowndresse of Commonwealthes that Politique Vlisses utterith in Homer to the liking of the whole armye οὐκ ἀγαθη πολυκοιρανιη, &c. And alsoe I rember Mr. H. in a certayne methodicall abridgment which he made not long since of Aristotles Politiques, translated in a manner ad verbum, thus. Tis not a good state where many beare rule; lett there be on sovrayne kynge, on prynce.

Farewell my good masters and readers.

---

In the nexte seate to thes hexameters, adonickes, and iambicks, I sett those that stand uppon the number, not in meter, sutch as my lorde of Surrey[a] is sayde first to have putt forthe in prynte, and my lorde Buckhurste,[b] and M. Norton[c] in the Tragedye of Gorboduc, M. Gascoygnes[d] Steele Glasse, an uncertayne autor in certayne cantions agaynst the wylde Irishe, and namelye Mack Morrise, an invective agaynst Simmias Rhodius,[e] a folishe idle phantasticall poett that first devised this odd riminge with many other triflinge and childishe toyes to make verses, that shoulde in proportion represente the form and figure of an egg, an ape, a winge, and sutche ridiculous and madd gugawes and crockchettes, and of late foolishely revivid by sum, otherwise not unlernid, as Pierius, Scaliger, Crispin, and the rest of that crue. Nothinge so absurde and fruteles, but beinge once taken upp shall have sume imitatoures. The like veyne of those, that hunte the letter, and I heard one Mr. Willes,[f] a greate

---

[a] Henry Howard, Earl of Surrey, *circ.* 1516—1547. He translated Virgil's *Æneid*, books i. and iv. into English blank verse.

[b] Thomas Sackville, Baron Buckhurst, afterwards Earl of Dorset, *circ.* 1536—1608. Wrote, conjointly with Norton, *the Tragedy of Gorboduc*, first acted at Whitehall, 18 Jan. 1561—2.

[c] Thomas Norton, *circ.* 1532—1584, Remembrancer of the City of London; joint author of *Gorboduc.*

[d] Gascoigne's *Steele Glass*, a satire in blank verse, was published in 1576.

[e] Simmias of Rhodes, *circ.* B.C. 300.

[f] Richard Willes, M.A. of Oxford, Mayence, and Perugia, incorporated at Cambridge, 16 Dec. 1578. *See* Coopers' *Athenæ Cantabrigienses*, vol. i. p. 398.

travelour, very well lernid, and nowe of riper yeares and sownder iudgment, that hath usid them himselfe, call them meere fooleryes, vices taken upp for virtues, apish devices, frivolous boyishe grammer schole trickes.

And heare will I take occasion to shewe you a peece of a letter that I lately receyvid from the Courte written by a frende of mine, that since a certayn chaunce befallen unto him, a secrett not to be revealid, calleth himself Immerito.[a]     f. 53.

"The twoe worthy gentlemen, Mr. Sidney[b] and Mr. Dyer,[c] have me, I thanke them, in sum use of familiaritye; of whom and to whome what speache passith for your creddite and estimation, I leave yourselfe to conceyve, havinge allwayes so well conceyvid of my unfainid affection and good will towardes yow. And nowe they have proclaymid in there $\alpha\rho\epsilon\iota\omega$ $\pi\alpha\gamma\omega$."

The same Immerito translated, He, &c. Catoni quæ edi, into these hexameters.[d]

---

The Schollars Loove, or Reconcilement of Contraryes. The very first Inglish meeter that ever I made.     f. 58.

The very first peece of Inglish Ryme that ever the autor committed to wrytinge: and was in a rage devised and deliverid pro and contra according to the quality of his first and last humor. Anno 1573, mense Septembri.

An amorous odious sonnet, intituled The Students Loove or Hatrid, or both or nether, or what shall please the looving or hating reader, ether in sport or ernest to make of such contrary passions as ar here discoursid. An owld newe cantion ffatherid uppon Sir Thomas More, and supposid to be on of his first youthfull exercises: but never before committed to prynte, nor ever heard of in Sir Thomas Mores dayes.

---

[a] Immerito = Edmund Spenser.
[b] Sir Philip Sidney.
[c] Sir Edward Dyer.
[d] The next seven pages, ff. 54-57, are headed by Harvey, "Fine Notes for mie Rhetorique Discourses." They contain nothing worth transcribing.

The Schollers Loove : or Reconcilement of Contraries (a few idles howers of a young Master of Art). A dayes correction woold sufficiently refine it. The meeter must be more regular, and the Inglish elocution more elegant. Fine and flowing as in posthast. (It was scribled at the first in a hurlewind of conceit).

### INITIUM.

Wheare, wheare, is there anye, for loove or for monye,
Can showe sutch a paragon as is my coonye.
Tell, floorishing youths, that to loove ar subiecte,
Did ever your cies behowld sutch an objecte ?
Queint Idees bemone your imperfections,
Or give me a type of such perfections ;
So divine, so fine, so wise, so nise ;
So bowntifull, so bewtifull, so charitable, so amiable ;
So feate, so neate, for Bewtyes seate ;
So lighte, so brighte, for angels sighte ;
So quick, so trick, for prize and prick ;
So rownde, so sownde, for vertues grownde ;
So lispering, so whisperinge ;
So whipping, so tripping ;
So blithe, so lithe, so sweet, so meet ;
So pretty a prim of every limme.
The streates to schim.
Her fellist fo speak of no moe,
From top to toe, wherever she go.
The minion foote of my harte roote,
It dooth me good, at the harte bludd.
Her legg, her thighe ! Alas, I sighe !
Till I come nearer, a litle higher.
Her waste so laste ; her fingers sutch wringers.
Her tender hart, the gentlest part of makers art.
Her loving harte, the sweetest dart of Cupids part.
Her swan white neck, her amiable beck beyounde all checke ;

Her loovely dugges, in spite of bugges;
Twoe precious Margarites, or rather Galactites; f. 57 b.
Sutch lippes, such teethe, as like none seeth,
The on of rubye, the other of ivorye;
Her fayer graye cies
Shininge christall wise.
Her nose in syse, as you woold devise;
The rose and the lilly mixte in her fisnomy;
Her milk-white skin, with a pitt in her chin;
Her breath-like baulme, her speache so caulme;
Her quickesylver tunge whenever tis runge;
Her heare to unfoulde like wyres of goulde;
A goulden fleece, a Jasons fees;
Her periwigges like corall twigges.
O gallant friseld pate; O miracle of fate.
Her angells face, her goddesse grace;
There needes no furniture to embellish nature;
No bombast or paintry to helpe deformity;
No cullors ought worth, to sett her cullor fourth;
No laanes or the like, to bewitch delite;
No perfume artificiall, like her breath naturall;
A frankincense tree, sweete rosemerie;
A bedd of cammomill, a right daffodill;
A braunche of lorix a very phœnix.
Etch part and every parcel
For dainty features doth excel.
On hunnysuckle kisse, worth a lordshipp, I wisse,
All proovith licorisse whatsoever she doth kisse.
A meere quintessence of favours and bewtyes.
Where her grace hath residence, there soiorneth all bowntyes.
Passing delicate beyond womans state.
A diamond girle, a pierles perle,
A shiny marke of heavenly sparke,
A piece of warke to pose a clarke,

Amongst all other I knowe not sutch an other
For favour or savour, or for behaviour.
A geme of virginitye, a starre of curtesye,
A laurell of governement, a myrrour of intertaynement,
A verie A per se A, not her fellowe in Europa.
Parisses Helena not like my Ellena.
A primrose with a witnesse, a heavenly demigoddesse
Descended from the sky, in æthereal bravery,
To ravish every eie that regardith her bewtie.
I dare bowldely sownde it, as sum eies have fownde it.
Her very excrementes nothing but incrementes
Of pothecarye restoratives, to comforte yungemens lives.
No shame at all to tell such a tale.
Her spitt is Hypocrasse, the rest I lett passe,
The dunge of a muskecatt not like unto that.
A compownde of marchepane, a very Diane.
Nowe maye I well bragg of my piggesnye,
The sunne did never her like espye.

f. 58. Or she is matchelesse, or I am senselesse.
The oddist wight, in my eiesight,
That ever man begatt of woman.

  I never wente to riminge schoole,
   Yet nowe must needesly rime,
  What thowghe I seeme to fooles a foole?
   Nothinge but hath his tyme.

I crye the amercy, most gentle poetrye,
That I the so longe accountid vanitye,
The extremitye of affectionate passion
At last hath browght me into loovers fasshion.

I imagined there was never substaunce
So uncapable of any circumstaunce
As myself of that accident,
Since ower Lady Day in Lente,

Yet nowe a loove in superlative degree
Scarcely sutch an other in Spayne or Italie.
Hayehoe my sweetist hallidaye,
I beseeche you marke my roundelaye;
Looke for no measure in my ryme,
Passions, you know, observe no tyme.
I thought myself as cowlde as on
    From scorching flames of fiery loove;
Yet am I nowe as woe-begon
    As if I fried in sweating stoove.
Did you never see a flye in y<sup>e</sup> nighte
Dally so longe with y<sup>e</sup> candle lighte,
Till at last she was burnid all to nothinge,
Paying her foolish selfe for that peece of lerninge;
Tis my particular case for want of better grace
Like the venomous salamander,
Alwayes to feede on fyer.

Loove is my life,
Loove is my deathe;
My makynge
And my marynge;
Etch byrde a doove,
Etch house a stoove.
What call you this but burninge?
What call you this but burninge,
And in fier to be ever groovelinge?
O scalding heate,
O cruell seate.
No marvell thowghe the poets owtdo,     f. 58 b.
Fayne Venus, Vulcan's wife.
In fyer he lyes,
In fyer she fryes;
In fyer is all there lyfe.

A likely tale,
And smells of ale:
That Venus cam of water.
Likelier it is,
And yet amisse,
That whott wine was y<sup>e</sup> matter.
If I can gesse the reason whye,
Me thinkes, is mente the contrarye.

Fyer was father,
Fyer was moother,
Fyer was nurse and all;
Fyer was the matter,
Fyer was the manner,
Fyer was y<sup>e</sup> cause finall.

Can cowldnes heate?
Can water burne?
Doth sea ingender flame?
You gabb fonde poetts, or in bowrde,
You blason Neptunes name.

A strange effecte
If it were true,
That water showlde inflame.
Ile sooner howlde,
The fyer is cowlde,
And pleade it with lesse shame.

'Tis but madd poetts pritle pratle,
Or but fond womens title tatle.
There can be (I trowe).
Nether affinity,
Nor consanguinity;
Nether alliance,
Nor dalliance;

Nether agreemente,
Nor reconcilemente;
Nether frendeshipp,
Nor kyndeshipp,

Betweene whott loove, whott as y<sup>e</sup> fiery elemente,
And the cowlde water, where Neptune hath regiment.
Even as likely it were Heaven and Hell to accorde,
Or God and Mammon coosin-germanes to recorde,
As these twoe to linke in chaynes of amitye,
Or fetch them by descent from the selfe same Petegrye,

Howbeit peradventure I maye venture to farr,
I dare not avowtche it, as my assertion,
(Which possibely schooleman will call in question),
That they ar so immediately and extremely repugnant,
But thoroughe the favorable mediation of sum gentle starre
They may at last be agreeid peeceabelye,
And ever after live togither curtuouslye,
Uppon sum indifferent and reasonable covenant.

And then why not confederacye,
Where afore was conspiracye?
There maye a fierye water be,
Or waterishe fier haply,
That skaldes, and boyles, and rostes so longe,
Till water getts the victory;
And then whye not humble and dutifull submission,
Where before was continuall warre and rebellion?

Tell me mistrisse     f. 59 b.
Tell me sweete nowe
Have you a gesse
More or lesse
At sutch a game

And yet at laste
Prooves but a blaste
Within halfe an hower
A coulde shower?
I saye a game
That itselfe doth tame
Death and life
In y$^e$ same knife,
Sea and lande
In y$^e$ same hande,
Fier and water
In one platter?

That is y$^e$ matter
That poetts clatter,
Venus cam of sea,
And thither shall agayne
To litle Cupides payne
When twill no otherwise be;
The riddle showith,
And every on knoweth,
She prooves as she is
But water and pisse.

A wonderment straunge
And miraculous case;
I feele Ætna at my harte,
And yet there tooe
Before hence I goe
Nilus must playe his parte.

Sweete hoony, sweete hoony,
Mine owne marchpane coonye;
Haye didle didle,
Give me heere the fidle,

A sugrid rosewater kysse
  Of the very best fasshion,.
And every thing else Iwisse
  To interteyne my passion.

Beseeminge enowghe for so precious a perle
The royall skyecolorid saphire,
Over base for the ringe of her finger;
God regarde her merits and rewarde her accordingly,
Newe stuffes and kindes of apparell must be devised presently,
That there may be a certain proportionable analogye
Betwene her gorgeous vesture and most noble bodye;
And yet impossible it were the on so to invente
That to the other it should appeare æquipollent.
Shall I make comparison
Accordinge to her perfection?

No glittering aglettes or purles of purle,
No crimson velvett gownes
Chose they never so many crownes;
No furres of sables or foynes
Worthy to cum neere her loynes;
Damaskes and cuffed taffatyes
Ar for other meane ladyes;
Not the very princiliest araye,
  Be it never so sumptuous, seme it never so gaye.

Twere pitty she should eate
Any other meate
But patriche, quayle, and fesaunte:
Or else the ambrosia
Thats præserv'd for Minerva,
She is so divinely pleasante;
And as for gallant araye,

As were convenient
For a starre so splendent.
And methinks Ipocrase
Is a wyne over base,
Considering y<sup>e</sup> noble currage
Of her gratious personage,
Nectar the drinke aloane
For so portely a paragone.
Manna were most fitt, for everry bitt
A heavenly diet for her better quiet.
No enammeled chaynes, no spangels of goulde,
No embroderid sylkes that ar to behoulde;
No tinseld satten or clothe of tissue,
Statelye enoughe for her fathers issue.
Her maiesties soveraine grace
Thrise dulcer then hypocrase,
To this corps gives place.
Her sugarcandye harte
Yeeldith at my starte
In every parte.
If any singuler delicacy I happen to demande,
Do but bould upp my finger, all y<sup>e</sup> graces at commande,
No comfitts so comfortable
As her grace is pleasurable.
She feedes me with sirruppes of delighte,
And makith me smyle day and nighte.
A saynte at my laye,
Letts make it hallidaye;
The happiest alive
So God me thrive.
I challenge the, Aretino,
Or any other Unico;
Nether thy Angelica,
Nor Petrarches Lauretta,
Nor Catullus Lesbia, alias Clodia;

Nor Tibullus Delia, alias Plautia;
Nor Propertius Cinthia, alias Hostia;
Nor Oviddes Corinna, alias Martials Julia;
Nor any other famous Donna
Comparable with my Ellena.
No, not Paris Helena
Comparable with my Ellena.
No, not Hercules Deianira
Comparable with my Ellena;
No, not Joves Europa
Comparable with my Ellena,
A most incomparable creature
For singular feature.
A most divine girle,
And inestimable perle.
I defy ye all
That her miscall,
And counte her not the glory
Of Inglishe bewtye.
A geme alone,
An union,
O delicate mistresse,
O very goddesse,
O heavenly wighte,
O blissfull sighte,
Such a semblaunce of Deity
Must needes provoke idolatry.
Sutch so rare so admirable perfection,
Often the cause of such imperfection;
A smaradye for myne eie,
With a sympathye.

And myselfe the lapidary.
Owte and alasse,
Howe I played the asse?
O fortune harde,
O cooling carde.
O horrible mischaunce,
O monstrous traunce.
Never miserable Villacco,
Surprisd with y$^e$ like Cammassado.
What so colorable pretence,
Whate halfe sufficient defence;
Ether my harteburninge to ease,
Or to countervayle and appease
So detestable and haynous offence,
So excessive and intolerable greevance?
Would not sutch outrage
Make a saynt rage?
I am more then a furye
To thiuk of such villanye.
I wante millions of tunges
To ease my lunges.
No eloquence can accomplishe
The tone half of my wishe.
Not if I were very Rhetorick herselfe
Could I sufficiently display sutch an elfe;
Nether hardhearted Gibiline nor desperate Guelphe
Made ever profession of so wicked pelfe.
Thowghe I were a volume of most exquisite orations,
Or a whole worlde of patheticall affections,
It were impossible ether to decipher her fasshions,
Or to mitigate and assuage myne own passions.
Tis only mallancholy
Must salve my malladye.
And yet this on worde,

And there a borde.
The worlde is tickle,
And loovers fickle.
Ile say no more,
But phy on her hore.
You that ar wery of your life,
For Goddes sake take my good wife;
Or else y$^e$ divell divorce his dame,
And marry her in y$^e$ divels name.
Ten divelles not enowghe
Her grownde to plowe
Sutch terrible plaguye furrowes,     f. 60 b.
Sutch infinite cunny burrowes.
Not y$^e$ like agayne, I weene,
In y$^e$ whole erthe to be seene,
A heavenly wighte?
A hellish kyghte,
A gemme of virginitye?
A sinke of strumperye,
The very quintessence
Of carnall concupiscence,
An union?
An Oonnyon,
Not garlick fayer
So bestinches the aier.
Not all y$^e$ kannals and pryvies
Betwene this and S. Davyes.
A primrose with a witnesse?
A dimigoddesse?
A beastely rannell,
A filthy cannell.
An insatiable rampe,
Of Messalines stampe;
A bitchfoxe jade,

A nastye bade;
A roynish hagg,
A common nagg,
More common then the common ooven house,
More vile then the vileste body lowse,
My cordiall?
My corsiveall.
A serpentine brood,
A poysonous tode;
A harte hewen forth of y$^e$ marble rock,
A stony minde as passionlesse as a block.
Phy on thy skurtes,
Gilleon flurtes.
A murron and a pockes
Consume thy guttes.
They call the Nell,
Thy name is Hell;
Thou warte my Helena,
Be the divels Proserpina.
If ever there were shee Divells incarnate,
They ar alltogither in the incorporate.
No hellish sprite,
So hellish a wighte,
Be it spoken, to y$^e$ honour of thy bone grace.
The very furyes to the give place.
And as for the Syr Lowte
That playdst inne and owte;
A dogg in y$^e$ maunger,
A very ranke raunger;
A squrvy knave skratch the,
And all y$^e$ divells go with the.
Thou hast woone her—weare her;
Rubb her oute and teare her.
Trye her and tyre her, and ty her to a tree,

Till she fries and dries, and cries benedicite.
And then at thy pleasure give her the slipp,
Complayninge she is trowbled with the pipp.
Shall I tell you a litle more of my proper owne selfe? f. 61.
O, most fortunate infortunate, happy most unhappy elfe!
A foole crampe me by the great toe,
For heatinge and coolinge and foolinge soe.
A wonderous greate exchaunge, a miraculous metamorphosis.
Who ever sae, who ever harde, who ever redd the like to this?
Whattes now my gallantist bravery
But reprochefull slavery?
My lustiest iettinge
But mallancholy frettinge?
My delicatist feastinge
But miserable fastinge?
My youthfulliste hollaes, hussaes, and sahoes,
But wretchid allasses, godhelpes, and woes?
My queyntist and most epicurelike confections,
Sugettes, ypocrase, and marchepane;
But over sensible and venemous infections,
Poysons, gaule, and rattesbane?
My deintiest conserves and restauratives,
But peremptory torments and corsives?
All y$^e$ rest of my trimmest, tricksiest, gingerliest ioyes,
But very tædious and most odious toyes?
Sweet meates, quoth good owlde Master Dawse,
Do crave, and must have a sower sawce.
A marvelous instance
Against all dalliance.
Good Lorde for thy mercy,
**Pardon my follye.**
Did not Empedocles,

Or some other archephilosopher,
Saye all thinges were create
Of contraryes by Fate?
Withoute all exception
I subscribe to his opinion.
In honour of humanity
I reverence contrariety.
Such irregular accidentes, and fittes of apostasy,
Will teache a saynte to forgett all regularity.
Myself have abandonid all former delightes,
Synce I was encounterid of so huge despytes.
Truste me no better axiomes in topicis,
Than those same be De oppositis.
A mistereye of lerninge,
Most worthye the scanninge,
For him that would blowe $y^e$ bellowes,
To owterunne his fellowes.
I must bewraye a scholler,
I spite of my coller.
And to make you beleeve it,
I will pawne my creddit,
Not sutch a principle agayne in all Aristotle or Boetio,
As is that same on maxim, Contrariorum eadem ratio.
Sum translations have, Disciplina,
But those two, I take it, are Synonoma.
Then of contraryes must we have $y^e$ selfesame regarde,
And per consequente bestowe on them $y^e$ selfesame rewarde.
In arguing the hoursesonnes stande so mutch upon their identity,
That in fine I præsuppose they will conclude an unity.
No heavenlier intendemente
Under this element
Then so sett uppon unity

Manger contrariety;
A goodly truce
If it were in use;
A brave poyute of logick
Whilst y$^e$ world is so quick.
No diviner melody
Then when consente and dissent
Do give there assente
To make a pleasant harmony;
A musicall experiment
Inferring y$^e$ former consequente.
Com to matters of pollicye and state,
All societies consist of contraryes
After on and the very same rate;
Our most sumptuous and floorishinge cities
Ar like dissonant and iarring dittyes,
Good and badd,
Merry and sadd, sober and madd,
Ar there to be hadd;
Ritche and pore
Of ether great store
Lordes and potentates,
Vassals and rubnegates,
Gentlemen and lawiers,
Coblers and colliers.
Fayer gallante ladyes as brave as the sunne
Lowte il-favorid drapsocks died into dun.
Here dwells a matron as honest as Lucretia;
There at the next dore
Dwelles as arrant a hore
As ever was Mistresse Dodecomechore.
I coulde make you laffe

Is as contrary to her selfe
As all these togither
That dwell altogither.
But mutch pleasant geere
I must kutt of heere;
In every vocation
And occupation
A wonderfull alteration
And contrary fasshion;
Yet on comonwelthe and all on bodye,
Under on heddes governement and principality.
The very semblable contraries
Ar residente in private families.
Listen what a storye Jacke Simkin made to his mother
Of his masters howseholde, and many an other.
Here goes my master, there runes tother man;
Here ruckes my mistrisse makinge cleene the pan;
I had ni forgott our mayde that is serving the hogges,
We all agree togither like kattes and dogges;
Yet dine we togither and supp we togither,
And sumtyme lawghe togither, and sumtyme crye togither.
And lye we togither, and keepe alwayes togither;
And never agreeing togither, ever agree togither;
Esspecially in the night when we ar fast sleepinge,
You shall not heere on aungrye worde sturringe.
My master and my dame which ar over hedd,
Agree passinge well when they ar abedd;
As soone as they ar upp this is his songe,
Marry gupp, hore, gupp, all the daye longe;
Sumetyme mi mistrisse singes the like note,
And sometime she getts me him fast by the trothe;
And sumtyme thesame canvasse my better blue coate,
And sumtyme Nell and I fall skouldinge by roate.
And yet still on howsehowld, you knowe,

Sumtyme amongst ouer selves
And allwayes against other elves,
Must needes togither howlde, I trowe,
Whensoever we have to deale with ower peevish neigbours,
It stands us then in hande to steke togither like burres.
This is y$^e$ deformitye, mother,
And this is y$^e$ conformitye, brother,
Of my masters familye and sum other.
Wel, sayd Jack Simkin, I have heard a better tale
Preachid ere nowe over a pott of ale.
And yet, berlady, thy brothers conformitye
Howsoever its temperid with thy mothers deformitye,
Makes well enowghe, me thinkes, for my uniformity,
Theres many a parte of my induction behinde,
But what nedes more where none of us is blinde?
Tell me nowe in good soothe, masters, ar not both your eares full weary,
Then I beseech you harken a litle to y$^e$ rest of my ditty,
He that did maynetayne,
In defence of rayne,
That water was cheefist elemente,
Wantid not reason,
Albeit were geason
To argue uppon that argumente,
And he that made fire
In defence of ire,
The only principle in effecte,
In my simple imagination,
Made good his probation
In many a weighty respecte.
And that same owld huddle
That sayd all was on
Hadd a parlous odd brayne
For sutch an hourseson swayne,

f. 62.

Take heede of sike a fellowe
That is allwayes mellowe
And never rotten,
However y̎ worlde kotten
Hese A per se A, a ladd for the nonse,
I, quoth Jack a napes, by these ten bones,
Nothinge happens amiss to a præparid minde,
Tis good philosophy, katt will to kinde.
Twas ill dun, Aristotle, to constute such a lore
As world withoute ende wilbe followid more,
Then any other secte, seeme it never so probable
That thou or thy schollars thowght most allowable,
Did not on defende,
God him amende,
That snowe was blacke?
Myselfe knowes $y^e$ wighte
That calles pepper white,
In honour of $y^e$ loovely smack.
Myne owne fier is water,
What needes more?
Ile saye it agayne,
Thowghe it be to my payne,
My fier is water
Woe is me and no more:
I tooke her for a saynte
She rimes to a dore,
But all is on masters
I am of his secte,
Concorde and discorde
Do well enowghe accorde;
We ar fraamde of contraryes,
Thats my suspecte.
You have hearde of the jacinct and jasper
As mutable as these is every jasker.

Many a precious knave is precious for this property,
As the better of them bothe for all their precious qualitye,
Men I warrante you can conforme themselves to the aiers disposition
As well as they or any other precious union,
Nowe whott, nowe cowlde,
And sumtyme lukewarme tooe,
And neutrals belive
The better to thrive
By dooinge as others dooe,
Nowe cruelly bente,
Now y$^e$ gentelist in Kente,
Nowe as holy as S. Pawle
Anone worshippers of Ball,
Our tomorrowes idolatrye
Controwles yesterdayes pietye,
As variable creatures
As y$^e$ cameleon or polypus,
Locke on ower features
There neadith noe overplus.
Woone with a napple and loste with a nutt;
As highe as y$^e$ hedd, as lowe as y$^e$ futt.
Frende and foe at pleasure,
This is the worldes measure.
Mistrisse Ellena is myne when her nowneselfe list,
By and by an other hath her cloake by y$^e$ fist.
Faste or loose, mine owne tender barne;
A kaste of leeger de mane, I the forwarne,
Cunninge is no burden and pretty sleights do no harme,
As good sumtyme over cowlde as over warme.
Every on conformable
To every gaerishe bable.
The worlde is a center and hypocrisy y$^e$ circumference,
The lives ar amongst us that therein have residence,

Twoe faces under on whood,
And possibely nether of both good.
Theres many a thowsande here of y<sup>e</sup> travelers moulde
That whilom Æsoppes satyre expellid his cave
For breathinge and blowinge both whott and cowlde,
And playing y<sup>e</sup> cownterfett dissemblinge slave.
But maye it please you, gentlemen, to heere the late apologye
Of a gentlewoman not far hence, on Mistrisse Infirmitye?
The eloquentist lerniddist hore, by reporte,
That ever pleadid in comissaries courte.
So nothinge but hath his qualification,
And who seeth not in me a grate alteration?
I once offendid against my conscience;
The next trespas shall never coste me so many pense,
And yet nothinge, my cownsell tells me against nature,
What needid so rigorous and severe a censure?
The best of ye all may committ a skape;
Was never Master Comissary charged with a rape?
I acknowledg my folly and protest repentaunce;
Nowe, I praye, whereto servith any other penaunce?
My heate is well coolid,
And myselfe better schoolid.
Theres a tyme for every thinge,
And why not then for foolinge.
I remember full well the time once was
That Master Comissary himselfe cried Alasse,
When the very principallist parte of his apology
Was fleshe and bludde, and mans imbecillitye.
Iwisse, Master Turnecoate, you neede not be so whott,
I knowe in whose dayes you were as cowlde as a blocke;
And maye well enough crye, Peccavi, agayne;
When fewe enowghe perhappes shall pitty your payne.
Meete the same measure unto others in your iollitye
That you will call and crave for in your owne misery.

I have heard lernid men talke of a circular motion,
And of y<sup>e</sup> naturall course of action and passion.
These mysteryes ar mystes to us silly fooles,
Wee ar better acquaintid with threefootid stooles;
But they beare us in hande, this on thinge is mente,
All thinges are allowable in Christendom and Kente.
Then, good Master Comissary, be compassionate,
And remember that all thinges being governid by fate
Your good selfe may cum on daye to like estate.
This was the defence of Mistrisse Infirmitye,
Being putt to her purgation before Master Comissarye.
Of all likehood her counselour was a naturall philosopher,
Or else, peradventure, had a physician to her brother.
I dare not avoutch any great certaintye,
But, berlady, she was behowlding to naturall philosophy;
She lernid beate and cowlde were thinges accidentall.
Nature, they tell us,
Doth nothinge in vayne;
And wheretoe serve contrary
Humors in mans boddy,
But to make us appliant
To every descant?
Dry, moyste, indifferente,                                                      f. 63.
Whott, cowlde, indifferente,
Good, badd, indifferente,
Honest, indifferente,
A good fellowe, indifferente,
For all thinges indifferente.
(Savinge that she countes it a most horrible wounde
To howlde with y<sup>e</sup> hare and run with y<sup>e</sup> hownde);
Thats Master Commissarys fault, not mine,
I appeale to his neighbours all in a line.
Whot planett reininge,
As whott as a coale:

Cowlde starr prædominante,
There goith y<sup>e</sup> goale.
In sommer season,
When buttarde peason
Ar eaten for deinty meate,
Cowldist of complexion,
And best of condition,
Complayne of extreame beate.
In winter nightes,
When fyer and candle lightes
Ar more chargeable to my cofers,
Then my dinnars and suppers,
The case is quite alterid,
My heate is qualified.
When Jove and Venus
Challenge domination,
What marvell thowgh nature
Be incensde to generation?
If Saturne be kynge and Luna empresse,
Tis nothinge as it was: I pitty her distresse;
Heat and cowlde ar thinges accidentall,
And nether of them both simply materiall,
But as other indifferent thinges that ar usuall.
An exchaunge of elementes she sae every daye,
A mutation of states every tragicall playe,
Sum extremely miserable, sum excessivelye gaye;
And there she supposid wente the heare awaye.
Erthe proovith aier and water fyer,
And why not whot, cowlde, and amity, ire?
Reatche me my hyghe shooen, Ile daunce in y<sup>e</sup> myer.
Nowe, I beseech you, seemith that so foolish a ieste
In good soothe, tis but like all the reste.
He that is in a traunce,
Makes many a glaunce.

The glosse
Is grosse:
The texte
Is nexte.
All in the ende, sooner or later,
Cummes to on reckoninge, it makith no matter.
When Ellena was myne
She was none of thine;
Take her for me, brother,
I knowe wheres an other;
As diamonde a prim
Of every limme;
A nobeler witt
Then that daggiltayld skitt;
An other manner of peece
For Jason to fleece;
A goulden girle
A purlous perle;
A damaske rose, a sweete budd,
Withoute pricks or thornes in hir whudd;
An alabaster neck, a turcois eie:
Who ever a clearer cooler did spye?
Her heare softe as sylke,
Her skin white as mylke;
Every thinge in printe
Withoute and withinte.
A very S. Kateryne,
I would she were myne.
And yet if she will none
All is still on.
I knowe twooe or three
**Full as fayer as shee;**

Yet will I defende it
Whoever gaynesaye it;
Theres no greate deyntye,
Where is sutch plentye.
Three, fowre and five till I cum to twentye and tenne,
Is not this reasonable choyce for halfe a scoare men?
I weene there was never any derth
Of maydes or wives in y^e erthe.
Theres many a lady of pitty
In every large citty;
And many a commoditye
In every ritch seigniory.
Take him for a ioultehedd and a senseless brute
That knowes not which waye to comense his sute.
At laste this or that
Will make him fatt;
If nether the on nor the other prævayle
As good or better may haplye avayle.
Tis a written veritye,
Quoth owlde Senior C.,
All prooves on whether you speede or misse,
In the mayne sea theres good stoare of fishe,
And in delicate gardens and in gourgeous bowers,
Theres allwayes greate varietye of desirable flowers.
Mye very mistrisse her nowne propper selfe,
Moughte yit be woon agayne, like a slippery elfe.
But seing all is one
I will letter her aloane
A lamentable victorye.
Where triumphe is misery,
And yit let me see,
Why maye it not bee?
The name of a conqueror
Were a title of honor.

And wheres reconcilemente
Theres hope of amendemente,
And no better confirmation of amity,
Then for frendes nowe and then to disagree.
Tush, frendes? thou arte worse then madd,
In the shawe there lurkes an ilfavorid padd.
A thousand to on, quoth owld Huddle,
No sweete rosewater in filthy puddle.
Not a dramme of newe honestye,
In an owlde shopp of impietye.
And besides this, every odious jarr,
Take it for a generall rule, leaves behind a skarr.
I have knowen ere nowe a greater clarke
Not by a span and a halfe cum so neere the marke.
My determinate resolution,
Never to be credulous:
He bazardes his owne confusion,
That is over venturous.
And I take him very slenderly and simpely wittid,
That may the seconde tyme be iustly twittid;
Ile sooner, Ile sooner,
Heare my knell:
And downe and downe
Descende into Hell;
Then lerne, then lerne,
Agayne to spell
A, M, O, Amo,
With Mistresse Nell.
Phy, phy on the beaste,
I loathe sutch a geaste,
The divell and his dame
Bringe the to shame;

Swallow her erthe
For fear of a derthe;
Choake her, good aier,
Lest she the empayer;
Twoe pestilent packes
She never lackes,
A close stoole in her teethe,
And a whot house beneathe.
And the thirde as ill or worse then y$^e$ worste,
Beshrewe me but the shrewe is shrewdely accurste.
Lett me rounde ye a litle in y$^e$ eare,
That all the worlde and no more maye heare,
Berlady they saye her best sylke netherstockes
Savour of a certayne thinge, callid y$^e$ Frenche pockes.
I marvell, the elemente
Can abide sutch a sente.
The este be her preiste,
The sowthe stopp her mowthe,
The northe and y$^e$ weste
Dispatche the reste.
Gentle sonne and moone
Destroye and consume her soone.
Raynye clowdes above,
Extinguish and quenche her stoove.
Highest heavens and starres by yer motive influence
Deprive y$^e$ erth of sutch a plague and pestilence.
I am over tædious,
In a poyute so frivolous.
On pore simple versicle
Had bene too mutch for such an article.
Nowe devower her, good hell,
And so farewell good Nell,
And, savinge my quarrell,
Once agayne farewell:

You take me Iwisse
Farr amisse,
If you call this
A Judas kisse.
A gentle farewell   f. 65.
At the ende doth well.
Anger muste go to bedd
When the sonne hides his hedd.
Tis nighte tenne a clocke,
Farewell, gentle French pock.
Now in y<sup>e</sup> divells and his dammes name
Letts to bedward, be freuds for very shame.
All is on, in conclusion:
And unity, you wott, is better then confusion.
Give me thy hande,
Ile forgive thy enormity,
But not for all Englande
Can forgett thy trechery.
And yet be we frendes, and frendes as you see,
In y<sup>e</sup> very hyghest superlative degree.
I remitt and pardon thy impietyes every chone,
Nowe, I pray you, what needes more betwixte John and Jone?
Lett no scruple of conscience disturbe thy hedd,
Thy trespasses and transgressions ar buried in the bedd.
A Plaudite and Deo Gratias for so happy an evente,
And then to borrowe a napp, I shalbe contente.
To-morrowe morninge exspecte y<sup>e</sup> reste,
After fower and fower howres reste.
In the meane while, gentle bedd of downe,
I beseech you give me leave to play my laying downe.

His Epiloge in y<sup>e</sup> morninge next his harte.

The peece of doctrine
Ye hearde yesternight
Was never myne.
By this fresh sunne lighte.
My good Mistresse Experience
Tawghte it me for twooe pence;
Her ladisship proov'd unto me by flatt demonstration
That there mought be established a perfitt reconciliation
Betwene all y<sup>e</sup> contraryes under y<sup>e</sup> cope of heaven,
Naming fyer and water and other aleaven,
With all the planetts, notwithstandinge there opposition,
And all y<sup>e</sup> prædicaments that ar in John Seton;
A generall edicte of pacification,
In despite of all partiality and faction.
A gratious and thrise blessed intendemente
Uppon so solemne and sacrid agreement,
In detestation of future revengement,
To vowe and proclame everlastinge reconcilement.
No treasure under y<sup>e</sup> highest skye,
So precious and inestimable as unity;
And where is unity, there is amity;
Farewell and adieu contrariety.
All nowe is on,
Quoth y<sup>e</sup> father to the son;
And Jack Simkins conformity
Is proov'd a notable story;
And Mistresse Infermity, for her good naturè,
Deservith to be reputid a gentle creature;
And therefore I must needes commende Master Comissary
That acceptid her repentance and dispensd with her folly.
To make shorte worke,
Thus goith the reporte,

Ten thousand Jack Simkins and Mistrisse Infirmityes
Mought be alledgd in defence of uncontraryed contraryes.
O noble philosophers, Melissus and Parmenides,
That iumpe so rightly and equally with all these ;
And by cause I am proceedid thus farr,
I will tell you my dreame before I sturr.
Loe the effecte of my yesternightes exercise,
In my very sleepe I was adrempt in this wise :
First, I considerid that every thinge was finally to be resolvid
Into y<sup>e</sup> selfe same matter whereof it was naturally com-
  poundid ;
And thereaboutes many a physicall sutteltye
Exceedingly busied and occupied my fansy ;
At laste I lett secundary causes aloane,
And mountid thoroughe y<sup>e</sup> skyes to the Almightyes throane ;
He, me thoughte, had the gloabe of y<sup>e</sup> worlde in his hande,
And turnd it at his pleasure like a hasell wande ;
Of a suddayne me thought he lett it fall,
And then to my thinkinge it seemed a ball ;
Twas reatchid him agayne by a glisteringe angell.
It gav then sownde owte like a paultery bell.
The noyse not pleasinge, he layde it up his legg,
And nowe to my seeming it was becum an egg ;
And so methought it continued full stowte,
Till by a mischaunce the yelke runid owte.
Then was there nothinge lefte but the shell ;
Better still have indured a paultery bell.
Give me here that shell, quoth God to a cherubin,
Twas streite wayes as litle or lesse then a pin.
And so I dremd,
**To me it seemd,**
**He stooke it a side,**
**A waye it did glide ;**

Twas suddainly vanisshed
As if it had bene perisshed
Quite owte of my seinge
As a thinge of nothinge.
Mie next imagination was a huge ilfavorid misshapen heape,
That had bene and should be agayne at a leape,
The very selfe same that poetts chaos do cleape.
The tale is too tedious: me thought y<sup>e</sup> worldes ending
Was iumpe all on with the beginninge
And then from chaos whereon I bussid over longe,
Me thought first all thinges was on thinge to make good my songe;
And by and by on y<sup>e</sup> suddayne, all thinges nothinge,
Creatid at y<sup>e</sup> first of nothinge,
Dissolvid at y<sup>e</sup> laste into nothinge.
Many an other shape
I over scape;
But these ar sufficient
To argue my intent.
To be accountid nothing else but nothinge,
A very nothinge, A childes say nothinge;
And then, in a fantasticall fitt,
I cried owte, Ex nihilo nihil fitt.
And therewithall very passionate and begininge to weepe,
I gan suddainly to awake owte my sleepe.
I committ the whole to your worshippes discretion;
Whether you creddit it or skorne it, all is on
Ever since goodly Mistrisse Ellena playd y<sup>e</sup> Jone
All was and is and shalbe on.
Gramercy my good loovinge
For this poynte of lerninge;
No arte nor article
Matchable with this versicle.
I see a foolish fitt

Maye sumtyme do good;
If the marke I not hitt
Saye he is starke wood.
This is y<sup>e</sup> wurste
That I am thus accurste.
A penalty for my excesse
Beyonde all redresse.
Somtyme my booke is unto me a god,
Sumtyme I throwe it from me a rodd.
On while I studdy as thowghe I were madd,
An other while I playe y<sup>e</sup> ungracious ladd.
To daye as merry and lusty as a crickett,
To morrowe as mallancholye and waspish as a wickett.
Robbin, good fellow, when I liste,
With in lesse then an hower all is whiuste.
Uppon every light occasion,
Contrary to all reason,
I helpe to make a ludent,
And nare a student.
I am shaken, like a kixe,
With a thousand sutch fittes;
And yet returne at laste
To my accustomid taske;
As close at Tullyes Orations and Aristotles Politickes,
As on that never hearde tell of other trickes;
And but for sleepinge and playinge, Iwisse,
I had kund them both by harte longe ere this.
All on the suddayne offendid with those,
I strayte gett me Plato or Xenophon by the nose,
Twoe excellent fellowes in every circumstance,
If ether of both had sufficient maynetance.
Incredible it is,
What in those twoe is.
Within a daye or twoe immediately followinge,

f. 66.

At Petrarche and Boccace I must have a flynge.
Every idiott swayne
Can commende there veyne.
Nowe and then a spare hower is allotted to Gascoyne, *Chaucer,*
And sum time I attende on gentle Master Ascham. *sage  Gower.*
They sownde well enowghe withoute makinge ryme
That iumpe so well in cuntry, tunge and tyme.
Would God Inglande cowlde afforde a thowsande sutch and better,
On condition my pore selfe kuewe never a letter.
Sumtyme of warr and sumtyme of peace,
And sumtyme of this and sumtyme of that
(And yet many a good booke
I warrante you unlooked).
I reade and I reade, till I needes must cease,
And insteade of drye studdy fall to gentle chatt.
Had I forgott Aristophanes and Lucian,
In fayth the hourson madd knaves ar unchristian.
Livye, Cæsar, Salluste,
Heredote, Thucidides;
Marke me now the reste,
Those thre ar ever beste.
Sumtyme of lawe I bestowe a daye,
And sumtyme Master Physician I playe.
And sumtyme I addresse myselfe to divinity,
And there continue till I gin to be weary.
All kinde of bookes, good and badd,
Sayntish and divelish, that are to be hadd.
Owlde and yunge,
For matter and tunge,
Wheresoever they dwell,
In heaven or in hell;

*f. 66 b.*

Machiavell, Aretine, and whome you will,
That ar any waye renownid for extraordinary skill;
Ether with myne owne familiar aloane,
Or when twoe of us, like dogges, strive for a boane,
I reade and reade till I flinge them away,
And then godnight studye, tomorrowe is hallidaye.
Be bowlde,
And behowlde,
A very compounde of contrarietyes
In thinges indifferent and medietyes.
And yet I overslipp
Many I pretty whipp
For fear of a quipp,
As ill as a nipp.
Before I gan loove twas far otherwise,
In nise poyntes and quillityes none more præcise.
This only vile property I cannot yet digest,
To winke on y$^e$ ewe when y$^e$ lamme is opprest.
Before God it is odious
To be so trecherous.
Will you have all in a worde and a halfe,
Foes mustbe frende, quoth an Essex kalfe.
Since I lernid to loove I have forgotten to hate,     f. 67.
Nowe God aboove sende me as looving a mate.
She cannot bestowe
Her loove, I trowe,
Where she shall mowe
And I will sowe.
And yet tarry a while,
I am not there by a mile.
Venus and Pallas
Agree not alasse;
Jove and Mercury
Dwell not in on allye,

And yet they doe,
I have proov'd it soe.
The goulden age
Is returned in a cage,
There is excessive unity
In extreme contrariety.
All is on,
And I have don.
This is the songe
Of him that did longe
To discharge his simple conscience.
Not halfe a word more but mumme,
And the divell be her bridegrumme.
Theres better choyce not a mile hence,
And yet charce too for many an ill property,
And yet yes tooe for many a good quality.
Gramercy my good unity at laste,
In this contrariety amongst y$^e$ reste.
Nowe, gentle fayer mistrisse, for a thousand A Dieus,
I wish thou were empresse and quene of the stewes.
I like not those same congyes by Bezo las Manos,
Or that same stale fareweth with Succado dos labros.
Savinge your Reverence, thats a fitter adieu,
Till ower nexte meetinge Boos mun kue.

FINIS.

---

f. 67 b.

O that I were a christall glasse,
For her to behoulde her angells face
   Continually in :
O that I were sum princely vesture,
Her most noble bodye allwayes to cover,
   And ever to be neare her skin.

Withowte any mocke,
Woold God I were her smock;
Else woulde I were a bathe,
Or sweete compounde water;
Her delicate limmes to baathe,
Both sooner and later.
On condition her grace would dayne
To weare me and not teare me:
God forbidd, I should disdeyne
To becum her pantocle.
I would wish to be her very shooe,
Wheresoever she chance to gooe.
Or any other thinge,
And specially her best ringe,
To be allwayes in præsence,
Where herselfe hath residence.
My sovraigne fælicity,
With her allwayes to be,
Whether she eates or drinkes,
Or swimes or synkes,
Or sleepes or playes,
Both nightes and dayes.
And yet what greate wonderment
Though I thus miscontente?
Was not Salomon wiser,
And Sampson stronger,
And David holyer,
And Job pacienter,
Then I?
And yet yow wott all these,
And thousand thousands more then these,
Both in scripture recordid,
And elsewhere reportid,
Betwitchid as well as I,

f. 68.

Beguilid as ill as I.
Then, seinge I have so good cumpanye,
In this miserable extremitye,
I will saye no more,
But gupp ill-favored hore.
And curse all of thy sexe under thy selfe
In despite of so mischeevous an elfe.

---

## To be Inserted in Contra.

What marvell thowgh after ther very frendlyest coniunction,
The sonne and y$^e$ moone mayntayne an opposition?
Suger proovith sault ; and hoony hath a faulte ;
The sweetist tastinge is not longist lastinge.
In the skalldinge dogg dayes the best venery soone decayes.
Flyblowen nor tayntid fleshe comm not in my messe.
And yet can the yuth haply tell
What hath unhappely befell
To as dainty mowthes as his
So many thinges be amisse.
I warrant you there be not so many gentle radiations,
But there be thrise as many cruell consollations.
For every sextile there is a quadrate or two at y$^e$ least,
And can you show me a trine but hath opposition for his gest?
I am none of y$^e$ deepelyest seene in judicialls of astrology,
Yet am I not to leerne that coniunction tooe hath his malady.
Venus is retrograde, and what a goddesname am I?
By my troth, at a resolute poynt whether I lyve or dye;
And yet longe I to lyve, but in fayth for no other ende,
But to be notoriously revenged on this vengeable feende.
By y$^e$ masse all, all is nawght,
Probatum est ; I teach as I am tawght.

To my only Loove and Mistresse, M. Anne,    f. 68 b.
  Yᵉ very ioye and conforte of my lyfe.

My only harte and lyfe, I have sente you here by my boye, a lytle small enamelid, I had lyke to have written enamorid, ringe for a token, whose inscription wyll bewraye my whole errande and suyte in fower doosen capitall, or rather cordiall, letters, for every letter is a syllable, and every syllable a worde, and every worde wrytten with yᵉ quintessence of myne owne harte-bloodd; and my lyfe lyeth in your I, and my deathe in your Noe, and all runnith in termes of on syllable in honour of unity, which wante but on mayde virgins subscription or twoe H. H.'s, that is her hande and harte, to knitt upp yᵉ knott of on man virgins perfection and blisse. If you dare not venture to subscribe till you heere the contentes and mysteryes of yᵉ fower doosen letters revealid, do but laye your right hande faste on your harte, and your left hande twyce as faste on yᵉ token, till you fall a sleepe; and behowlde in your dreame there shall soddainly appeare unto you a lively and cheerefull wynged boye, callid of sum "cupide," of other "loove," you will take him for sum heavenlye angell at yᵉ leaste, that shall præsente you with a fayer peece of very fyne vellam, in fourme and proportion of a harte, as naturally framid as ever was harte, wherein you shall reade the interpretation or exposition of those letters, with a blanke beneathe purposely lefte for your twoe H.'s, my only twoe restoratives. Thynke not any worde here, or anye peece of a worde wrytten in a fonde and counterfett dalliaunce, after yᵉ manner of sum phantasticall loovers. It is yᵉ verye hande and verye harte of him that cannot possibely be his owne till he is actually youers and you his. The inscription of yᵉ ringe in four lines:—

  I. A. R. A. Q. A. W. T. H. T. B.
  A. M. N. L. T. H. T. W. W. I. C. I.
  O. E. A. H. W. F. M. P. A. D. I. S.
  O. L. N. S. S. K. A. P. S. T. A. E.

Cupides Interpretation.

I am a rynge
As quicke as wynge,
True harte to bringe.
And must not lin
Tru hart to win,
Where I cum inne.
Or else a harte
Will from me parte,
And dy in smarte.
Oh, lett not smarte
So kyll and parte
So true a harte.

---

f. 69.            Add to y$^e$ first comendation of my loove.

So many influences and triplicityes of loove
Never ioyyned, synce bewty cam first from above.
The prowdist of woomen cum neere my queene,
And alasse what a shame by her to be seene.

ff. 69 b, 70.          To be insertid in y$^e$ fittest place.

Lord, what a queynt fellowe was Momus for conceyte,
That founde the wante of a wyndowe into the clossett of deceyte?
Thereby to discrie ower corrupte thowghtes, and divellish trecherye,
And whatever mischeif is cooverid with y$^e$ cloake of hypocrisy.
Had Apollo, or Mercury, or Pallas spyed y$^e$ defect,
Or any other God or Goddesse of semblable respect,
I am fully persuadid and sett it downe for my opinion
This devise woulde have karried y$^e$ creddit from any invention
That Polydore or any other ever commendid,
Whatsoever now to y$^e$ contrary is prætendid.

A most delicate imagination and no oracle Iwisse,
No apothegg, no emblem comparable to this.
O that I might have openid y<sup>e</sup> casement of her harte;
How easely might I have præventid so intolerable smarte?
What other apology needes Momus devise?
Were I wiser than Salomon, I woold count him more wise.
All shoold ly open, that now fosterith such villany,
There shoolde not neede any figure to disclose disloyalty.
Pravum cor hominis et inscrutabile,
The horoscope not halfe so certayne as this memorabile.
O that there were a wyndowe in to y<sup>e</sup> breastes of such falsaryes,
The woorld should not be pesterid with such millions of miseryes.
It is a world to enter into y<sup>e</sup> windowles mynde,
What remedy but pacience and fast bynde, faste fynde?
Had the byrd bene traynid to this suspicion in tyme,
He coold hardly have bene so intanglid with y<sup>e</sup> twigg and y<sup>e</sup> lyme.
Nowe in supply of Momus honest casement,
Mistrust and ielousy must lerne to be provident.
Take heede, they say, is a fayer thinge:
Nowe fye on all fylthes, quoth y<sup>e</sup> karte to y<sup>e</sup> bullringe.
The kage and y<sup>e</sup> cooking stoole procleame no lesse;
And all to lytle in good sooth for my sweetharte Besse.
Nell, I would have sayd, but for rymes sake;
A small fault where her mistrisship doth brue and bake.
There is not a Besse or Jone in this londe all abowte,
That hath such iadysh qualityes within and withoute.
My moother tawght me once to beware of such stuff:
Try them farther that lyste: I have enuff.
Wooinge and woing differ not muche:
Yet had I rather serve Hecate then any sutch.
The only good I have gotten by this hatefull loove,
I can give a shrode gesse at a serpent and a doove.
**No plague in y<sup>e</sup> world so horrible as this:**
**To have a bedlom in bed and a tode to kisse.**

Purgatory a jest,
To such unrest:
The black deepes of hell
Less wofull to dwell.
If any negotiation requires advizements,
None more then matrimony by my advertisement.
If you happen aright, and fortune be your friend,
The tresure inestimable,
The plesure inseparable,
From wynter to wynter unto your lives ende.
If crooked be your chaunce, and lottery badd
No luck so unsufferable,
No estate so damnable,
As good dy betimes as lyve to be madd.
And yet what shoold carcase of miserable wight
Hunt after tresure or dreame of delight?
All in the windeuppall cummith litely to on reckoning,
The surist accountant faylith commonly ere y$^e$ parting.
A straung world and a queynt and of a mad fasshion;
Who knowith in wysshing how to order his passion?
Not myself I feare me when twenty yeares to cum,
Of forty with advantage shall make upp the summ.
Notwithstanding peradventure a man may plodd on
With other good fellowes, and not be over gon,
Happy man, happy dole; and all is but happ;
Who but happ hazarder in Madame fortunes lapp?
I rove at all aventures, but so much perchaunce
The nearer to y$^e$ marke may I happen to glaunce?
In truth it is not y$^e$ reason or y$^e$ cunningist bente
That ever succedith best in event.
Tyme and fortune master every circumstaunce:
Nothing fadgith, that with them is at variaunce.
Now good tymes and good fortune do me reason and right;
Especially in matters of choyce and ensight.

Howbeit still all is ace,
And there still a fayer chace.

Certayne younge conceytes and poeticall devises, copied owt of a schollars paperbooke, and publisshed by a gentleman of his acquaintaunce, who first borrowed them of y^e author as once his private exercises of pleasure at idle bowers, and now lendith them unto y^e reader as still appliable to lyke publique use of recreation at vacant tymes. ⸺ Not a worde more by any meanes. In this on treatise all the poeticall devises that ever I made in Inglishe sett in as witty and fine order as may be, Aretinelyke.

---

1. A Sundaie supper at Mr. S.
2. The first meating in y^e feild a litle straunge, mooving y^e matter a far of, without offer of anie thing, uppon y^e Munday sennight after.  f. 71.
3. The 2 meating in y^e feild more plaine, with wines, cakes, glooves, girdell, y^e next Tuesday being halliday, a halliday breakefast.
4. A thre or fower dales after at J. R. y^e small inamleld ring with a ribben of urring tanye.
5. Milord and his man P. y^e next Weddensday presently after five a clock in y^e evening (a marvelous foggie mistie eveninge) came up y^e streate purposely to speake with y^e maide, and seing y^e dore ope, stepd in; but P. spying in y^e maulthowse (P. had on foote in y^e mault howse) y^e maides mother and sister with sum of ther servantes, sum turning y^e mault, sum steaping, sum looking on, they were faint to get them homewards, as wise as thei cam. A great iorney lost. Milord swore to P. he had rather have ridden fortie miles then have taken sutch a iorney in sutch a mistie night.
6. Hereuppon y^e maide writt her first letter then on uppon an other as thei followe in order. With y^e "thirde" seconde letter

of Milords cam a prettie bowed goulden ring, which P. swore Milord tooke from his owen fingar to sende her.

All this time of letters sending had P. manie a shrode wettie iorney, and evermore in y$^e$ evening, nether could he speake with y$^e$ maide, but thurrough a pale, for all this while he never cam in her fathors howse nether could he cum to y$^e$ speach of her, everie time he cam, but nowe and then lost his iorny.

---

f. 71 b.

## A NOBLE MANS SUTE TO A CUNTRIE MAIDE.

First his man P. bad her to y$^e$ eating of a coople of cunnies in y$^e$ towne, which y$^e$ yung lord was privie too, as P. swore afterward.

With in a sennight after, P. watchd her going a milking a mile from y$^e$ towne, having with him a bottle of mamsey and short chakes, to moove her appetite.

The mamsey was drunk of, and y$^e$ chakes eaten in a wood they passid thurrough, none being there but P. and y$^e$ maide and a pore woman that bare y$^e$ maide cumpanie.

The woman going a litle aside to gather upp sticks that lay scattering in y$^e$ wood, P. began to commense his masters sute, marry not so flatly as afterwarde, to feele of a like y$^e$ maides minde. The maide could not be brought to beleeve his master ether knewe her, or would motion any sutch sute to any other, having so goodlie a ladie of his owne.

f. 72.

P. was well providid to answer to all sutch doubtes, and swore deeply to y$^e$ maide, that both his master knewe her (by that token, that she passing once by him, when he was bowling in sutch a place, her hatt blue of, and she therewith sumwhat chaungid her colour) and set more by her than he did by his owne ladie.

She still was unbeleeving, saying she knewe well Mielord passid not for so homelie wenchis, that she was but a milkmaide, and a plaine cuntrie wench, and if Mielord were so disposid he might have manie a on at commaundiment far more likelie then she.

P. notwithstanding all this continued his sute, and would needes make her take a good faier sylk girdell and a hansum paier of glooves that Mielord, he said, had sent her, prommising her, with many a lustie othe, that if she would graunt Mielord his request, she should not neede to care for y<sup>e</sup> leefist frende she had, but should be thus and thus maintainid. Still y<sup>e</sup> maide kept aloofe, and made verie straung, taking it to be P. owne sute, and not Mielords. Whereuppon P. swore he would bring sum other token from Mielord, that she should not choose but think it was he, and no other, that desirid her cumpanie.   f. 72 b.

Within a daie or twoe after he brought her a prettie inammeld ring with this posie, DON JAMYE, which he swore Mielord took from his owne hatt not two howers before, whereon it was sowen, given him by his awnt, Mieladie of W       , saiing Mielord would as leeve have sent her half a score ould aungels, but that those might as likely cum from sum other man.

These thinges seemid marvelous straung to y<sup>e</sup> cuntrie wenche, in so mutch that she was half amasid at y<sup>e</sup> matter, and therefore could not well tell what answer she should returne to Mielord. Only, like a good plaine wench, she saied she could not but thanke him for his looving tokens. Marry, yeeld unto him she durst not in aniewise. And so pleadid for hir honestie as well as she could; nether would give anie signification of graunting his request.

Whereat P. saied he marvelid mutch, having so faier offers of  f. 73. Mielord; swearing that if she were his owne sister he would counsell her, and desier her too, to yeeld unto him. Yea, saith he, by the bodie of God, you make more straung than most gentlewomen would do of five hundrid pounds a yeare. And assure yourself Mielord maie have manie a good gentlewoman and ladie tooe at commaundiment; by the Mas, if you denie him his request, you ar the veriest foole in y<sup>e</sup> world; with a manie sutch whot and ernest wordes. Whereto y<sup>e</sup> maide knewe not well what to say,

CAMD. SOC.           U

but wild him to desier Mielord to be contentid, she could not in that case fulfill his minde. Marry, any other way she thought her self bownde to his Lordship in respect of sutch kindnes. Still P. laied at her to appoint sum place where Mielord might meete with her, for Mielord was marvelous desirous to speake with her.

Alas, said she, I knowe not in what sort to behave mieself before his Lordship; what should he so desier to speake with me?

f. 73 b. Well, in the end, the maide being thus importunately laied at, that at y<sup>e</sup> lest Milord might cum to y<sup>e</sup> speach of her, prommisid that if he would cum over to her fathers howse, in sutch a streat, uppon sutch a daye towards the evening (this day was Weddensday, almost a sennight after), she would be there to speake a word or twoe with him. This day cam, and Milord and P. cam according to ther appointment. But in steade of the maide her self, which was not there, there were as it happenid in y<sup>e</sup> maulthowse the maides mother, her sister, and two of her fathers servants, and in y<sup>e</sup> parlour on of her bretheren, that sae them cum faier and softly upp y<sup>e</sup> streate, and stay a prettie while at y<sup>e</sup> dore, looking of a like to be interteinid of y<sup>e</sup> maide, but she not being at hande, as thei hopid for, thei steppid both prettely in to y<sup>e</sup> entry, and P. went pering to y<sup>e</sup> maulthowse dore to spie if she were there, but having on of his fitt in y<sup>e</sup> maulthowse, he sae that he lookid not after, and missid that he came for. Whereuppon thei conveied themselves away as hansumly as thei could, and were fainte to gett themselves homewards as they cam, being well mirid and weried for ther labour, besides that it was the mistiest and foggiest night that was that winter.

f. 74. Notwithstanding this, P. usid meanes to speake with y<sup>e</sup> maide againe within a day or two after, telling her howe Milord was disapointid, and what a werisum and toiling iorny he had taken in vaine, saiyng, moreover Milord did half suspect she mockid him, &c.

The maid quitt herself as hansumly as she could of the præsent, saying that she could not possibely be there at that time as things fill owte: and if she had bine there, there had bene no speaking with Milord at that time, &c.

Marry to satisfie Milords mind, who, as P. saied, thought himself deludid, she prommisid with in a daye or twoe to purge herself to Milord by letter. Which was as P. would have it, for then he thought her deade suer.

P. cummes me the next night for her letter.

It was not finnishid.

He cummes againe y<sup>e</sup> next daye.

She could not be spoke with all.

Bye the third day she had addressid " her " this letter, and gave it unto P. at his cumminge:—

Milord, thowgh mie bringing upp hath bene allwaies so homelie and milkmaidelike, that I know not in what sort to behave mieself towards your lordship, ether for talk or for other seemelie behaviour; yet to satisfie your lordships minde (having receivid your loving token, which notwithstanding I allwaies dourid was sum other mans that bore me gud will) I was mindid truly to speake with you y<sup>e</sup> last evening, had there not bene sutch blocks in y<sup>e</sup> way that I could not possibely do as I was mindid. I beseech you, good Milord, pardon me; truly if I would never so faine, I could not at that time, as it fill owte, have spoken with you. And yit, alas, what is in me, pore wench, that Milord A. S. should desier to speake with me? The thing you wot of, Milord, were a great trespas towards God, a great offens to the world, a great greif to mie frends, a great shame to mieself, and, as I thinke, a great dishonor to your lordship. I have hard mie father saie, Virginitie is y<sup>e</sup> fairist flower in a maides gardin, and chastitie y<sup>e</sup> ritchist dowrie a pore wench can have.

f. 74 b.

These things, Milord, and sutch other make me aferde to yeeld to your request; though truly I am verie sorie your lordships request is sutch that I may not safely yeeld unto it. I beseech you, good Milord, have me excusid, though I make straung with youer lordship in so daungerous a matter. Thus, hoping your good

f. 75.

lordship will take all in as gud part as it is ment on mie part, I take mie leave most lowly and humbly of you.

Your lordships anie way els at commaunde,

PORE M.

I pray, Milord, rent this paper alltopeesis, lest it chaunce by sum mishap to cum to light, and so turne to your dishonor, which I would be loth.

To this letter Milord returnid an answer y$^e$ next evening as followith.

Fearing, as P. said, that she had her secretarye, and desiring an answer to his letters y$^e$ next daye.

f. 75 b.

### THE YUNG LORDS FIRST LETTERS.

I have receivid your letters. I do not anie thing mislike of your great showe of chastity, and yit I hope that you wil be none otherwise unto me then I looke for. I did thinke it mie great goodhap that it was mi luck to make choise of the above y$^e$ rest, both bycause I kuewe nature hath delt better in fashioning the then with any other here about, and also that being so given I might more safely dele with the then with many other common gallantes, by whome I might reape that frute which hardly while I livd I could recover. I protest here before God, and vowe to the, whome I love best, that.I was never of that unconstant minde to deceive any woman, nether can I be of that dissembling nature to profess great loove where I do not like.

f. 76.

The next day after save on, y$^e$ maide answerid by letter in this wise:

Milord, if I did nether feare God, nor stand in awe of mie frendes, nor passe what report went of me, then sutch letters, from sutch a man, so lovingly written, so full of lavish prommises and rewards, might perhaps allure me to yeeld unto you. But God forbid, Milord, that anie perswading words or faier prommissis should prævaile with me in that matter, wherein I should so greevusly offend so manie, and so shamefully cast away mieself. Chastitie, they say, is like unto time, which, being ons lost, can no more be recooverid.

Good Milord, pardon me, though I deale plainely with you. It is no showe of chastitie, as your Lordship imagin, but chastitie indeede, that I care for. You may have other gallants, I know, at commaundiment. I pray, mielord, spare me, and make your sute to sutch as wilbe as reddie to take as you to offer.

Alas, Mielord, what talk you of crueltie on mie part in not graunting your desier, or of unhappiness on your part in not enioying your desier. Iwis, Mielord, it wilbe y$^e$ best for us both that I be thus cruell, and you thus unhappie. And, howsoever it be, truly I cannot yeeld unto you. And this is all y$^e$ answer I can make to your long letters. I pray your lordship be contente.

Youres as before and no otherwise,<br>
Pore M.

Use this paper I pray, as you did y$^e$ other. I can keepe youer counsell, though I cannot fulfill your request.

Milord replieth y$^e$ next day at night on this manner.

And for his farewell sendith a small gould ring from his owne fingar.

## THE MAIDES FAREWELL.

Milord, if youer sute were as honest as it is ernest, truly you shuld not be so reddie to make it, but I wuld be as willing to graunt it. For I cannot nowe but think youer lordship hath sum fansie to me in deede, not only in showe, that have so oft sente your man to me to intreate for you, lost ons a iorny yourself in a mistie foggie evening to speake with me, and nowe last of all writt two sutch larg and loving letters, all to be spicid with sugrid words and honysweet offers. For which tokins of gud will I cannot for manners sake but thanke you, though I dare not, for mine owne sake, yeeld unto you. Good lord, that you shuld thus seeke after so base and cuntrie stuff abrode, that have so costly and courtlie wares at home. You loove me best, you say, and præfer me in loove before any other, and esteeme me more then you esteeme yourself. Alas, Milord, howe can you; I being so base and abiect in comparison of your lordshipp? You have answerid mie thre pointes at large, but not at full. I still feare y$^e$ worst. I would be loth to yeeld to you in a madnes, and ever after sorrowe to mieself in good sadness. You knowe well, Milord, the matter must needs brust owte in y$^e$ end on mie part, beit clokid never so lordly on your part.

And then were I, pore wench, cast up for hawks meate, to mine owne utter undoinge, and mi frendes exceeding greef. And yit ar there a manie things mo to be fearid. Good Milord, wey mie case a litle better, and you will leave of your whot sute, I doute not. And thus I take mie farewell of your lordship, after y$^e$ best fashion I can for mie bringing up, prommising you unfainedlye never to bewraye your secrets, but to give you mie gudd word wheresoever I becum. As your letters beare me in hande, I have gudd cause to doe.

     Your lordships, as afore,
      Seing you will needs call me so,
        CRUELL M.

I knowe not I, what you meene by your conquest, but it matterith not greatly.

Milord culd not quiet himself with this farewell, but settes upon her with a fresh reioinder, as followithe.

The maide being resolvid to write no more, yit uppon y$^e$ receipt of so looving a letter, thought good to make an ende with these fewe lines. f. 78.

You knowe full well, Milord, faier words make fooles faine, and you weene of a like. Maides will refuse and take; but I would not you should thinke me a chaungelinge. Wary would I faine be: cruell can I not be; and your Lordship is unsatisfied, but not unhappie. Unhappie am I rather, that ———, but there a strawe. Tis not inke and paper, your man telles me, that can content Milord.

> What, then, but put up mie pen,
>  And pray God amende you?
> An that be crueltie tooe, I knowe not what to dooe,
>  But pray God sende you.

> Yours as she may,
> And not as you say,
>  Though it greeve ye.
> Yours as she can,
> And not as you scan,
>  You may beleeve me.

> And thus I pray you stay.
>             PORE M.

f. 78 b.  To this letter Milord made no answer by writinge, but sent his man P. to deale with her, that he might speake a word or twoe with her as shortly as might be. Whereunto with mutche adooe y<sup>e</sup> maide grauntid.

This was y<sup>e</sup> Thursday before Christmas Day (1574), Christmas Day being uppon y<sup>e</sup> Satterday. And the maide appointid Sundaye to meete with Milord againe.

And prommisid to speake with him upon sutch a day, at sutch a neighbours house. Milord was there at y<sup>e</sup> day and time appointid, and sent for y<sup>e</sup> maide by on of y<sup>e</sup> house. The maide with in les then a quarter cam, and spake with him. Milord stud reddle in a litle parlour in his dublet and his hose, his points untrust, and his shirt lying out round about him. And after a short salutation, and a twoe or thre kisses would needs have laid y<sup>e</sup> maide on y<sup>e</sup> bedd.

The maide would none of that, but bad him fie for shame, and so by struggeling shiftid as well as she might.

The good wife of y<sup>e</sup> howse, perceiving y<sup>e</sup> winde in that dore, gat me her self owt in to y<sup>e</sup> streate at a side dore, and cam and knockid alowde at her owne dore, and tould on in y<sup>e</sup> howse M mother had sent for her in all hast.

f. 79.  This was M. own devise beforehand, that if y<sup>e</sup> gentleman, that would be heere uppon sutch a night to speake with her, should stay her never so litle, that y<sup>e</sup> woman would præsently knock at her dore, and say she was sent for.

M. hearing y<sup>e</sup> knocking, saied she was suer it was for her, and therefore tould him she must needs begon præsently.

Whereuppon mi yung lord fill to swaring, and praied M. very instantly to yeeld unto him.

M. made hast awaye, and saied she durst not tarry any longer.

Heare was good M., good M., and a great deale more. God confounde me, God confounde me, if thowe wantes, while I have, &c.

Milord, seeing it would not be that time, desirid her that she would appoint sum other day, when he might talk longer with her, and have his request, protesting unto her that he would be true unto her, and use her as his wife, and have to dooe with no other, but only her and his wife. And swearing that she should have any thing he had at commaundiment, and use him as familiarly and bowldly at any time as her owne brother; with a many sutch goodly supplicamussis; besides that he put his hand into his pockit, and pullid owt at a venture sutch moony, as ether he had put there for y$^e$ nonse or as cam next to hande, which he would needs make y$^e$ maide fingar whether she would or noe. The maide tould him she had deservid no sutch giftes at his hands, nor none would take; she had, she thankid God, enough to serve her tarne, and needid to take none in that sort, and so would needs begon.

Milord swore she should not choose but take it. (It was iust 13$s$. in testers and shillings). The maide seing him so ernest, and being verie desirous to be gon, tooke y$^e$ mouye, and at y$^e$ lenght, with much adooe (only, as she saied, to be rid of him at that time), promisid to meete with him there againe on Sunday next, which was y$^e$ next day to Christmas. This Sunday was a marvelous wet day, and suddainly there arose great waters, by reason of y$^e$ raine and snowe, that fill togither. f. 79 b.

Notwithstandinge, y$^e$ maide purposely tooke a iorny a seven miles of, in y$^e$ morning before six a clocke, dreading y$^e$ wurst if mie lord should chaunce to cum. The raine continued y$^e$ whole day, and yet P. in y$^e$ evening cam to y$^e$ place appointid (he was fajnt to cum on pattins, bycause of y$^e$ great wett), thinking verely to have y$^e$ maide there. It was tould him the maide was gon to a frendes of hers this Christmas, to make merrie. But they thought she would be here again by Neweyeares time. And this was all y$^e$ newes P. had to his master.

The Thursday before Neweyeares day (being on y$^e$ Satterday), the maide, by counsell of on she trustid well, excusid herself on this wise to Milord :— f. 80.

Milord I thanke you hartely
For your late liberalitie;
I would I were hable to requite
Your lordships bowntie with y^e like.
Marry, mie hart is not so franke
But mie habilitie is as scante;
Therefore, in steade of a leifer gift,
I bequeath you this paper for a shift.
You se I am disposid to rime,
Though it be eleen out of time.
I hope your L. will have me excusid
As longe as you feel not yourself abusid.
To be short, Milord, thus it is, Iwis,
I could not be at home according to prommis.
I would not, perhaps it may to you seem;
I pray you, Milord, do not so misdeem.
Truly I was sent for to spend this good time
A fewe miles of with a kinsman of mine.
Whether mi father in hast wuld so faine have me goe,
That I could not nor durst not for mielife say noe.

   So that I was faint
    At his commaundiment
   To take a iornye
    That I litle ment.
   I pray you, Milord,
    Have me excusid,
   Though by mie frends
    I be thus rulid.

The truth is, I am not mine owne maide,
My frends to disobey I am afraide.

>     An other time as good
>     To speake your minde;
>     In y^e meane time if you seeke
>     You can not but finde.
>   Your honors to commaund
>   In anie honest demaund.
>                 M.

Milord, if you will any thing with me, ether concerning your letters (for your man telles me you looke for them againe), or concerning mie breaking prommis with you, or your next speaking with me, or anie thing els that shall seem good to your L., you may safely, I warrant you, write your minde, and send your letters by P. to y^e pore womans you wot of, to be broute me on Friday next in y^e morning by on that can not reade himself, and that I will charg to bring me in his purse sutch a letter that I had forgott in sutch a place; which to be suer I will say I wrote to be sent mie brother of Cambridg concerning his cumming downe into y^e cuntrie, the day before he cam downe of his owne accord unsentfor.

And therefore I take it not amis, Milord, you seale your letter, and write thus in y^e backside, in a small raggid secretary hand,—

To mie loving brother, Mr. G. H., on of y^e fellowes of Pembrook hall, in Cambridg. As I use to write to mie brother there, when I write unto him, that if y^e simple fellowe chaunce to offer me y^e letter before cumpany, I may say it was a letter I had writt to be sent my brother Gabriell at sutch time as he cam home to mie fathers, and so kept it still, and by chaunce left it in sutch a place, and therefore sent nowe for it, being loth it should cum in any others hands. Thus, Milord, in mie foolish fansie you may write most safely, an you be disposid to write. Marry, I pray do as it shall seeme best to your L. If you write I will answer you ether by pen or tunge, as shortly as may be.

Thus ons againe I take mie leave of your L., having no other new yeares gift, but this sillie sheete of paper to bestowe uppon you. And so I wish you many a good newe yeare.

Which letter mielord answerid præsently uppon y$^e$ deliverie thereof, so that y$^e$ bearer was desirid to tarry awhile and take an answer with him, which he did.

The answer was superscribid thus, in a small counterfet secretary,—

        To my loving brother,
        M$^r$. Gabriell Harvey,
        Fellowe of Pembrook
        Hall in Cambridg.

And y$^e$ letter itself was as followith.

The letter was mett withall by y$^e$ waye, whereuppon this letter was addressid to Milord :—

Milord, it was mie hap on new yeares even, as I was riding towards Cambridg, to overtake by y$^e$ way a cuntrie fellowe that I had ofttimes seen long since at mie fathers here in Walden. The plain fellowe amongst amanie other goodly matters tould me he had a letter in his pocket, that should ons have bene sent me to Cambridg, but that I cam home to miefathers that verie time it should have bene sent me. I pray the, said I, from whome? I warrant you, syr, quoth y$^e$ fellowe, from on that loovith you full well, your sister Marcie. And her letters, said I, ar sumwhat daintie, they cum so sildom. But I prythe lett me see y$^e$ letter, for, being written to me, as thou saist it was, there can be nothing in it that I may not knowe of. Indede, syr, quoth he, who should see it, if you might not see it? But by y$^e$ Mariegod I was straitly chargid by mie yung mistres, that noboddie, in anie case, should see it. Whie, foole, said I, I am nobodie, thouh I see it, thou maist say; and vowe too, if need be, nobodie hath seen it. You schollars be merrie gentlemen, quoth y$^e$ fellowe; but seing you will needs see it, you shall see it indeed for me, a Gods name, and with that he put his hand in his purse, and gave me y$^e$ letter to peruse. I sae it superscribid to me jndeed, and therefore made nothing daintie at y$^e$ matter, but broke it up. At y$^e$ verie greating, to tell you y$^e$ troth, Milord, I was sumdeale abasshid, but more astonied at y$^e$ processe, and finally, most of all, moovid at y$^e$ subscription. The greeting was, Mine owne sweet Mercy, as if it had bene addressid to mie sister from sum loover of hers, and not scriblid from mie sister to a brother of hers. The processe, a verie amorous and glosing discours touching her suddain departure, her speedie return, y$^e$ want of her præsens, y$^e$ pleasure taken in reading her letters, y$^e$ possession of her according to prommis, with a menie goodlie faier words of allurement and persuasion to that effect. The subscription was in your lordships owne name, as I remember me, thus—

Thine more then his owne,<br>PHIL.

Meethouht, Milord, this was wunderfull straung geare, and full mutch adooe had I (God wot) to dissemble mie suddain fansies, and comprimitt mie jnward passions. Notwithstanding I sett as good a countenaunce on y$^e$ matter as I miht. And I prey the, what have we here beside (an God will) in this prettie paper? said I to y$^e$ fellowe. Marry, syr, I wud it were an ould angell for me, quoth he. Na then, for me, said I; but I feare me, when all is dun, it will rather proove sum crackd grote in y$^e$ opening; take it thou for a tester at all aventure. Not so, Master, quoth he, Ile none of y$^e$ pig in y$^e$ poke, I thanke you. Well, then, Ile unpoke y$^e$ pig for this ons, said I; and before y$^e$ fellowe, contrarie to mi exspectation, found there a Gods name a faier Inglish crowne, appointid as should appear for a neweyeares gift. The pore fellow lauhid out, and askid me what I had gottin, if I had gon thorouh with him aforehand. I tould him I should have bene faint to have made sum backreckning with him again. And so, to be short, I bore the sillie fellow in hand I would ease him of that burdin, both y$^e$ letter and tokin too, being sent to me as they were. Na, by y$^e$

Mariegod, syr, quoth he, I would not for y<sup>e</sup> best coate to mie back you shuld serve me so. Your sister, I dare sweare, wuld trust me y<sup>e</sup> wurs as long as she should knowe me. I pray ye nowe give me them again, and if it be her mind you shall have them, you may better have them at her hands then at mine. Thou saist troth indeed, quoth I, and seing thou wilt needs purse them up again, take them here with the for me, and mutchie godditch her good hart with them. But I prey the have me commendid to her, and tell her, I am a storer of hers for a twoe or thre crackd grotes and bowd testerns, but y<sup>e</sup> devill a crowne of gould of hers I could fingar before, and now an God will must I part with it tooe. And for a tokin, will her in my name to looke ere she leape. She maie pick out y<sup>e</sup> Inglish of it herself.

f 84. And this be all, God be wye, M. Harvey, said y<sup>e</sup> pore honest fellowe, I shall do your commaundiment an God will within this fewe howers.

Thus it was mie hap, Milord, by a meere chaunce, to liht on sutch a letter and tokin, sent, not from you, as I take it, but in your L. name, from I knowe not whome, to a sister of mine. Whereuppon I was sumwhat straungly affectid on y<sup>e</sup> suddaine, musing greatly whoe this lustie suter should be, and what should be ment by y<sup>e</sup> loftie subscription within, and y<sup>e</sup> suttle superscription withoute. In so mutch that I was now fully resolvid at mie returne, which should be y<sup>e</sup> next day, to make sum arrand to mie sister by y<sup>e</sup> way, being so little way of, and so to boult out y<sup>e</sup> matter. The next morning, contrarie to mie overnights forecast, it was mie illluck to stumble on sutch cumpany to Walden warde, that I could not possibely cumpas mie purpose, unles I would have lingerid a day or twoe longer in Cambridg for y<sup>e</sup> nonse, which I could not nether conveniently do, mie busines lying as it did. So that I was faint nowe to quiet mieself, as well as I miht, and, seing this would not fadg, to do an other. I thowht best to spur cutt and make y<sup>e</sup> more speede, that as soone as I cam at Waldin, I miht huddle up a word or twoe to mi sister by sum of y<sup>e</sup> markit folks.

Here the letter-book is resumed from p. 54.

### To Dr. Young, Master of Pembroke Hall.

It mai seem straung unto you, riht wurshipful, that I, whitch am accustomed to write lattin epistles unto you, do now, contrary to mi manner and your exsspectation write in Inglish. But if it mai pleas your wurship to consider the caus, I hope you wil accept as wel of it, as if I had writ in lattin. I have often and sundri times, as gud reasun wuld, and mi duti requirid, given you most harti and special thanks both for your great and manifould bennefits, and also for your singular and fatherli gud wil towards me. This I dout not but your wurship did wel think and like of: considering that there was no other means to show how mindful I was of your gudnes towards me, and how desirus I wuld be to do you servis. And in ded mi mening was alwais to let your wurship understand, that as I was greatly bound unto you, so I did indevor mi self to be, and sem thankful towards you. Notwithstanding becaus it is commonly the manner of schollars, to write more in there lattin epistles, then thai profes in there commun talk, or show in there outward doings, and mani things often times mai sem to be spoken rather of cours and custum, then of ani inward affection, I thouht it not amis, or rather I thouht it mi duti, plainly and simply in flat Inglish to utter mi mind. If I do not wel, I besech you pardon me, for that I men wel. It mai like your wurship to cal to your remembrans how easly, uppon none or smal occasion, without ani great labor of frends, you ware furst inducid to be gud patron unto me: and then how largly and lovingly you bestowid your bennefits uppon me, and, last of al, how duly and constantly you have ever sins unto this dai continued them. As concerning the first, I must nedes sai and confes, that it was not so mutch the liking of ani thing in me, whitch was then and am yet both rude in talk and simple in behaviour, as a plain and evident token of a great gud nature and wunderful kindnes in you, whitch were as willing to bestow, as I was reddie to aske,

f. 85.

f. 85 b.

and nedi to have the bennefit. And therefore it was then and is now so mutch the more to be estemid and accountid of, in that, that I, unto home it was thus frely grauntid, miht in al respects be thouht most unwurthi of it. For in what other consideration could I or mi freuds hope to obtain ani thing at your hand, saving only for names sake? And alas what was this to procure so great and special frendship; considering that there were mani mo of the name, and I as litle, or les known unto you, then ani other? So that there is gud cause, whi first in this respect I shuld shew mi self both greatly mindful of sutch a bennefit, and verry thankful to sutch a frend. And as herein I have iust occasion to commend your gud and loving nature, from the whitch, as from a clear spring the bennefits them selvs did flowe; so by reasun of them, I have as iust occasion to commend of your excellent liberaliti and singular gudnes. Whereuppon if I wuld contend to discours at larg, and you could intend to peruse it, I could easely and miht iustly write a great deale more, then I purpose to speak of at this time. And therefore now I have in most humble manner to request your wurship, that this mai suffice, to acknowledg your bennefits frely, to thank you for them hartely, and to submit mi self unto you dutifully.

f. 86. And if mi servis at ani time mai stand you in ani stead (althouh I cannot tel how possibely it shoold, so far am I from requiting ani part of your kindnes), yet if it mai ani wais stand you in stead, I am yours alwais to commaund in dead and word to the uttermost of mi power; if it mai pleas you so to accept of it. And this I speak, God is mi witnes, not for fasshion sake, after the manner of sum schollars, and mo courtiers; but for your deserts sake, and mi duties sake, after the manner of thos, that account wel of wel doing. As for your constancie and continuanc in deserving so wel continually of me, whitch is the third point that I purposid to touch: I must neds, and ouht of duti make as great, or greater account of it, then I have or can make of y$^e$ rest; for so mutch as it is an harder matter and a hiher commendation to continu wel, then it is to begin wel; as that spring is more wurth that alwais runmith then that whitch is soone dried up. Therefore as before I was occasionid to think and speak wel of your good nature in the graunt, and of your great liberaliti in the perfourmanc of it, so now I cannot but prais and extol your wunderful constanci in persevering. So that this great constanci of yours in doing so wel bi me must at the lest bring forth no les constanci in me, in speaking as wel bi you. But alas what is speaking to doing, if a man wil but speak uprihtly? Yit this wil I sai, and I mai sai it truly, if I were as wel hable to deserv wel of others, as I am reddi to speak wel of them, I wuld then ful plentifully perfourme in ded, whitch now so couldly is utterid in word.

And if you amongst sum others shal ever have occasion to tri me, whitch amongst al others have deservid best of me, (as God knowith whether ever you shal, or no, so litle hope there is hereof, and yet I wuld to God it miht be so) I wil speak it here bouldly, whitch I wil then proove gladly, you shal find me as trusti to mi power as I have found you beneficial to my proffit. But it is no better then folli on mi part to talk of ani sutch matter, when as it is past al hope that my habiliti shoold ever proove sutch, as that in ani point I miht stand you in stead. And yit suerly I cannot choose but write thus fondly, whitch I mind unfainidly, and profes that in mi letters whitch I purpose in mi hart. I beseech you bare with mi rudenes: How so ever undiscretly I write, I men with the best. But I have alreddi bene over tædius to your wurship, and therefore I wil here rest to trubble you, making this prommis, that as you have duly and daily dun for me, so I wil duly and daily prai for you.

f. 86 b.

Your wurships ever at commaundment,

GABRIEL HARVI.

CAMD. SOC.      Y

## To Sir Thomas Smith, of Audley End.

When I call to remembraunc, riht wurshipful, the special frendship that I alwais hetherto sins mi first cumming to Cambridg have found at your hands (as suerly I do, and must neds remember it often, having continually had so ful trial thereof) it puttith me in mind of as special a duti towards you ; and causith me to make a veri great account of your furtheraunc, in whatsoever thing mai concern mi commiditi. It is not past thre yers, as you wel remember, sins I trubblid your wurship with laboring to our Master about a fellowship; wherein the event did declare how mutch you prævailid with him. And not long ago, thorouh the importuniti of a few, I had like to have stud in nede, and would suerly have præsumid of your frendship, had not our Master himself takin the hole matter uppon him at the first, and dispatchid it so in the end, that the busiest and lustiest of them al was ashamid of y$^e$ enterprise. Now being willid by mi freuds, and set on bi others example, to determin with mi self to what kind of studdi I were best to betake me to, and having a great gud liking of the Civil Law, whitch I know to be so hihly commendid of y$^e$ worthiist of men, and namely of Tulli; and therefore intending bi the grace of God, if not præsently altogither, yit partly now, and fully hereafter to make it mi studdi; I thouht it most convenient, and so did thai too, to make you privi to mi purpose before I went ani further, and to crave your wisdums advise in this behalf, meaning not to enterprise so serius and waihti a matter without your assent. For both first I am suer, that nothing can concern a man more, then to forese in time, whereuppon to stai himself, and to considder advisedly of y$^e$ end, whereunto he purposith to direct his studdies: And then I know wel both your wisdum to be sutch, that you can easly discern what is best for me, and I assure mi self your gud affection to be sutch, that you wil gladly counsel me for the best. He that intendith to proove a gud artificer, wil betake him self to that occupation which he and his frends iudg him aptist for. If a man have a count to give up, it behoovith him to kast al things beforehand lest he fail in his reckning, when time cummith, and so leave himself in the lurch. It standith him in hand that wilbe a bilder, to know in what order he were best and mai fitliest appoint his roomes; or els he mai perhaps tast what diruit, ædificat meanith. Yea not so mutch as the archer that hath ani regard ether to wæne the match, or to purchis himself creddit, but wilbe wel advised at what mark he shoote, and wilbe suer to choose out that mark, if he mai, whereat he takith him self best. Everi schollar must make his reckning to be a thrifti occupier, a wise countkaster, a wari bilder, and a cunning archer. He must appli and conform himself to that trade wherein he mai do most gud another dai. He must provide to give up sutch a reckning as wise lookers-on mai like and commend of. He must order and convei his bilding so that the cunningist workmen mai rather follow him then flout him, and his neihbors rather prais his devise then pitti his los. And finally he must appoint to shoot at sutch a mark as he is fully able to reach, or els short shooting mai loose his game. And no dout that schollar that takith rashley uppon him ani profession without ani great forecast of his own or advise of his freuds, mai perhaps fli at a pie, as y<sup>e</sup> proverb is, but he is most likeli to catch a dawe. And therefore I, for mi part, althouh I am verri wel bent of mi self to give mi self wholy in the end to the civil lawe, which I se to be groundid wholy ether uppon Nature, or custum or good deeres, and therefore cannot be but a fruteful and commodius studdi; yet knowing your scil and experienc in this behalf, and assuring mi self of your favorable counsel, I thouht it best to let you understand mi mening, bi home I owht esspecially and wil chefly be rulid in the case. Crassus, a notable lawier himself, in the first book of Tulli de Oratore, commendith the civil law for these three points: that it is facile, iucundum, and dignitatis plenum. Inded Antoni doth afterward confute him; but so that a man mai fitly appli the common saiing, Scientia non habet inimicum nisi ignorantem. Nether stekith he to confes so mutch

f. 88.

him self, that he was nothing sen in the faculti. But it is nether Crassus commendation greatly, that I build uppon; althouh I cannot think but it is sumwhat, that so famus a civilian allegith for his profession; nor Antonies confutation nether that can withdraw mi mind from the studdi, althouh he arguith probabely after his manner. Only that which he speakith de antiquis legibus that thai were then wel ni grown out of use, and therefore the knowledg of them to be the les profitable, mai sem now to be a more forcible and more effectual argument with us, that have so smal use in comparrison in our common welth of great part of the cjvil lawes, by reasun that the common law, to speak præcisely, is our civil law; aud $y^e$ civil law takith place only in a few matters, and meddlith but with certain cases. And it mai be in time also, that the common lawiers wil handle the matter so, as I have hard sai a great number of them do alreddi go about, that even thos few cases too mai daily be more and more abridgid, and in the end altogither be utterly remoovid out of Ingland. And to sai troth, this is the chefist, or rather the onli dout, that I steek at, althouh indeed I am partly resolvid both to studdi the hole for $y^e$ use of the part, and to abide the venture with so mani mi betters, what soever hereafter do befal. And so mutch $y^e$ rather bicaus I am not ignorant what a great plesure I shal take, and what a ripenes of iudgment and discretion I mai grow unto, in perusing the laws, and acquainting mi self with the state of that empire, whitch hath bene the most florisshing empire in mi iudgment that ever was, far surpassing the auncient Greek Commonwelths, of whitch notwithstanding it borrowid good part of thos laws, wherebi it was governid. For it is verri tru generally in things not yit perfitid, that Tulli applieth particularly to Nova Academia, recentissima quæque esse correcta et emendata maxjme. So that I am now almost determinid, notwithstanding al douts, that miht hinder or slack mi purpose to be shortly novus Justinianeus, as mi other busines wil suffer me, if your wisdum shal think good or not mislike of the matter. Inded ons I suppose verrely Christ Collidg fellowship, whitch I had over great a fansi to. miht have drawn me in to the minnisteri, as it hath dun a great mani mo, and as I remember I tould your wurship so mutch at that time.

But suerly in this, and in sum other respects, I thank God as mutch that I was not chosen fellow there, as I have caus to do that I was chosen in an other place. Marry yit to speak truly I have not travailid ani thing at al in the studdi to talk of; but as I have red in Tulli de legibus, and in his Toppicks, and in sum of his orations, certain laws and cases and examples to this purpose: besides on law logick, that I have run over of Hegendorphinus [a] doing, and a two or thre set orations in the commendation of the studdi. As for the institutes I have scars yit gon thorough the first book; and therefore am as nu to begin in law as he is in philosophi, that hath onli stumblid uppon a few principles, scatterid here and there in poets and orators, and never yit laborid in ani on sett tractate of ani professid philosopher.

f. 89.

Marry now I intend, God willing, as I mai have convenient leisure (for yit I cannot so thorouhly as thos that make account of no other studdi) to take sum pains, or rather sum pleasure that way, and therefore am thus imbouldnid to use you as a Crassus, or a Scævola in the matter, uppon hose advise, as uppon an oracle, I am to set down mi staf, both what wai I were best to turn me to, and how to cum most conveniently at mi iurnies end. Wherein I beseech your wurship to shew me that favor and friendship, that both for your wisdum you can and for your good wil ar wunt to shew me. And thus præsuming thereof, I rest to truble you.

[a] Christoff Hegendorff, German philologer; born at Leipsic in 1500, died at Lunebourg in 1540.

## To　　　　Harrison.[a]

f. 89 b　　Salutem in eo, qui est vera salus. Master Harrisun, I have now at the last sent you Plutarch, according to your request; and had in deed sent him thre weks sooner if ether the owner or I had bene hable to have redemid him sooner out of prison. For to sai troth he was fast in our treasure hows, a good while before the first time you sent for him, and hath bene lodg there ever sins, til within this thre or fower dais. So that he is bownd of duti to do you what servis he can, thorouh whos procurement esspecially he was so soon set at libertj; otherwise, perhaps, he had been like enouh to have winterd there, where he summerd. And therefore you of al men shal have him now at a beck, I dout not, that after so hard and uncurtuous handeling so gladly, and frendly voutsave him herburrouh. Notwithstanding when he hath dun you al the servis he can, I prai you return him over to his ould master again. For althouh he punuishid him a time, when in ded he culd not wel otherwise choose, yit his servis heretofore hath bene sutch, that he wuld be loth so lithly to kast him of. Marry in the mean while, if ned be, for a munth or twoe, you mai put him hardly to what wurk you wil, if it be but to help you with a few stones, or sum gud pees of timber, towards that wide and costly building, whitch I hear sai you have in hand. And suerly I take him so mutch the meter man for your purpose, for that he hath bene countid heer, how iustly you mai now have trial, a πολυίστωρ, and in deed is so commonly termid amongst us.

f. 90.　　In gud sadnes, M. Harrisun, I am verry glad to hear of your purpose, and cannot but commend of your paines, and trust ere long to thank you for your wel deserving this wai. In mi simple judgment that studdi of al others is most frutefully and commendabely emploied, that is emploied to a common use, and the bennefit of a great mani. Sed γλαῦκ' εἰς 'Αθήνας, qui ad te hæc.

[a] ? Jacob Harrison, of Christ's College.

God be with you, good Mr. Harrisun, and give you good succes to your good enterprise, for it is not so common, but it is as tru a saiing, Θεου διδοντος ουδεν εστι φθόνος, καὶ μη διδοντος ουδεν εστι πόνος. In hast.

From Pembrook Hall.

## To Arthur Capel.[a]

M. Capel, I dout not I, but you have ere this sufficiently perusid or rather thurroughly red over thos tragical pamflets of the Quen of Scots, as you did not long ago that pretti elegant treatis of M. Chek[e] against sedition: and verry lately good part of the Mirrur for Magistrates,[c] thre books iwis in mi judgment wurth the reading over and over, both for the stile and the matter. Now, if your leisure wil serv you (for truly I præsume of your good wil) to run thurrough ani part of M. Ascham[d] (for I suppose you have cauvissid him reasnably wel alreddi), or to hear the report of the furius outragies of Fraunc in Inglish, or to read over the Courtier in Lattin[e] (whitch I would wish, and wil you to do for sundri causis), or to peruse ani pes of Osorius, Sturmius, or Ramus, or to se ani other book, ether Inglish or Lattin, that I have, and mai stand you in stead, do but cum your self, or send on for it, and make your ful account not to fail of it. Perhaps you wil

f. 90 b.

f. 94.

---

[a] Afterwards Sir Arthur Capel, Sheriff of co. Hertford, father of Arthur, first Baron Capel.

[b] Sir John Cheke, 1514-1537. *The hurt of sedition hon grievous it is to a Commonwealth*, London, 1576. 8vo.

[c] Thomas Marshe's *A Myrrour for Magistrates*, London, 1578. 4to.

[d] Roger Ascham, 1515-1568, Præceptor to Queen Elizabeth. *The Schoolmaster*, London, 1570. 4to.

[e] *Balthasaris Castilionis Comitis de Curiali sine Aulico libri quatuor ex Italico sermone in Latinum conversi, Bartholomæo Clerke, Anglo Cantabrigiensi interprete*, London, 1585. 8vo.

marvel at the sudden proffer. In good sooth mi purpose is nothing els but this: I wuld have gentlemen to be conversant and occupied in thos books esspecially, whereof thai mai have most use and practis, ether for writing or speaking, eloquently or wittely, now or hereafter. Fare wel, good M. Arthure "Capel," and account of lerning, as it is, to be on of the fairist and goodliest ornaments that a gentleman can bewtifi, and commend him self with al. Th<sup>i</sup>s morning. In hast.

There is a frend of mine that spake unto me yesterniht for mi book of y<sup>e</sup> Quen of Scots. If you have dun withal, I prai you send me it præsently, otherwise he shal for me tarri your leisure; or if you send it now, assure your self to have it again at your pleasure. Iterum vale.

---

### To Sir Thomas Smith, of Audley End.

f. 91 b.    Mie dutie in most humble sort remembrid, riht worshipful, with most harti and esspecial thanks for your continual goodnes towards me, thes shalbe to let you understand that, first mi busines, and then mie helth hath bene sutch, sins mi last being with you, that according to your wil and mi desier I could not wel cum unto you. I have bene il at ease this thre or fower wekes, and am yet as il almost as ever I was, or els I had trublid your worship long ere this. But as soone as I shal recoover mi helth, and begin to stur abroad again, I purpose, God willing, to crave your favorable and gentle furtheraunc. Suerly I took wunderfull pleasure and great profit bi your last frendli or rather fatherli taulk. I thank your worship most hartely for it; and I thouht it sins a singular bennefit and blessing of God, that I had sutch a patron, or rather a father, to resort unto. And as for y<sup>e</sup> points you stud uppon, I did so mark them at y<sup>e</sup> præsent, that I am suer I shall never forget ani on of them as long as I live. 1. Towching y<sup>e</sup> studdi of the law generally. 2. Towching the necessit. of Civilians in Ingland. 3. Towching the compendious utilitie of y⁶ Institutes. 4. Towching the easines and hardnes of y⁶ Institutes. 5. Towching y⁶ differenc betwene lawe and physick for y⁶ studdi and practis. 6. Towching y⁶ daili perusing of sum part of y⁶ Institutes. 7. Towching conferenc with others for y⁶ better deciding of douts. 8. Towching y⁶ keaping of a man to on and the same book. 9. And last of al, towching y⁶ over hasti proceeding of sum yung Civilians in Cambridg, that think thai should bi and bi commens doctors, if thai ons have time sufficient, how insufficient so ever thai be for there scil in law. Whitch points as thai were verri diligently and attentively notid of me at the first; so I dout not but in time hereafter I shal have verri special use of them. I can but thank your worship for al; and after the manner of pore men, prai God reward you when I can not mi self; to whome I commit you both now and ever, trusting that you wil continu your ould liberaliti towards me. For suerly I stand in as great and greater neade of it, even now, then ever I did.

f. 92.

From Pembrook Hal.

---

Ad D. H.[a]
Ips[is] Calend[is] Januar[iis].
Pleraque sunt moris, sed amoris xenia quaedam,
En tibi xeniolum moris, amoris, Ave.

Qui novos tibi annos
multos optat
non novæ, sed notæ
beneficentiæ ergo,
G. HARVÆUS.

[a] Probably Harvey's own father.

## To the Riht Worshipful and mi verie good Ladie, mj Ladi Smith.[a]

f. 92 b.   Madame, I hope your good ladiship wil pardon mi bouldnes, if at the instant request of mi speciallist freuds and nearist kinsfolks, I præsume so mutch this ons of your ladiships gentle favour, as without ani farther means by others, to moove an ernest sute unto you mi self, in the behalf of a pore sistar of mine, which for sundri good causis, and esspecially uppon the excellent report she hath oft hard of your Ladiships singular goodnes, is marvelous desirous to do you service. Whitch sute notwithstanding 1 durst not now in any case have commensid, had I not ons mi self, about a seaven or eight yeares ago, had sum tast, and proof of your loving and gentle nature, being then occasionid to repaier unto Sir Thomas Smith, about a litle busines I had of his. So that being first ernestly requestid hereunto by mi veriest frends, and calling then to remembrauns that excellent ingraftid kindnes and rare bownti, whitch so long ago I notid in you; I was now the easier set on to adventure the mooving of your ladiship in this matter. And so mutch the rather too, bicaus I am alreddi veri greatly and nearly bownden unto Sir Thomas, as unto on, whome I ouht of duti and wil alwais for sundri special causis reverens, and honour, and serv too, if occasion serv, as far forth as possibely I mai. And suerly I trust his honours bowntiful goodnes towards me heretofore, wilbe a means unto your Ladiship now, both to conceive y$^e$ better of mi bould request, and to do the rather for mi sister. Besides that I hope, that litle acquaintauns whitch I have with

f. 93.   M. Wilford, bi meanes of his son, mai be an occasion, that your Ladiship wil bare the more with mi over sawci petition. For so in deade it must neads have bene thouht; but that partely Sir Thomas his wel deserving of me, and partly mi acquaintauns with sum of

---

[a] Philippa, 2nd wife of Sir T. Smith, of Audley End, and relict of Sir John Hampden.

his and your kinsfolks, but principally your Ladiships own good nature miht emboulden me to undertake the attempt of this enterprise with you, being otherwise scarsly known and perhaps quite forgottin of you. Marri now, considering thes and the like incurragements, and being so importunatly urgid unto it bi mi frends, I supposid I miht sumwhat the more bowldly adventure and assai the matter; besides that, having a special regard and brotherli consideration of mi sisters welfare, I was after a sort violently moovid hereunto, thurrough a certain inward affection of mine own. Wherein notwithstanding I am most humbly and dutifully to request your ladiship to pardon mi unadvisednes, if in ani point I seem to have passid the bownds of modesti, or limitation of good manners. But I have reposid mi whole confidens and affiauns in your good Ladiships favorable and gentle acceptation, with this hope, that you wil præsently voutsafe mi sister your long wisshid and desirid service; in whos behalf thus mutch I dare assuredly prommis, that you shal have a diligent, and trusti, and tractable maiden of hir, besides sutch service as she is able to do in sowing, and the like qualities requisite in a maid. But I feare me I have trublid your Ladiship over long; and therefore I wil now most humbly take mi leave of you, and so commend you unto God, whos you ar. From Pembrook Hal, in Cambridg, this xxix of March.

Your Ladiships ever at commaund,<br>G. H.

### To Luke Gilpin.[a]

Syr, you maie count me verie impudent, that uppon so smal acquaintaunce as I have with you, præsume thus sawcely to trubble you with mie letters, and namely in sutch a matter as maie not wel

---

[a] Luke Gilpin, of Trinity College, Junior Proctor in 1574.

be moovid to anie but a special frend. Notwithstanding y^e case being nowe, as it is, and y^e onset given alreddie, as you might partly lern bi M. Proctors sute, I hope you wil impute it rather to y^e præsent necessiti, then to ani want of modesti, if herein I seem to do otherwise then becummith me. The enterprise I knowe is veri great, and I cannot but acknowledg mine owne insufficiencie, but thus it is. I have bene willid by mi frends to sue for y^e rhetorick lecture, and sum of them, I thank them, have labourid y^e matter, and sollicited ther frends alreddi, in so mutch that it is wel knowen abroade in y^e town that I am purposid to stand for it. And in deade sum have askid me the question. So that y^e matter being grown thus far, as I understand it is, I am now enforcid to be as importunate in y^e cumpassing thereof as, thurouh there persuasions, I have bene venturus in y^e attempting thereof. In deade it were more meet, I graunt, for mi self, that I were an auditur rather then a lecturer, and more convenient for the Universiti, that sum on of longer studi and riper lerning shuld suppli the room: but, seing it hath so ffallin out, that I shuld be namid unto it, I would now be veri loth to take the foile. And therefore, I trust, syr, you wil beare with me in præsuming thus bouldly to request your favorable furtheraunc in y^e matter. But that is not al. Qui verecundiæ fines semel transilierit, eum naviter esse oportet impudentem. I am to beseech you furthermore to deale with your frends, as you mai conveniently, in mi behalf. I could not sai so mutch to your face without blussing, but literæ non erubescunt. I prai you pardon me this ons.

f. 94.     A certain exceeding feare, lest short shooting shuld loose mi game, maketh me thus unseemely to overshoot mi self. Marri I have reposid mi whole affiaunc in your gentle and favorable interpretation. God be with you, good M. Gilpin, and I beseech you consider of mi sute.

I had cummen unto you now mi self, but that I have hurt on of mi legs with a fal, and cannot without sum paine stur abroade. But I hope, as Tulli saith of his brothers ring, Sit Annulus tuus, non tanquam vas aliquod, sed tanquam ipse tu, so this letter, if it deserve y<sup>e</sup> name of a letter, shalbe non tanquam schedula aliqua, sed tanquam ipse ego. Albeit I have bene driven to huddle it up in as posting hast as might be; but so I trust, that mi importuniti wil prævail with you. Iterum vale.

## The Answer.

Before your letters cam, your request was grauntid. Notwithstanding, lest you should think your labour herein altogither spent in vaine, I wil in your cause step on foote further than I purposid. Be bould with me, and use me in what I maie pleasure you. I am not, nether would I be thought, to be sutch an on, as should drive mi frends to blush in a request so reasonable. For smal sute servith in an honest cause, præsertim movid by a frend. Commend me to your self, and in y<sup>e</sup> meane time I wil commend your cause unto God, and mi freuds. Vale.

Yours unfainidly in what I maie in domino,

L. GILPIN.

## To Richard Bird.[a]

M. Bird, I hope I mai præsume thus mutch of your freudship, as to request your furtheraunc for y<sup>e</sup> obteining the Rhetorick lecture. I confesse I am unmeet for y<sup>e</sup> place, but y<sup>e</sup> matter is gon so far aireddie, and y<sup>e</sup> sute so wel knowen (not bi mi meanes, but bi mi freuds), that I would be loth now to be set beside y<sup>e</sup> chussion.

In whitch respect I am to desier you to deale with your frends, as you mai conveniently in mie behalf. And if so be at ani time it

f. 94 b.

---

[a] Richard Bird, Fellow of Trinity College, and, in 1576, Curate in the neighbourhood of Saffron Walden.

shal li in me to do you, or ani frend of yours, y$^e$ like good turn ani wai, you shalbe suer to have me alwais as redi to pleasure you, as now I am bould to trubble you. I must prai you to make that account of me. God be with you, good M. Bird; and assure your self to have me at commaund in a greater matter, if so be, but I sai no more. I trust there shal neade no ifs or ands betwene us. Only I prai you return a word or two what you minde to do in the matter; and recount me

Yours to mi smal power in<br>
what I may requite your curtesi,<br>
G. HARVEY.

---

Mr. Harvey, I veri wel accept of your letter, ful of curtesi and good wil; having alwais had, since mi first acquaintaunce with you, sutch conceite of you in respect of your curtesi and towardnes, that I have often wisshid sum opportuniti, wherein I might ani wais do you good. Touching y$^e$ furtheraunce of your sute, you shal find me as redie to pleasure you, as you have frendly conceivid of me.

And thus fare you wel.

Your veri frend,<br>
RICHARD BYRDE.

---

To    REMINGTON.[a]

f. 95.   M. Remington, you remember I was in hand with you not long agoe for your Machiavell, y$^e$ greate founder and master of pollicies. I praie you send me him now bi this schollar, and I wil dispatch him home againe, God willing, ere it be long, as politique I hope as I shal find him. For I purpose to peruse him only, not to misuse him; and superficially to surveie his forrests of pollicie, not guilefully to conveie awaie his interest in them. Although I

---

[a] ? Richard Remington, Fellow of Peterhouse.

feare me it had neede be a high point of pollicie, that should rob Master Machiavel of his pollicie, esspecially if the surveier be himself a straunger in y^e Italian territories. Howe often shal he be trubblid with meeting il Duca I knowe not whoe, il Signor ——, Messer ——, and a cumpanie of sutch Italian magnificoes, ranging and stalking up and down y^e forrests, and almost conntinually in siht? Marry, if thai haunt me over mutch, I wil ether quite give over the enterprise, or repaier unto sum practised surveier that can thurrouhly and wil frendly informe me of there state and segniories. And perhaps unto you rather then to ani other, whome I take to be sufficiently studdied, to resolve me in most points. In good sadnes, M. Remington, if ani dout greatly trubble me concerning the state of ani citti, or the condition of ani person (for I understand Machiavel is altogithers in his Italian stories) I am purposid to make bowld of you, and to crave youer advise in the matter. I knowe I shal not be hable to requite youer frendship; but I dare prommis I wil be alwaies verri mindful of it, and ever most reddi to do y^e best I can. God be with you, good M. Rem[ington]. In hast.

But I had like to have forgottin mi chefist matter. I am purposid to be a laborer for y^e Rhetorick Lecture; unfit I graunt, but I am nowe purposid and have given the onset alreddi.

I prai you further mi sute, as you mai conveniently, by yourself and your freuds. You shal commaund me in a greater matter Iterum vale.

f. 95 b.

## To Richard Bird.

M. Bird, I understand bi M. Osburn that you were in our colledg yesterniht to inquier for me. I am verri sorie I was not then within to speake with you. If I could conveniently, I wuld sins have repairid unto you. As for mi sute, I can saie nothing but this, spero optima, metuo pessima. And indeed mi spero is growndid esspecially on the confidens and affiauns I have in Triniti

Colledg. M. Duffils[a] iolli and lavish vaunts make me distrust the wurst, for both in his letters and otherwise he assurith himself ot the victori; but you knowe what it is ædilitatem gerere sine populi suffragijs. Good M. Bird, do what you mai conveniently, that thos both be there and give there voices that have prommisid of your colledg. Unles there be a good meni, or rather an il meni fœdifragi, I hope M. Duffild, for al his fiaunting præludium, shal have no great cause to exsult. I dout not but mi, or rather mi frends auxiliariæ copiæ ar able to encounter with his, and as for legionariæ I beleeve his mai soone be numberid without ani deep siht in arithmetique. Wel there is now no remmedi; I must stand to y$^e$ adventure, and hazard the succes on y$^e$ maine chaunce. I prai you commend me to M. Gilpin, with special thanks for his frendship, and tel him but that I trust verri mutch to his warrant, I have sum cause to mistrust sum that have geven there word in your howse. Vale. Tuus et tuorum.

---

## To Sir Thomas Smith.

Your wurship mai marvel mutch that I have absentid mi self thus long time from you, having so great and iust occasion to resort unto you, as I have had. But suerly, sir, mi lets and hinderaunces everi wai have bene sutch, that I could not possibely do that I purposid fully, and wuld willingly have dun for mi better proffiting in the civil lawe. It were too long a thing to declare them al severally and at larg; but truly, what for sicknes and private busines, I could scars reade over thre titles in Justinian before Lent, and ever sins y$^e$ beginning of Lent, at y$^e$ instant and importunate request of M. Church,[b] mi verri frend, I have red y$^e$ rhetorick lecture in y$^e$ schooles; so that y$^e$ providing for mi

[a] John Duffield, of Peterhouse.
[b] ? Robert Church, B.D. 1579, Fellow of Caius College.

lecture, togither with yᵉ reading to mi pupils, yᵉ doing of ordinari acts in yᵉ howse, and disputing in yᵉ schooles, have made me so unprovidid for Justinian, that, to sai troth, I have bene asshamid to cum unto you. Thinking alwais to get ere it wear long sum vacant sennight, or other, wherein I miht studdi him thurrouhly, and do nothing els, and then præsently to repaier unto you. And so lingering of from on week to an other, I have thus long, to mi great shame, but greater greef, absentid mi self, mutch like an idle and untoward schollar, that when he hath once plaid yᵉ trewnt is as hardly afterward brouht to schoole as a bare to yᵉ stake. Notwithstanding nowe douting not but you have conceivid the best of mi long absens, and having a special sute unto you (as I am alwais inforcid to crave your furtherauns in my need) I have at the last thouht good, rather with blusshing to cum unto you, then thurrough slouhth and bashfulnes to mis of mi purpose; for thus it is, syr, I am mindid to sue for yᵉ rhetorick lecture, and sum of mi freuds have laborid yᵉ matter alreddi, in so mutch that it is noisid about yᵉ town that I am purposid to stand for it. The matter being now so far gon and a good mani voices prommisid me thurrouh others procurement, I wuld be veri loth to have the repulse. Considering also both yᵉ bennefit of the stipend, and having tried the profitablenes of the exercise. Marry, I can not se how I shal be hable to cumpas it by mi self, or mi other frends, unles your wurship stand mi frend in yᵉ matter, and deale with yᵉ hed in mi behalf. For it lieth in them wholy and not in the regents (as you yourself know better then I) to have home they list to be readers. Thai neade not prick but what twoe thai wil, and on of thos two, if it like them, mai be as like too perhaps to be rhetorick lecturer as I am fit to be the lawe lecturer. The case standing so, I am to beseech your wurship to talk with M. Vice-chauncelour, and sum of the other doctors in mi behalfe; as I dout not, but at your request thai wil deale as reasnably, or rather as favorabely with me, as thai maie. Thus I make bould **alwais of your wurship, in what soever I persaive you mai pleasure**

f. 96 b.

me, being hable to returne nothing els at ani time in respect of your goodnes, but only bare thanks, utterid of a sillie sheet of paper. Nether am I able ani other wai to requite your liberal newyearesgift (whitch suerly at that time stud me in verri great stead), then bi renuing mi ould ditti of gratiarum actio. But it wuld requier over larg a discours to run thurrough your particular bennefits; and when al is dun, I have nothing els to sai, but gratias ago habeoque, referat Deus, utinam par pari, and the like, for you ar well acquaintid with the stile. Nowe, as concerning mi studdi of the civil law, whereof I can scarcely make mention without blusshing, the next quarter, I hope, being a vacant quarter, and I then fre from so mani businesses, I shal find leisure to plie it as diligently as hetherto I have bene constrainid to pas it over slackly. Althouh in this meane while (as I have dun al this terme, marry with smal proffit, I must needs confes, for want of a booke) I purpose to heare M. Doctor Bing,[a] and "get" gleane as mutch as I can bi snatches, for suerly I have yet no on hower that I can wholy and constantly imploy that wai in mie studdi; but after midsummer I trust I shal have more spare daies and weeks then I have nowe bowers. There is at this præsent a fellowship voide at Christs Colledg for Essex, and sum of the fellowes have desirid me to stand for it; but I am now and have bene long resolvid to make the Civil Lawe mi profession, how slowly yet soever I go unto it; and therefore it would not quite the cost to get that fellowship, whitch I shoold be faint to loose at y$^e$ years end, unles I shoold make the meanes to keape it bi a dispensation, as M. Lewen did. But I am so far from sturring in the matter, that indeade, if I were chosen unto it of there owne accords, I woold refuse it, unles thai themselves woold warrant me a dispensation. And thus, having concealid nothing from you whitch I thouht miht concerne mi commoditi, I cease to trubble you.

[a] Thomas Byng, Master of Clare Hall, 1571-1599, and Regius Professor of Civil Law, 1574-1594.

## To Sir Thomas Smith.

Debui quidem ad te iampridem, ornatissime vir; nunc etiam vellem, si liceret, quod sane liberet scribere; sed ijs vel verum asperitatibus vel angustijs temporis sum implicatus, ut, quod maxime velim, non queam certe in hoc tempore ullo modo præstare. Rogo, ut ignoscas occupatissimo, scribam profecto posthac diligentius fortassis etiam elegantius. Itaque superiora iam cuncta omittam; neque ullam tuæ vel communiter in omnes studiosos humanitatis, vel in me privatim beneficentiæ mentionem faciam. Debeo quidem, ut magister, gratias, et debeo recte, fateor, singulares (meministi enim quibus sim fluctibus iactatus), sed debeam etiam ad huc necesse est. Persolvam uti spero, aliquando tandem cumulatius. Nunc bona cum venia tua aperte dicam, quod res est; Rhetoricus prælector esse cupio, pudet dicere, sed esse cupio, non ut alios doceam, qui enim possim indoctus? Sed ut discam ipse rhetoricam. Tuam hic opem imploro, tuam inquam, id est, et Doctoris Binge, et Procancellarij opem etiam, atque etiam imploro, obsecroque. Dicerem pluribus, et urgerem vehementius, si per tempus liceret; sed verbum cum sapienti, tum benevolo, qualem ego te cognovi, sat esse spero. Ociosus forsitan quanquam quid dico forsitan? Ociosus, mihi crede, non epistolam bene longam, sed πανηγυρικον aliquem, et quidem cum calamistris quibusdam inustum concinnabo; qui et debitas tibi gratias persolvat copiosissime, et iustissimas laudes studiosissime persequatur. Interim tu quæso τὸ παρὸν εὖ ποιεῖν ut ait ille nescio quis græcus. Neque enim vel plura iam possum, vel accuratiora. Vale, optime et ornatissime vir; . et petitioni meæ tantum tribue, quantum humanitati et prudentiæ tuæ videbitur.

Tui multis nominibus observantissimus,

G. H.

f. 98.

### From [? Richard] Remington enclosing one from John Duffield.

f. 98 b.

M. Remington, I know not how to præsume of your favour, if your prommis have passid to M. Harvie, nor yet to want it, for that I am a Peterhowse man or els of this house, the whitch thei say you loove no les. I prai you considder with your self M. Harveis case and mine; how wel he mai tarri an other yeare, and how il I mai want the recooveri of mi creddit, sumwhat crackd by our broiles at home. I hope wel of your frendship this waie, and if you knew mi case as wel as I you would tender it charely. Good M. Remington, let me have sum frendship amongst you, and I dout not but to obteine this sute.

Youers, JOHN DUFFEYLD.

M. Har[vey] yesterniht I receivid this letter from M. Duffild, concerning his sute, whereby you mai partly gather in what case yours doth stand. And therefore I have sent it unto you. He seemith to have sum good hope, and therefore it standith you in hand more forcibely to deale against him. And your cheef labour in mi opinion had need be to the hed for propounding. Among the rest I thinke there is smal dout, by reason that M. Proctor doth so diligently labour for you.

---

### To [? Humphrey][a] Hales.

f. 99.

Syr Halles, I am not a litle glad, I assure you, to heare what paines you take with your schollars; nether doubt I but thai proffit and go forward accordingly. Whitch if thai do, as I hope verrely thai do, you cannot think your travail better emploid ani other way to my iudgment. Nihil enim Reip[ublicæ] utilius prudenti

[a] Humphrey Hales, B.A. 1572, of Pembroke Hall; afterwards York Herald in 1587. He died 16 June, 1591.

et compendiaria Juventutis institutione. To whitch effect you and I ons, as I remember, had sum conferens. I suppose your self remember the time when, and the particulars whereuppon, as well, and parhaps better then I. At this present I cam sai no more ; but Macte virtute: mi laisure is so smal from other necessarie and urgent busines. At sum other time, it mai be, I wil not steek to open mi mind and fansi unto you, touching y$^e$ most commodius and compendius way of teaching. In the mean while let this suffice, as y$^e$ speciallist properti of a good schoolmaster, to teach none but y$^e$ choisist and purist autors, ether for prose or verse; that is, in y$^e$ lernidist mens iudgments, for th'on Tullie and Cæsar, for y$^e$ other Terens and Virgil. Whereunto if you have that regard that I trust you have, and therewith use sutch discretion in reading and teaching them as I knowe you maie, and hope you doe, no dout you must needs proffit both your self and your schollars exceedingly. I had thought to have sent you a pretti treatise of Henricus Schorus [a] touching y$^e$ ordering of his schoole, being in a manner an extract of Ramus worthie oraticn pro philosophica Parisiensis Academiæ disciplina; but suerly it was not to be gotten amongst all our stationers, and mine owne I gave away to a frend of mine above a munth ago. Wherefore, in steade thereof, I thought good to bestowe uppon you those two bookes, whitch in mie iudgment might stand you in singular steade for y$^e$ better understanding and resolving of all good autors ; and whereof Schorus in his treatise

[Cætera desunt.]

f. 99 b.

[a] *" Specimen et forma legitima tradendi sermones et rationis disciplinas ex P. Rami scriptis collecta,"* Strassburg, 1572. 8vo.

---

The next three pages contain theological notes of no interest in another hand, the volume being reversed.

## To Wood.

f. 101 b.
Good Mr. Wood, communicate sum part of your courtly affayres, and esspecially newes, if ye have any, with your poore freinds in Cambridg. Inioyne me twise as mutch any way, and I will do my endevoyr to requite your courtesy. Schollars ar now Aristippi rather then Diogenes; they would fayne be sumwhat more then schollars, if they could tell howe. And of all things we cannot abide that spitefull proverb of y$^e$ Greatist Clarks. The date whereof, I take it, was out when Duns and Tomas were abandonid y$^e$ schooles. Marry yet (we must not deny it) we ar to take instructions and advertisements at you courtiers hands, that ar better trainid and experiencid in matters of counsell "wisdum" and pollycy, then we schollars ar. For my self I take it on great part of my fælicity, that I have a Mr. Wood in y$^e$ Court that can sufficiently and will gladly, &c.

I woud fayne have endid this period at y$^e$ least, but y$^e$ tyme curtolid it of in y$^e$ midst. Habes non copiæ sed inopiæ nostræ cornu.

## To Arthur Capel.

### Raptim.

f. 102.
But that I prommis myself to see you at London very shortly, truste me I would not nowe write so shortly at any tyme unto you as I do. Good Mr. Arthure " Capell " let this suffice. He that writeth these fewe lines unto you nowe will not steek to write whole volumes and iliades to do you good. I assure you and in good faith, Mr. Capell, you shall alwais finde G. H. the selfe same man that you fownd him by y$^e$ fierside in his pore chamber y$^e$ night before your departure from Cambridge, when you knowe what secrets and privityes he revealid unto you. Verbum tibi sat. Et mihi sat tua salutatio. Si me verbo quoque dignatus fueris, id mihi quidem sat erit, superque. Sed non exspecto literas nec

literatas quidem; tantum verbum si placet si vacat; aut etiam literam. Quicquid ab Arthuro proficiscetur, id mihi erit jn delicijs. Syllabam si miseris aut literam equidem exosculabor. Delegi præsentem præsens, quem diligerem absens absentem. In cæteris rebus Cameleon esse possum : jn amore non possum. Non videor amare multos ; sed quos amare videor, eos plus amo, quam videor. Ex ijs etiam, quos amo, alij apud me primus, alij secundus, alij tertius obtinent. Tu quidem certe, Arthure optime, (id tibi epitheton optime convenit) cum primis, et in primis es. Non dicam quod statueram ni videar novam, et octavam artem, quæ dicitur, didicisse. Sed quid si dicam, ita te apud me primus obtinere, ut primorum sis facile primus. Mihi crede, mi Arthure, ita est, etiamsi non dicam. Sed quorsum hæ jneptiæ? Quasi non novimus nos inter nos. Quamdiu tu Arturus eris, tamdiu me Gabrielem senties; qui (pace tuorum amicorum quos habes alios) et esse et videri cupit

Alter Arturus.

Non statueram, verbum addere; sed vide, quam sim fantasticus. Utinam tibi liceret esse non meo sed mecum

ALTERI ULISSI.
JAM DIXI.

### To his Brother Richard.

Brother (all other thinges layd asyde), you ar præsently in all reason and pollicy to sollicite and importune your Master for your present restitution; alleging that you cannot quyet your mynd or settle yourself to your book, untill his Woorshipp hath taken certayn order for your better assurance; or whatsoever else your self can best devise to insinuate why you shoold the rather so instantlie urge his W[oorshipp] in so greate haste. In very deed this is my opinion, that as in meates, dum calent, valent; so such matters, depending uppon other mens curtesyes, especially not of y$^e$ frend-

f. 102 b.

lyest, ar ægerly to be prosecutid, whilest they ar whottist; lest space and farther deliberation chaunce to yeeld new matter of greevaunce, or at y^e least by renuing y^e memory of owld sores, obdurate your hartes, being as yet a lytle mollified (perhaps) with y^e late suytes of your frendes, your owne humble submission, open confession, pænitentiall prayer, and so many voluntary protestations and offers of any reasonable satisfaction, enioynid you by themselves. Which all notwithstanding wyll soone (God wott) weare owt of exulcerate and spytefull myndes, unles they be præsently taken at y^e most advauntage. Our Canon law sayeth, Mora sua cuique nociva est; and you know y^e proverb, In mora periculum. Opportunityes ar not allwayes alyke favorable; and it is wisdom to take them at y^e best, that ar rather inclining to y^e worst. Insipientis est dicere, Non putaram; and how many have payed (with a witnes) for their simplicity and levity in being over credulous without sufficient assuraunce? Wherefore, no dowte, your best and surist way is immediatly by all meanes to dispatch yourself atonce of this care, and then rowndly to settle yourself abowt your other businesses, esspecially your Astronomicall Dialogues, which I would have more perfetly finisshed in as quick speede as conveniently you may, sine præcipiti negligentia. Vale.

---

Reversing the book, ff. 103 b, 104, contain theological notes in the same hand as those on ff. 100, 100 b, and 101.

FINIS.

# INDEX.

Æschines, Harvey imitates his "reading to the Rhodians the Oration of Demosthenes in defence of Ctesiphon," 82

Æsop, allusion to his Fables (1573), 122

Agrippa a Nettesheim (Henricus Cornelius) conjuror; mention of as the ill-favoured conjuror, 71; meaning of the word "farewell" according to, 78; attributes infectious air and plagues to the influence of devils, 90

Alexander the Great, inspired to greatness by Homer's writings (1579), 65

Allen, Walter, of Christ's College, Senior Proctor in 1572, dispute on his attainments between G. Harvey and T. Nevil (1573), 7, 8

Amyot, Jacques, his "Plutarchi Vitæ et Moralia, Gallice," in vogue in Cambridge, 79

Anne, mistress of G. Harvey, letter to, with posy, 139

Aristippus, scholars in Cambridge more Aristippi than Diogenes, 78, 182

Aristophanes, study of, by Harvey (1573, 1579), 81, 134

Aristotle, notice of his works in use at Cambridge (1573), 10; maxim not to be found in (1573), 116; blamed by Harvey for founding a school of philosophy (1573), 120; study of his politics by Harvey (1573), 133; his "Organon" little read in Cambridge (1579), 79; study of, by Harvey, when engaged in philosophy (1579), 81; longing of Harvey for his subtle and intricate acumen, 71

Arius, of Alexandria, allusion to, as a noble heretic (1573), 11

Ascham, Roger, study of, by Harvey (1573), 134; study of his "Schoolmaster," 167

Athens, Ancient, no fitting example for England (1579), 66

Bartholomew Fair, allusion to (1579), 59

Bear Inn, at Cambridge, mention of (1573), 33

Beatrice, Dante's mistress, meeting between her and Gascoigne in Hades (1577), 58

Becon, John, Fellow of St. John's, Cambridge, public orator in 1571, comparison between him and W. Lewyn, public orator in 1570, 7

Benevolo, v. Spenser, Edmund

Bibbiena, Bernardo, Cardinal, alluded to as the "pleasurable Cardinal" (1579), 68

Bird, Richard, Fellow of Trinity College, Cambridge, correspondence with, 173-6

Bishops Stortford, co. Hertf. allusion to the fineness of the wheat-meal in, 92-3

Boccaccio, study of, by Harvey (1573), 134

Bodin, Jean, his "De Republica" in vogue at Cambridge (1579), 79; opinion as to the golden and other ages (1579), 85

Boethius, maxim not to be found in (1573), 116

Bovington al. Buffington, Edmund, Vicar of All Saints, Cambridge, longing of Harvey for his profound learning, 71

Bradford, John, Prebendary of St. Paul's, martyred in 1555, praise of, as the ornament of Cambridge and glory of Pembroke Hall (1573), 53

Brown, Lancelot, Physician, Fellow of Pembroke Hall, opposition to G. Harvey (1573), 21-54, *passim*

Buckhurst, Lord, v. Sackville, Thomas, Baron Buckhurst

Buffington, M. v. Bovington, Edmund

Busbye, Humphrey, Regius Professor of Civil Law, and Fellow of Trinity Hall, longing of Harvey for his disputative appetite, 71

Byng, Thomas, Regius Professor of Civil Law, Harvey attends his lectures, 178; Harvey seeks his help for the Rhetoric Lectureship, 179

Cæsar, Julius, comparison of his writings with those of Cicero (1573), 7; inspired to greatness by Homer's writings (1579), 65; study of, by Harvey (1573), 134; considered the choicest and purest prose author, 181
Caius, John, M.D., founder of Caius College, longing of Harvey for his trim Latin phrases and witty proverbs, 71
Cambridge, University of, correspondence of G. Harvey during his residence at Pembroke Hall (1573), 1-54, 159-184; letter on the study of civil law in, 167-8
Capel, Arthur, father of Arthur, 1st Baron Capel, letters to, 167, 182
Carlile, Christopher, Fellow of Clare Hall, Cambridge, note on Grouchius' correction of Perionius' translation of Aristotle (1579), 63, 75
Carneades, of Cyrene, Greek philosopher, allusion to (1573), 39
Carr, Nicholas, Regius Professor of the Greek at Cambridge, praise of as ornament of Cambridge and glory of Pembroke Hall (1573), 53
Casa, Giovanni della, Archbishop of Benevento, his work, "Il Galateo," in vogue at Cambridge (1579), 52, 78
Castiglione, Baldassare, Count, his work, "Il Cortegiano," in vogue at Cambridge (1579), 78; study of Clerke's Latin translation of his "Il Cortegiano," 167
Catullus, challenge to, from Harvey (1573), 110
Chaucer, Geoffrey, study of, by Harvey (1573), 134; meeting between him and Gascoigne in Hades (1577), 57
Cheke, Sir John, study of his treatise against sedition, 167
Chesterton, co. Cambridge, allusion to the fineness of the wheat-meal in, 92
Chilo, of Sparta, one of the seven sages of Greece, quotation from (1573), 38

Christ's College, Cambridge, Harvey nearly accepts a clerical fellowship in, 164, 178
Chrysippus, Stoic philosopher, allusion to (1573), 39
Church, Robert, Fellow of Caius College, Cambridge, procures Harvey to read in his place the rhetoric lecture in the schools, 176, 177
Churchyard, Thomas, poet, mention of (1579), 68
Cicero, comparison of his writings with those of Julius Cæsar (1573), 7; study of, by Harvey (1573, 1579), 81, 133, 165; longing of Harvey for his brave eloquence, 71; commends civil law, 162; considered the choicest and purest prose author, 181; quotations from, 163, 164, 172
Civil law, letter on the study of, in England, 168-9
Cleobulus, one of the seven sages of Greece, allusion to his counsel (1573), 40
Clerke, Bartholomew, of Cambridge, study of his Latin translation of B. Castiglione's "Il Cortegiano," 167
Comines, Philippe de, Seigneur d'Argentan, his "Memoirs" in vogue at Cambridge (1579), 79
Courtier, the, v. Castiglione, Baldassare, Count
Ctesiphon, Harvey imitates Æschines reading Demosthenes' oration in defence of, 82

Dawse,... Master, proverb by (1573), 115
Dee, John, conjurer, Fellow of Trinity College, Cambridge, longing of Harvey for his mysticall and supermetaphysicall philosophy, 71
Demosthenes, study of, by Harvey (1579), 81; Harvey imitates Æschines reading Demosthenes' oration in defence of Ctesiphon, 82
Diogenes, scholars in Cambridge more Aristippi than Diogenes, 78, 182
Dorrington... of King's College, visit to Harvey's house at Saffron Walden (1573), 27
Drama, mention of the different companies of players and of the theatre near Shoreditch (1579), 67

INDEX. 187

Dudley, Ambrose, Earl of Warwick, mention of his company of players (1579), 67
Dudley, Robert, Earl of Leicester, exerts his influence in behalf of Harvey (1578), 88; mention of his company of players (1579), 67
Duffield, John, of Peter House, Cambridge, opposes G. Harvey for the rhetoric lectureship, 176, 80; letter to R. Remington, 180
Duns, Joannes, Scotus, his "Quodlibet" little read in Cambridge (1579), 79; expulsion of his works from Cambridge, 78, 182
Dyer, Sir Edward, the poet, dedication of Harvey's verlayes to, by E. Spenser, 89; familiarity with Harvey and Spenser, 101

Elderton, William, Master of the Company of Westminster Boys, mention of (1579), 68
Empedocles, allusion to his philosophy (1573), 115
Erasmus of Rotterdam, quotation from his epistles (1579), 66
Essex, county of, vacancy of an Essex fellowship at Christ College, 178

Farre, Henry, Fellow of Pembroke Hall, junior proctor in 1586, opposition to G. Harvey (1573), 3, 17, 48
Foxius Morzillus, Sebastianus, tutor to Don Carlos, opposition to Aristotle's philosophy, 10
Frontinus, Sextus Julius, his "Stratagems, Englished by R. Morysine," in vogue at Cambridge (1579), 79
Fulke, William, Master of Pembroke Hall, letter to the Fellows in behalf of Harvey (1578), 88

Gascoigne, George, poet, study of, by Harvey (1573), 134; elegies on, by G. Harvey (1577), Lat. and Engl. 55-58, 68-70; allusion to his comedy of "Supposes" (1579), 85; allusion to his satire "The Steel Glass" (1579), 69, 100
Gaubert, . . . Pensioner of Pembroke Hall, opposition to G. Harvey (1573), 20, 27, 41, 42, 44, 45, 49

Ghibilines, the, allusion to (1573), 112
Gilpin, Luke, cf Trinity College, Cambridge, correspondence with G. Harvey, 171-173; thanks sent to, from Harvey, for his patronage, 176
Girlington, Anthony, Public Orator at Cambridge, afterwards rector of Tilney, co. Norfolk; praise of, as the ornament of Cambridge and glory of Pembroke Hall (1573), 53
Gorboduc, tragedy of; allusion to the joint authorship of (1579), 100
Goter, . . . apparently the same as Gaubert, q. v.
Gower, John, poet, study of, by Harvey (1573), 134; meeting between him and Gascoigne in Hades (1577), 57
Griffin Inn at Cambridge, mention of (1573), 45
Grindal, Edmund, Bishop of London, afterwards Archbishop of York and Canterbury, praise of as the ornament of Cambridge and glory of Pembroke Hall (1573), 53
Grouchy, Nicolas de, professor at Bordeaux, note on his correction of Perionius' translation of Aristotle (1579), 63, 75
Guazzo, Stefano, his work "La Civil Conversatione," in vogue at Cambridge (1579), 79
Guelphs, the, allusion to (1573), 112
Guicciardini, Francesco, his "History of Italy," in vogue at Cambridge (1579), 79

Hales, Humphrey, Fellow of Pembroke Hall, afterwards York Herald, refusal to join in opposition to G. Harvey (1573), 46; letter to, 180-1
Harrison, Jacob, of Christ's College, letter to, 166
Harvey, . . . ropemaker, of Saffron Walden, co. Essex, letter to, from his son Gabriel (1573), 40-43; a new year's greeting to, from his son, 169
Harvey, . . ., sister of Gabriel, recommendation of, as a handmaid to Lady Smith, 170, 171
Harvey, Mercy, sister of Gabriel, lovesuit with a nobleman (1574), 143-158
Harvey, Richard, letter to, from his brother Gabriel, 183

Hegendorff, Christoff, study of his Law Treatises by Harvey, 165
Hercules, meeting between him and Socrates in Hades, 56
Herodotus, study of, by Harvey (1573), 134
Hesiod, meeting between him and Socrates in Hades (1577), 56
Hexameters, English, copy of, by Harvey, 97, 98
Homer, study of, by Harvey (1579), 81; meeting between him and Socrates in Hades, 56; inspired Alexander, Scipio, Cæsar, &c. to greatness by his writings, 65
Horace, allusion to his poems (1577), 57; study of, by Harvey (1579), 81
Hortensius, Quintus, study of, by Harvey (1579), 81: longing of Harvey for his gallant pronunciation, 71
Hoult, . . . M.A., of Pembroke Hall, opposition to G. Harvey (1573), 3, 17, 48, 49
Howard, Henry, Earl of Surrey, meeting between him and Gascoigne in Hades (1577), 57; allusion to his blank verse translation of Virgil (1579), 100
Hutton, Robert, Rector of Little Braxted and Wickham Episcopi, co. Essex, praise of, as the ornament of Cambridge and glory of Pembroke Hall, (1573), 53

Immerito, v. Spenser, Edmund
Innocent III. Pope, quotation from his "De Miseria Humanæ Conditionis" (1579), 63, 76

Jackson, . . . Butler of Pembroke Hall, tolls the college bell for G. Harvey's Greek lecture (1573), 47
Jackson, . . . Fellow of Pembroke Hall, opposition to G. Harvey (1573), 5, 43, 46
Jovio, Paolo, Bishop of Nocera, his work "Raggionamento Sopra i Motti et Disegne d'Arme et d'Amore. Con un discorso di G. Ruscelli," in vogue at Cambridge (1579), 79
Justinian, Emperor, study of the Institutes by Harvey, 165, 168, 176, 177
Juvenal, quotations from (1573), 5, 37, 53; praise of, as a poet (1573), 53

Katharine, S., comparison of Harvey's mistress to (1573), 125

Lawherne, . . . ., Fellow of Pembroke Hall, opposition to G. Harvey (1573), 2, 26, 28, 33, 35, 36
Leicester, Earl of, v. Dudley, Robert
Le Roy, Louis, Professor of Greek at the College Royal, Paris, his work, "Les Politiques d'Aristote," in vogue at Cambridge (1579), 79
Lewyn, William, Fellow of Christ College, Junior Proctor in 1568, Public Orator in 1570, comparison between him and J. Becon, Public Orator in 1571, 7; dispensation for keeping a fellowship without taking orders, 178
Livy, study of, by Harvey (1573), 134
Lucian, study of, by Harvey (1573), 134
Lucretia, allusion to the rape of, 1573, 117
Lydgate, John, meeting between him and Gascoigne in Hades (1577), 57

Macchiavelli, Niccolo, study of, by Harvey (1573), 135, 174, 175; his works in vogue at Cambridge (1579), 79
Marshe, Thomas, study of his "Mirror for Magistrates," 167
Martial, praise of, as a poet (1573), 53
Mary, Queen of Scots, study of the "tragical pamphlets" of, 167-8
Melanchthon, Philip, opposition to Aristotle's philosophy, 10
Melissus, of Samos, allusion to his philosophy (1573), 131
Messalina, wife of the Emperor Claudius, comparison of Harvey's mistress to (1573), 113
Midsummer Fair, v. Stourbridge Fair
Mirror for Magistrates, study of, 167
More, Sir Thomas, poem by Harvey, fathered upon (1573), 101; meeting between him and Gascoigne in Hades (1577), 57

Nestor, meeting between him and Socrates in Hades, 56
Nevil, Thomas, Fellow of Pembroke Hall, Cambridge, afterwards Senior Proctor and Dean of Peterborough and Canterbury, opposition to G. Harvey (1573), 2-54, *passim*

Norton, Thomas, Remembrancer of the city of London, allusion to his Tragedy of Gorboduc (1579), 100
Nuce al. Newce, Thomas, Fellow of Pembroke Hall, Prebendary of Ely, and Vicar of Gazeley, opposition to G. Harvey (1573), 2-54, *passim*

Omphalius, Jacob, Professor at Cologne, study of his works, by G. Harvey (1573), 11
Osburn . . . , Fellow of Pembroke Hall, opposition to G. Harvey (1573), 2-54, *passim*; informs Harvey of inquiries after him, 175
Osorius, Hieronymus, Bishop of Silves in Algarve, study of his works by G. Harvey (1573), 11; recommendation of the study of, 167
Ovid, challenge to, from Harvey (1573), 111
Oxford, Earl of, *v.* Vere Edward de, 17th Earl of Oxford

Parmenides, the philosopher, allusion to his philosophy (1573), 131
Patch, jester to Cardinal Wolsey, mention of (1579), 70
Pelagius, allusion to, as a noble heretic (1573), 11
Pembroke Hall, Cambridge, correspondence of G. Harvey during his residence at (1573), 1-54, 159-184; letter from the Master to the Fellows in behalf of Harvey (1578), 88
Perionius, Joachim, note on Grouchius' correction of his translation of Aristotle's works (1579), 63, 75
Petrarch, challenge to, from Harvey (1573), 110; study of, by Harvey (1573), 134
Phaer, Thomas, physician, of Kilgerran, co. Pembroke, allusion to his translation of the Æneid, 72
Philebert, de Vienne, his work, "The Philosophy of the Courte," in vogue at Cambridge (1579), 78
Pietro Aretino, challenge to, from Harvey (1573), 110; study of, by Harvey (1573), 135; mention of, as "Unico Aretino" (1579), 68, 110; imitation of the order of his works by Harvey, 143

Plato, study of, by Harvey (1573, 1579), 81, 133; longing of Harvey for his divine notions and conceits, 71
Pliny the Elder, mention of, as an orator (1573), 53
Pliny the Younger, mention of, as an orator (1573), 53
Plutarch, mention of, as an historiographer (1573), 53; "Plutarchi Vitæ et Moralia, Gallice," in use at Cambridge (1579), 79; loan of, by Harvey to J. Harrison, 166
Polyænus, his "Stratagems" in vogue at Cambridge (1579), 79
Pomfret, . . . delivers, through his man, a token from Spenser to Harvey, 77
Præcisians, allusion to (1573), 30
Propertius, challenge to, from Harvey (1573), 111
Puritans, allusion to (1573), 30

Quintilianus, Marcus Fabius, praise of, for his oratory (1573), 53

Ramus, Petrus, opposition to Aristotle's philosophy, 10; recommendation of the study of, 167; notice of his oration "Pro Philosophica Parisiensis Academiæ Disciplina," 181
Remington, Richard, Fellow of Peter House, correspondence with G. Harvey, 174, 175, 180
Rich, Robert, 2nd Baron Rich, mention of his company of players (1579), 67
Ridley, Nicholas Bishop of Rochester and London, praise of, as an ornament of Cambridge and glory of Pembroke Hall (1573), 53
Rome, Ancient, no fitting example for England (1579), 66
Ruscelli, Girolamo, *v.* Jovio, Paolo, Bishop of Nocera
Rydge, . . . . of Pembroke Hall, teaches Spenser and Harvey, 75

Sackville, Thomas, Baron Buckhurst, afterwards Earl of Dorset, allusion to his Tragedy of Gorboduc (1579), 100
St. Davids, co. Pembroke, mention of (1573), 113
Sallust, study of, by Harvey (1573), 134
Scholar's Love, a poem by Harvey (1573), 101-143

Schorus, Henricus, notice of his Treatise, "On the Ordering of his School," 181
Scipio Africanus, inspired to greatness by Homer's writings (1579), 65
Scogan, court fool to Edward IV., meeting between him and Gascoigne in Hades (1577), 57
Scots, Mary, Queen of, study of the "tragical pamphlets" of, 167-8
Seton, John, of Cambridge, allusion to his "Dialectica" (1573), 130
Sidney, Sir Philip, familiarity with Spenser and Harvey, 101
Silius Italicus, Caius, praise of, as a poet (1573), 53
Simias Rhodius, allusion to his Emblems (1579), 100
Simkin, Jack, his tale (1573), 118-19
Skelton, John, poet laureate, meeting between him and Gascoigne in Hades (1577), 57
Smith, Dame Philippa, 2nd wife of Sir Thomas, of Audley End, letter to, 170-1
Smith, Sir Thomas, of Audley End in Saffron Walden, Dean of Carlisle, Ambassador to France, visit to his house, by G. Harvey (1573), 19; advice of M. Yale to G. Harvey to procure letters from, to the Master of Pembroke Hall (1573), 32; letters to, 162-5, 168-9, 176-8, 179; acquaintance of Harvey with, 170
Socrates, survey of the ghosts of Homer and others, in Hades (1577), 56; longing of Harvey for his moral and philosophical wisdom, 71; study of, by Harvey, when working at philosophy (1579), 81
Sommers, Will, v. Sumner, Will
Sophocles, quotation from (1573), 39
Spenser, Edmund, letters to, from G. Harvey (1579), 58-63, 70-88; humorous bond with G. Harvey (1579), 64; dedication of Harvey's Verlayes by, to Sir E. Dyer, 89; note of a translation from Latin into English hexameters by, 100; fragment of letter from, to G. Harvey, 101
Steele Glas, a satire by George Gascoigne, allusion to (1579), 69, 100

Stella, Julius Cæsar, praise of, as a poet (1573), 53
Stourbridge Fair, near Cambridge, allusion to (1579), 59, 61, 74
Strozzi, Ercole, poet, of Ferrara, comparison between him and G. Gascoigne, by G. Harvey (1577), 55
Sturmius, Joannes, Sleidanus, recommendation of the study of, 167
Suetonius Tranquillus, Caius, mention of, as an historiographer (1573), 53
Sumner, al. Sommers, Will, court jester to Henry VIII. and Edward VI., allusions to (1573—1579), 5, 70
Supposes, a comedy, by George Gascoigne, allusion to (1579), 85
Surrey, Earl of, v. Howard, Henry, Earl of Surrey

Tacitus, mention of, as an historiographer (1573), 53
Tarleton, Richard, court jester to Queen Elizabeth, allusion to (1579), 67
Terence, considered to be the choicest and purest verse author, 181
Theatre, the, near Shoreditch, mention of (1579), 67
Thomas Aquinas, expulsion of his works from Cambridge, 78, 182
Thucydides, study of, by Harvey (1573), 143
Tibullus, challenge to, from Harvey (1573), 111
Trajan, Emperor, quotation relating to, from Juvenal (1573), 53
Treacle, notice of (1573), 22
Trinity College, Cambridge, supports G. Harvey for the rhetoric lectureship, 175-6
Tyndale, Humphrey, Fellow of Pembroke Hall, Cambridge, afterwards President of Queens' College and Dean of Ely, letters to (1573), 20, 22; carries tidings of Harvey to Spenser, 70

Ulysses, meeting between him and Socrates in Hades, 56

Valerius, Cornelius, Professor at Louvain, opposition to Aristotle's philosophy, 10

Vaux, William, 3rd Baron Vaux of Harrowden, mention of his company of players (1579), 67

Vere, Edward de, 17th Earl of Oxford, apostrophe to, by Harvey, in his "Gratulationes Valdinenses" (1578), 99

Virgil, quotation from (1573), 17; study of, by Harvey (1579), 81; allusion to Dr. Phaer's translation of the Æneid, 72; allusion to the blank verse translation of, by Lord Surrey (1579), 100; considered the choicest and purest verse author, 181

Wale, . . . , carrier from Cambridge to Saffron Walden, delays his journeys owing to change of weather (1573), 22

Wilkes, . . . . of Trinity College, Cambridge, joins the opposition against G. Harvey (1573), 50

Willes, Richard, M.A., of Cambridge, opinion of emblematic verses (1579), 100

Williamson, . . . . barber at Cambridge, longing of Harvey for his "rolling tongue," 71

Wilson, Thomas, of the Queen's company of players, allusion to (1579), 67

"Wily Beguiled," comedy of, mention of (1573), 42

Withipoll, . . . . of Ipswich, meeting between him and Gascoigne in Hades (1577), 57

Wood, . . . a courtier, letter to, 182

Xenophon, study of, by Harvey (1573), 133

Yale, . . . Fellow of Queens' College, conference with G. Harvey (1573), 32

Young, John, S.T.B., Master of Pembroke Hall, Cambridge, afterwards Bishop of Rochester, letters to (1573), 1-20, 24-35, 35-38, 38-40, 44-54, 159-161